D0878685

The Big Hat Law

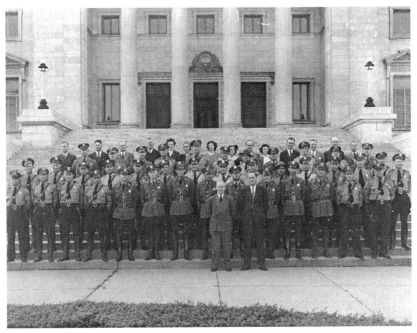

The entire Department of Arkansas State Police in 1945. Standing in front are Governor Ben Laney and Director Jack Porter. (Courtesy of Travis Ward)

The Big Hat Law

Arkansas and Its
State Police, 1935-2000

Michael Lindsey

BUTLER
CENTER

BOOKS

Little Rock, Arkansas

**BUTLER
CENTER**

BOOKS

The Butler Center for Arkansas Studies
Central Arkansas Library System
100 Rock Street
Little Rock, Arkansas 72201

First Edition, 2008

ISBN (hardback) 978-1-935106-01-2
Hardback printing: 10 9 8 7 6 5 4 3 2 1

ISBN (paperback) 978-0-9800897-4-5
Paperback printing: 10 9 8 7 6 5 4 3 2 1

Acquired for Butler Center Books by David Stricklin
Project manager: Ted Parkhurst
Book design and cover design: H. K. Stewart
Cover photograph: J. Stobaugh next to his State Police cruiser.

Photographs used in this book are the property of the author or were secured for use in this book by the author.

Library of Congress Catalog Card Number: 2008939482

Printed in the United States of America

This book is printed on archival-quality paper that meets requirements of the American National Standard for Information Sciences, Permanence of Paper, Printed Library Materials, ANSI Z39.48-1984.

Dedicated to the memory of

Sidney Pavatt

Ermon Cox

Harry Locke

Allen Bufford

Ron Brooks

Kelly Pique

Glen Bailey

Louis Bryant

Robbie Klein

Charles Bassing

Wilson Atkins

Clark Simpson

John Scarberough

Tom Craig

Herbert Smith

Jimmie White

Mark Carthron

Troop L's S.W.A.T. Team during their deployment to the CSA siege. From left to right, Bill Burnett, Les Braunns, Keith Ferguson, Charlie Brooks, Rocky Baker, Robin Casey, Joe Hutchins, Dennis Johnston. (Courtesy Win Phillips)

Table of Contents

Chapter One

The Creation of the
Arkansas Rangers

"They should be gentlemen, incorruptible, highly intelligent, good judge of human nature, self possessed, good listener, not too talkative, independent by environment and nature..."
—Governor J. M. Futrell's vision of Arkansas Rangers.

"This is a luxury we can't afford."
—State Senator Cowart
speaking against the State Police bill in 1935.

In October 1935, Arkansas Governor Junius Marion Futrell began to review the voluminous correspondence that poured in from his constituents on a daily basis. The letters and telegrams covered a litany of topics including requests for jobs, pleas for clemency, and requests for meetings. Of this correspondence, probably the most common motivation was to lodge a complaint. These complaints could run the gamut from trivial, like a woman whose daughter had eloped, to serious, like the charge made by an east Arkansas tenant farmer accusing his landlord of holding him in virtual slavery. For the most part, Governor Futrell took little direct action. Instead, he forwarded these letters on to the appropriate state agency and had his assistant respond to the complainant with a generic letter of receipt.

On occasion though, a complaint could raise the ire of the fiery governor and prompt his personal attention. Just such an occasion developed after Governor Futrell read a letter from a resident in Marion County. The man lamented the inability of local law enforcement to protect the peace and maintain order saying, "some Saturdays there is twelve or fifteen drunks in the streets of Yellville at once and no law to be found...we kneed [sic] protection."[1] Another problem Marion County farmers had to contend with during this time was a rash of cattle thefts.[2] The advent of the automobile coupled with an expanding state road network made cattle rustling a fairly quick, low-risk crime, and in 1935 a group of criminals were taking advantage of the lack of law enforcement in north Arkansas.

In the past, an Arkansas governor would have had few assets at his disposal to respond to such a complaint. A governor's traditional tool of dealing with civil unrest would be to call out the National Guard or state militia, but it would be highly unlikely that the governor would call out the Guard to arrest a group of unruly drunks and cattle thieves. By October 1935, times had changed and Arkansas had a new law enforcement agency available for its citizens: the Arkansas State Police and its Rangers—and the governor intended to try them out.

Futrell forwarded the letter to State Police Superintendent A. G. "Gray" Albright with a note requesting the State Police to look into the charges. Superintendent Albright dispatched the Ranger assigned to northwest Arkansas, Gene Mooney, to Yellville with orders to report back on what he found. A week later, Albright passed along Ranger Mooney's report to the governor, which confirmed the citizen's complaints and noted that it was a common sight for drunks to come into town on the weekends causing disturbances, insulting women, and just generally upsetting the right and upstanding citizens of Yellville. As for the sheriff, Ranger Mooney determined he was taking drunks home instead of arresting them because the county could not afford to feed them while they were in jail. Such actions allowed the county to operate within their limited budget, but it did little to deter these weekend rabble-rousers.

Ranger Mooney promised the county judge and sheriff he would arrest the drunks if they would find enough money to feed and prosecute the offenders. The county judge agreed to this arrangement, which prompted Ranger Mooney to predict a return to law and order "damn quick."[3]

Mooney was more concerned about the gang of cattle rustlers that was operating in the area. According to Mooney's investigation, one of the gang members named Kyles "goes armed all the time, shoots stores and homes at night, and is doing lots of stealing in the country."[4] In a short time, the gang had stolen almost 30 cattle and one horse, but residents were too afraid of violent reprisals from the gang to take any direct action.[5] Ranger Mooney was determined to stop the gang and told Superintendent Albright, "I think I can break up this gang in a few days, but I believe I'll have to kill Kyles before he will be caught … so don't be surprised at anything that happens."[6] Fortunately, Mooney, Albright, and local officers were able to arrest the gang members without bloodshed, following which the courts found the nine gang members guilty of cattle rustling and sentenced them to prison.

This early example of the State Police's role in Arkansas law enforcement does not involve the capture of an infamous fugitive, or a shootout, or a car chase. Ranger Mooney's efforts did not warrant any special mention in either the statewide or the local newspapers. What it does reflect is the impact a central law enforcement agency can have on the lives of the citizens. No longer would citizens' appeals for justice and fairness be limited to the sheriffs and local officers whose responses might be restricted by budgetary, political, or personal considerations. Over the course of the next 70 years, the Arkansas State Police would witness more than its share of high-profile investigations, shootouts, riots, car chases, and the capture of infamous criminals, but the vast majority of their time and energy, like Ranger Mooney's, would be spent in less high-profile activities whose importance was not diminished by their obscurity.

Today the need for a state police force appears obvious, and every state in the Union boasts at least some form of central law enforcement agency. Yet, the creation of a state police force in Arkansas faced enormous obstacles in 1935. Examining Arkansas' history, one finds several attempts to create a statewide law enforcement agency, but until 1935 none would prove entirely successful for a wide range of reasons.

Even though the Fiftieth Session of the Arkansas General Assembly faced most of those same obstacles when they convened in January 1935, a forceful governor combined with a unique confluence of events and issues, and pushed through the historically significant legislation that created the Arkansas Rangers. To fully understand the issues and events that culminated during the General Assembly's 50th session and realize the depth of opposition, one must trace the historic development of both the pro- and anti-state police movements.

The movements to create state police forces in the United States during the first four decades of the 20th century faced a number of practical and ideological obstacles, and nowhere were these hurdles steeper than in the South. Not only were southern states financially poorer than their northern brethren and thus less likely to absorb the added expense, but also, southerners' preference for local control reflected more than a century of practice by the time the first modern state police agency was established in 1905. This preference for localism (or "localistic republicanism," as Edward Ayers more specifically described it) opposed any attempts, no matter how noble minded, to empower an outside entity with authority over local affairs.[7]

Arkansans proved particularly stubborn in their adherence to localistic republicanism as a defining cultural trait. A belief partly exhibited by the fact that Arkansas remained one of the few states without a statewide law enforcement agency in January 1935. By tracing the repeated efforts to create a state police force in Arkansas, one is able to see just how deep this ideology ran even though a state police force, like many other progressive-era state agencies, had the potential to provide numerous benefits for the state's residents. Therefore, the ultimate success of the state police movement represented a significant turning point, both symbolic and actual, in Arkansans' perception of state government and its role in their daily lives.

As 1935 dawned, Arkansans' opposition to a statewide police force showed few obvious signs it would be overcome, especially considering the dire financial straits many of the state's residents were suffering through. Arkansas had never been a rich state, and the decline of cotton prices in the 1920s coupled with the advent of the Great Depression in 1929 had led to an economic and social disaster by the early 1930s. The outlook for these impoverished Arkansans darkened even further in late 1934 when the Federal Emergency Relief Administration (FERA) threatened to cut off all federal assistance to more than 400,000 people within the state unless the legislature committed $1.5 million in matching funds by March 1935.[8]

While resolving the state's financial crisis and locating matching funds were the most critical issues facing the governor and the General Assembly in January 1935, another issue promised to generate a tremendous amount of statewide interest and debate: the attempt to repeal prohibition within the state. For Governor Futrell, the issues of liquor and state finances were tightly intertwined. Legalizing the consumption, manufacturing, and transportation of alcohol had the potential to provide a tremendous influx of new revenue for the state's coffers without the political damage that a tax increase would inflict. Yet, he also realized the current judicial system's inefficiencies in adequately and impartially enforcing state laws, so he argued that the best way to correct it was through the creation of a state police force. He believed that a statewide police agency would be essential if the inevitable liquor law was to be enforced and widespread bootlegging stopped, but such an agency would tip the balance of power in Arkansas from counties and cities to the state. While centralizing power within the state government had the potential to make the enforcement of laws more efficient, effective, and equal, it also created fierce opposition from many Arkansans who clung protectively to their core belief of localistic republicanism.

Prior to 1935, the means and methods of law enforcement in Arkansas had remained fairly true to the state's Old South roots. Except in rare instances, local officials and citizens took responsibility for policing their own communities and maintaining their own standards of law and order. Most often, the local political and economic elites within a county represented the ultimate arbitrators of law and justice, either officially through an elected sheriff or unofficially through a vigilante group or lynch mob. These vehicles of "justice" squared with their belief in republicanism, which first found a voice in America through the writings and speeches of the fledgling nation's Revolutionary leaders who saw the centralization of power as the first step to a corrupt government and the destruction of a man's independence.[9] Any sort of standing force, whether it was a professional army or a uniformed police agency, symbolized a potential agent of repression, and thus these early patriots discouraged their formation.

A few minor encroachments on pure republican standards for law enforcement had appeared by the Civil War. The creation of a state penitentiary centralized the care and incarceration of the state's convicts while, in theory at least, improving the care and conditions for prisoners. Also, the city of Little Rock had created the first standing police force in Arkansas in 1859. This new agency boasted uniformed officers engaged in regular patrols within the city limits to "preserve order, peace, quiet, and enforce the laws and ordinances throughout the city."[10] Yet, even Arkansas' violent descent into lawlessness following the Civil War proved insufficient to convince most of the state's politicians that additional efforts at centralizing law enforcement within a state agency should be taken. The best way to stop violence and lawlessness, according to the *Arkansas Gazette*, was for citizens to take responsibility for bringing the offenders to justice, adding "whoever willfully fails to do this is scarcely entitled to the reciprocal benefit of protection."[11] Such a solution is classically republican, where the onus of stopping these acts is placed on the community instead of a strong, central law enforcement agency.

Not everyone agreed with the *Gazette*'s solution, but the group that advocated a different course was almost as hated by the old guard elite as the "viscous and desperate characters" that roamed post-Civil War Arkansas. The Republicans elected during the Reconstruction period in Arkansas elicited the undying hatred of most planters and many yeoman farmers due to their alliance with the newly freed slaves. The fact that the Reconstruction Republicans were so outnumbered necessitated a centralized approach to law and order.

It is from this desperate position that the first proposal for a state police force emerged. During the 1873 legislative session, Pulaski County Representative Joseph Murphy introduced House Bill 211, which sought a "more efficient administration of criminal laws of the state; the apprehension and arrest of criminals; and the establishment of a metropolitan police district of the state of Arkansas."[12] The plan divided the state into two districts: the city of Little Rock and the rest of the state, with each district having a separate organization of officers, sergeants, and captains. The police officers would hold all the law enforcement powers that a constable and a sheriff had except their jurisdiction extended throughout the state. A superintendent, who was appointed by the governor to a four-year term, would oversee day-to-day operations of both districts. A three-member police commission composed of the governor, the state treasurer, and the superintendent would provide administrative oversight of the agency.[13] To foot the estimated $40,000 annual budget, the state would levy a one-tenth of one percent tax on real and personal property.[14]

Despite vehement objections by the *Gazette*, which called the proposed agency "odious" and "pernicious ... to every municipal and state interest in every respect," the Republican-dominated House of Representatives looked as though it would pass the measure. The bill came out of the Judiciary Committee with a do-pass recommendation and came up for a vote on the House floor on March 22, but the Democrats were strong enough to force a two-week delay in consideration.[15] The bill came up again in early April where it sparked a heated debate over its implications and cost. Supporters pointed to a rash of politically motivated violence in Pope and Hempstead counties— which combined with a lack of punishment for the offenders and the refusal of the Democrats to support a call-out of the state militia—that produced virtual anarchy in those two locations. Eastern Arkansas

Representative V. M. McGehee loudly supported the bill and questioned its opponents, saying, "How can they oppose it when it gives protection to every citizen of the state, or are they in favor of riots and bloodshed?"[16]

The opposition remained unmoved by McGehee's plea and argued that he was exaggerating the current level of criminal activity. Representative C. E. Berry cut to the heart of the matter for the opposition by saying the bill "strikes directly at the liberties of the people."[17] Representative George Latta also voiced his concerns over the effectiveness of such an organization before arguing that the bill was improperly amended after it left the Judiciary Committee and therefore should be sent back to the Engrossment Committee. The House complied with Latta's wishes and sent the bill back to be properly engrossed, but with just a few weeks left in the 1873 session of the General Assembly, it never made it back to the House floor.

The next attempt toward centralization of law enforcement occurred in 1883 with the creation of the Arkansas Sheriffs' Association. In large part, the Sheriffs' Association reflected the improved methods of travel that had developed in the state, including river, road, and rail transport, which allowed criminals to enter and flee an area with unprecedented rapidity.[18] The Sheriffs' Association adopted as their mission "the protection of life and property and suppression of crime," which they intended to do by creating a main office in Little Rock that would store and distribute photographs and descriptions of wanted criminals.[19] Both the plan for creating a central records system and the Sheriffs' Association itself languished and never achieved any of their goals after even this limited attempt at centralization created controversy and charges of political abuse.[20]

By the early 1890s, the idea of law enforcement associations had gained favor throughout the United States. This national movement encouraged the state's sheriffs to try reforming the Sheriff's Association in 1893 with 26 sheriffs attending an organizational meeting in the capital city. Once again, they proposed to centralize their criminal records and disseminate wanted information around the state while also working to represent the interests of their office among legislators. City police and town marshals in Arkansas created a similar statewide association in February 1894 charged with "the betterment of the protection of the state from criminals and crime."[21] Few concrete results came from these early attempts to improve the efficiency of local law enforcement agencies through centralization. Yet their existence does show a slight bend in will by local officials toward a statewide entity.

As Arkansas entered the 20th century, the argument could be made that it was not that far behind the times in its methods of law enforcement. Throughout the United States, sheriffs represented the primary police agent in the rural areas, while constables or town marshals were elected to serve in small towns. In larger cities, professional, uniformed police officers walked a beat. Arkansas had a version of all of these agencies at the beginning of the 20th century, but in 1905 a major change in law enforcement would occur following the establishment of the first modern state police force.

A modern state police force is defined as an agency that holds general police powers, has statewide jurisdiction, and is responsible for enforcing all of the laws of the state.[22] The force should be uniformed, centrally controlled, and engaged in regular patrol. Statewide law enforcement organizations existed prior to the 20th century, but no long-term agency met this definition. The Texas Rangers were the first American organization with statewide jurisdiction, but their role was limited to frontier duty and protection of early settlers from attacks by Indians or Mexicans.[23] In 1870, Radical Republicans in Texas did create a true state police force to combat the explosion of crime and violence sweeping the state after the Civil War. The force had an authorized strength of 257 men, of which nearly 40 percent were black. These officers produced a credible record of enforcing the law and bringing criminals to justice during the agency's three-year existence, but as one student of the organization finds, "the State Police force was guilty of two unforgivable sins: it was part of Radical rule, and it armed the Negro and placed him in a position of authority over white men."[24] The demise of the State Police placed the onus of law enforcement on the Rangers in 1874, but they still did not wear uniforms or badges. Nor did they adhere to a centralized command structure or engage in regular patrols, all key symbols of a modern, professional state police force.[25]

Pennsylvania became the first state to create a permanent, modern state police force in 1905. The driving force behind this new agency was a series of violent confrontations between striking mineworkers and private police hired by the mining company. The inability of the local authorities to maintain order and the governor's reluctance to use National Guard troops, which would be taken from the same social class as the strikers, led to the call for a new force. This new agency was large (228 men), horse-mounted, uniformed, well armed, organized on a semi-military basis, and given general police powers.[26]

Between 1905 and 1935, Arkansas was not immune to instances of civil unrest, crime, and lawlessness that seemed to cry out for the creation of a state police force. The most infamous instance of unrest during this period happened in 1919 at Elaine. On the last day of September, members of an all-black farmers' union in Phillips County shot and killed two white men. These murders triggered a massive and violent response from many of the region's white residents, an estimated 500 of which gathered to seek revenge and forcibly squash any signs of a long-feared race war.

One segment of the white population that did not want revenge on the black farmers were the planters and businessmen who depended on a large and reliable pool of labor to pick the cotton crop that was currently in full bloom. It was this group that pleaded with Governor Charles Brough to send in soldiers to end the violence that was interrupting their cotton harvest. Depending upon the version of events, the arrival of federal troops in Elaine on October 2 either marked the end of large-scale violence and the return of calm or the beginning of a massacre of black residents.[27] Either way, the soldiers, who were less than a year removed from the carnage of World War I battlefields, were an inappropriate choice to act as impartial police officers, but without a state police agency, no other force existed for the governor to call for help.

A less deadly, but equally illustrative example of local unrest that might have been prevented by the presence of an independent state police agency occurred in 1923 at the Ozark Mountain community of Harrison. Harrison was a small town lying along the Missouri and North Arkansas rail line, which connected the rugged and relatively isolated communities in North Arkansas with Helena and Kansas City, Missouri. The railroad's union employees had been out on strike since 1921, and throughout the next year and a half they were blamed for repeated acts of vandalism and sabotage of company equipment, bridges, and rail lines that hindered the railroad's new non-union operations. Local authorities and citizens' protection leagues struggled unsuccessfully to stop these acts of sabotage, and on January 13, 1923, the railroad's vice president, J. C. Murray, warned that continued acts of sabotage would lead to a shutdown of the railroad. Murray made himself perfectly clear by stating, "It is now entirely with the public as to whether or not they desire the continued operation of this railway, and their desire will be expressed entirely in the protective measures they may and will take."[28]

The next day, an estimated 400 armed strikebreakers arrived in Harrison on an M&NA train to put an end to the strike by arresting its leaders, exiling those who refused to return to work, and even hanging one defiant union man.[29] At the same time, the anti-union leaders formed a "Committee of Twelve" who deposed Harrison's mayor and city marshal, and assumed the role of local government. In effect, the elected government of the city of Harrison had just been forcibly overthrown by armed insurrection.[30] The local paper explained that these actions were the result of the mayor being "out of harmony with the situation."[31] In Little Rock, Governor Thomas McRae pleaded with the sheriff to assert control and stop the vigilantism that had taken over the city or to call on the National Guard to intervene, but the only official law enforcement agent remaining in Boone County declined the governor's offer of outside intervention and even allowed his deputies to assist in the round-up of strikers.[32]

A more widespread and long-term phenomena that seemed to cry out for a state police force was the flaunting of state and national prohibition. Arkansas was a "dry" state even before the ratification of the 18th Amendment to the United States Constitution and the passage of the Volstead Act by Congress in 1919. A number of counties and cities passed local option laws in the 1870s, and prohibition was extended statewide following the passage of "bone dry" laws in 1915.[33]

As the 1920s melted away, it became more and more evident nationwide that local authorities were not enforcing the law and that people were not interested in following it. President Herbert Hoover responded by establishing the National Commission on Law Observance and Enforcement, known as the Wickersham Commission after its chairman George W. Wickersham, and ordered them to determine the state of law enforcement in America.[34] The Wickersham Commission released 14 reports in 1931 that focused on all aspects of American policing, including the enforcement of prohibition laws. The commission's report found Arkansas to be "chiefly dry," but identified several areas of the state that were not in compliance with the law.[35] The report referred to Desha and Crittenden Counties as being "especially bad" and noted that the continued production of moonshine in the Ozark Mountains was to be expected since it was a "specialized profession among the hill people before the Civil War."[36] Texarkana was also identified as a problem area due to the numerous oil field workers who exhibited a strong taste for liquor. The report saved its strongest criticism for Hot Springs where it found that "gambling houses and bootleggers flourished ... unmolested by city or county officials ... [and] in perfect harmony with the political ring."[37] As proof of this harmony, the report cited the employment of the police chief's son as a casino table attendant and an ex-sheriff as a casino doorman.

Even with so many instances of unrest and a blatant disregard for state and national laws between 1905 and 1935, the arguments against creating a state police force in Arkansas overwhelmed existing pro-state police sentiment. Still, public and political opinion gradually began to look upon a state law enforcement agency with more favor as the popularity of automobiles, changing perceptions of crime, and a national state police movement gained prominence.

The first of these pro-state police catalysts took root in 1913 when the legislature created the Arkansas Highway Commission. Such a move seems uncharacteristically farsighted for the General Assembly, since at the time the state had fewer than 4,000 registered automobiles. Yet it quickly became clear that Arkansans loved their automobiles. Over the next 20 years, automobile ownership expanded by more than 6,000 percent, and the length of paved highway in the state more than tripled.

Table 1.1–Arkansas Automobile and Highway Data, 1913–1936[38]

Year	Registered Automobiles	Total Highway Miles	Paved Highway Miles	Unpaved Highway Miles	Annual Vehicle Miles Traveled
1913	3,596	—	—	—	—
1916	15,123	—	—	—	—
1920	58,998	—	—	—	—
1924	141,888	6,718.55	612.56	6,105.99	750,920,000
1928	218,382	8,715.50	843.90	7,871.60	1,401,140,000
1932	142,873	8,841.50	1,781.56	7,059.94	1,119,079,000
1936	231,890	8,927.41	2,179.24	6,748.17	1,628,450,000

One consequence of this rapid expansion in automobile ownership and highway construction was the toll in human lives. The laws regulating drivers and their vehicles for most of this period were few and rarely enforced. As early as 1914, the *Arkansas Gazette* followed a national trend lamenting the carelessness of drivers and noting the dangers of automobiles.[39] Initially, these fears were a reflection of problems in other areas of the country, but by 1917, those problems had come home to Arkansas. In particular, the *Gazette* remarked that speeding "up to 30 miles per hour" caused vehicles to rock unsteadily due to the often rough Arkansas highways and crude automotive suspension systems. The editors theorized that this instability was the primary cause for many of the all too frequent automobile accidents in the state.[40] Speeding was not the only potentially fatal decisions the newly motoring public was making. The Highway Commission complained of motorists' glaring headlights, overloaded trucks, improper parking on highways, and the "failure to display a light at night on horse-drawn vehicles" as recurring actions that created numerous accidents.[41]

Table 1.2–Motor Vehicle Fatality Rates for Arkansas, 1923-1934[42]

Year	Deaths	Deaths per 100 Million Miles Traveled
1923	45	7
1924	111	15
1925	119	12
1926	155	13
1927	166	13
1928	213	15
1929	285	16
1930	285	17
1931	323	22
1932	266	24
1933	287	20
1934	347	24

Even as cars became larger and more sophisticated, accidents continued at an unprecedented pace. The main problems were high speeds, which combined with alcohol, bad roads, or just plain carelessness to take a growing number of lives throughout the nation. The outcry over the rising death toll was again reflected in the editorial pages of the state's newspapers, even leading one north Arkansas newspaper to describe the situation as a "great slaughter."[43] Such "slaughter" was occurring throughout the United States and even compelled President Franklin Roosevelt to urge states to pass stringent traffic laws and organize "proper agencies of administration and enforcement."[44]

Comparing contemporary fatality statistics with current rates reveals just how dangerous operating a motor vehicle was during this time. In 2001, 611 people were killed on Arkansas highways. This equates to a fatality rate of 2.08 deaths for every 100,000,000 vehicle miles traveled. In the same year, the United States averaged 1.52 deaths per 100,000,000 vehicle miles.[45] Arkansas' fatality rate in 1934 was twenty-four deaths per 100,000,000 vehicle miles or 12 times the current level. Applying the 1934 fatality rate to today's traffic volumes would result in more than 7,000 automobile fatalities in Arkansas each year. These high fatality rates and the publicity they garnered in the newspapers helped to convince many that the enforcement of traffic and public safety laws required a new organization.

Traffic deaths were just one factor working to change opinions toward a centralized enforcement agency. Another was the perception of crime and criminals during the 1920s and 1930s. The images of lawlessness during this period are numerous and wide-ranging. New York and Chicago became notorious for the violence and political corruption caused by organized crime's competition over the sale of illicit alcohol. In the Midwest, newspapers and magazines popularized bank robbers like Bonnie and Clyde Barrow, John Dillinger, and "Pretty Boy" Floyd, even prompting Governor Futrell to lament that "people like Dillinger can drive through our state with machine guns, shooting down law-abiding citizens, and we are powerless to prevent them from driving in Arkansas."[46] Additionally, the occurrence of high-profile crimes like the kidnapping of famed aviator Charles Lindbergh's baby in 1932 played on

Americans' fears of both crime and immigrants. All of these events led many to believe that the country was in the midst of a crime wave.[47]

Determining the actual presence of a "crime wave" for this period is difficult because of the inherent problems with crime statistics and the lack of reliable statewide data. The only source even close to providing a statewide picture of criminal activity in Arkansas is the number and type of indictments returned by the state's court system. Indictments do not represent a complete picture of crime in Arkansas because not all criminal acts result in the arrest of a perpetrator, but it can provide insight on whether crime is increasing, decreasing, or staying the same.

Table 1.3–Summary of Criminal Indictments in Arkansas, 1925-1936[48]

Year	Indictments	Robbery, Burglary, & Larceny	Homicide	Assault with Intent	Liquor
1925-1926	3,712	436	232	1,959	7,151
1927-1928	2,624	497	294	2,677	7,683
1929-1930	2,513	392	260	1,907	6,376
1931-1932	3,097	513	284	1,129	6,420
1933-1934	4,196	513	453	872	7,525
1935-1936	3,818	511	355	262	6,401

A review of this information confirms what historians have found throughout the country, that crime in Arkansas was not on the rise during the 1920s and 1930s and instead remained fairly level. For the two-year period of 1925-1926, the State Attorney General's Office reported that 7,151 people were indicted for felonies by Arkansas courts. Larceny/robbery/burglary (3,712), liquor (1,959), and homicide (436) topped the list of charges.[49] By the end of the 1920s, the number of felony charges decreased slightly to 6,376.[50] The two years prior to the 50th session (1933-1934) of the General Assembly did see a rise in crime from the 1925-1926 period, but it still remained within the upper and lower bounds of indictments during the 10-year period.

While these statistics do not reflect the presence of a verifiable crime wave, it does not mean that crime did not exist at high levels. In 1934, Little Rock had the 13th highest homicide rate in the nation with 37 murders per 100,000 residents. This ranking was an improvement from 1933, when Little Rock had the second highest homicide rate in America.[51] Another city with a high crime rate was Texarkana. The discovery of oil in southwest Arkansas in 1920 created a boom in drilling camps around the border city. These encampments led to increased crime which seemed to explode during the winter of 1933 as burglaries, assault, and drunkenness became commonplace. The situation became so desperate that city officials commissioned 100 citizens as "special officers" and asked for help from the Texas Rangers, which sent three officers across the border in February.[52]

The "crime wave" perception influenced American police reformers August Vollmer and Bruce Smith to search for ways to turn back the assault on law and order. Both came to believe that a statewide police agency provided a cost-efficient, honest way to enforce the law, and both wrote several books and articles during this period extolling the virtues of the State Police. Smith's The State Police, which was released in 1925, argued that urban criminals caused most of the instances of rural crime and then used automobiles to escape the clutches of sheriffs and city police.[53] In 1929, the Annals of American Academy of Political and Social Science printed a series of articles that spoke of the need for statewide bureaus to enforce the law and maintain a centralized database of criminals and crimes.[54]

The Wickersham Commission's findings also supported the creation of a state police force.[55] August Vollmer co-authored the commission's Report on Police, which recommended that states create a statewide agency to protect the public and investigate crimes. He expanded on these recommendations with his 1935 book, Crime and the State Police.

In this text, Vollmer argued that a well-trained, independent state police force was a "necessity" because of the improved mobility and firepower of criminals, the negative influence of politics in local law enforcement, and lack of training for local officers.[56] By the time *Crime and the State Police* was released, many states agreed with Vollmer and Smith and had created a statewide law enforcement agency influenced by the Pennsylvania model. Most of these new agencies were created during two time periods: 1915-1923 and 1929-1935.[57]

The first period witnessed the establishment of statewide law enforcement agencies in 27 states. A key impetus for this trend was World War I. The war not only raised fears of enemy agents committing acts of sabotage, but the call-up and overseas deployment of many National Guard units left governors with no one to call on in times of actual emergency or unrest. Even after the war ended and the Guard returned, the public continued to fear the existence of subversive agents, with the hidden specter of German spies replaced by Bolshevik agitators. These fears made a state police force more acceptable for many people.

The second period (1929-1935) found another 11 states establishing statewide police forces. For the most part, these agencies were created in response to the popularity of the automobile and the high accident rates that accompanied new drivers. This second phase finds most of the southern states joining the state police movement.

In Arkansas, the factors supporting the creation of a state police, which included motor vehicle fatality rates, crime rates, and a national movement in support of state police forces, met equally strong arguments against its creation. While the national state police movement had not borne fruit in Arkansas prior to 1935, this did not mean that law enforcement in Arkansas had remained unchanged.

The first effort in the 20th century to establish a state police force occurred on March 5, 1923, just three days before the end of the state's legislative session. Senator W. U. McCabe introduced Senate Bill 546, which called for the creation of an agency of state motor patrolmen.[58]

While it is interesting that a senator from north Arkansas would introduce a bill for a statewide police force in the same year of the civil unrest in Harrison, the actual intent of the senator remains unknown since the legislature adjourned before the bill could be debated and neither statewide newspaper considered the item important enough to warrant specific mention.

The next movement for a statewide law enforcement agency developed within the Arkansas State Highway and Transportation Department. In 1926, the Highway Commission recommended all motor vehicle rules be established as state laws and that the state provide funds for the Highway Department to enforce them "independent of the counties."[59] In the next legislative session, the General Assembly enacted all motor vehicle rules into law and provided the Highway Department with funding for license inspectors who were charged with ensuring motorists purchased new automobile licenses each year, but they ignored the commission's request for a statewide traffic enforcement agency.

This failure stemmed, in part, from legislators continued preference for authority residing within local officers. Even Governor John Martineau advocated the existing division of authority and responded to criticisms of the state's sheriffs by saying "It is unfair to thrust upon the officials the exclusive duty of maintaining peace and order. The citizen who has not discharged his full duty in aiding our public servants has no right whatever to complain of laxity."[60]

Not satisfied, the Highway Commission recommended an even bigger step in their next *Biennial Report*, which was released in 1928. Citing the dangers of operating an automobile in Arkansas and the unnecessary wear and tear on the state's highways by overloaded trucks, the commission recommended the creation of a state police force. The commission saw the New Jersey, Ohio, Illinois, and Indiana State Police as models for this new organization, which would be provided with full police powers and would be used as a "remedy for the flagrant violation of the automobile laws which are now written upon our statute."[61]

As one of the most powerful departments in state government, the recommendations and requests of the Highway Commission carried significant weight with legislators. During the next legislative session, two very different State Police bills were introduced. Phillips County Representative Jesse Booth introduced the first on January 29, 1929. House Bill 367 called for the establishment of a Bureau of State Police "to cover the entire state, [and] not to conflict with any local established law enforcement agencies, but to co-operate with all such agencies."[62] A four-member commission composed of the chief justice of the Arkansas Supreme Court, governor, lieutenant governor, and attorney general would oversee the proposed bureau, which would field 128 officers split into four platoons. In what appeared to be an attempt to justify the expense, Representative Booth proposed a wide range of responsibilities for these officers in addition to their main duty of enforcing state laws, which included acting as oil inspectors, fertilizer inspectors, game wardens, and forest fire fighters.[63]

Surprisingly, Representative Booth said that the Arkansas Sheriffs' Association endorsed the bill. This endorsement seemed to contradict the supposed preference by sheriffs to maintain local control. Although no direct evidence exists to indicate why the Sheriffs' Association may have endorsed this bill, some circumstantial documentation can be found. During the debate over State Police legislation in the 1935 session of the General Assembly, Governor Futrell complained that the state's sheriffs supported the organization of the State Police as long as they thought they would be able to control the officers. He argued that once bills proposing an independent State Police force were introduced and gained support, they became its "biggest opponent."[64] Booth's bill might have included provisions that subordinated the State Police officers to the sheriffs, thereby reconciling the endorsement by the Sheriffs' Association with their demand for local control. The sheriff of Jackson County and later superintendent of the Arkansas State Police, Gray Albright, agreed in part with Governor Futrell's assessment. He found that many sheriffs supported a State Police force as long as it was intended to help them during manhunts, for traffic enforcement, or in times of unrest, but greatly feared "that if some governor wanted to, he could use the authority of the State Police to embarrass him or interfere in his political affairs."[65]

Either way, this endorsement carried little weight with the judiciary subcommittee because six days after the bill was introduced it was returned with a "no recommendation" from its members.[66] A "no recommendation" by the subcommittee ended any chance of HB 367 even being brought up for a vote.

Three days later on February 21, Senator Duval L. Purkins introduced the second statewide law enforcement bill of the session. Senate Bill 359, which became known as the State Road Patrol Bill, asked for a very different force than Representative Booth desired, but it still met the minimum requirements of the Highway Commission's request. The State Road Patrol Bill granted general police powers to the Highway Department's license inspectors and assigned them the duty of enforcing motor vehicle laws and collecting delinquent motor vehicle license fees and gasoline taxes.[67] The bill came out of its subcommittee with a "do pass" recommendation and on March 6, the Senate voted unanimously to approve the bill.[68] The House would not be so easy on Purkin's bill. Its opponents argued that such a force undermined the authority of local officers and reduced the fees they received through enforcement of traffic laws. Also, they stated that the Road Patrol just represented additional staff positions that the state could ill afford.[69] These arguments failed to convince a majority of the representatives and the State Road Patrol bill passed by a vote of 57 to 26. Interestingly, Representative Booth voted against the Road Patrol bill.

On April 18, 1929, the Highway Commission formally organized the State Road Patrol by commissioning its 16 license inspectors as Highway Patrolmen.[70] Since the Road Patrol was not charged with enforcing criminal laws or assisting county or local officers in the enforcement of criminal laws, this new force cannot accurately be identified as a "state police" force, but its creation signified a big step toward such an organization.

Over the next six years, the Road Patrol had mixed success in enforcing the state highway laws and collecting delinquent license and gasoline taxes. In the Highway Department's *Biennial Report* for the period of 1928 to 1930, the patrol received high praise from the commission for improving public safety and enforcing revenue laws, which prompted the commission to ask for additional funding to expand the force. The *Report* also noted that because of this new statewide force "all matters of highway violation seemed to be passed on to the State Highway Patrol and little or no effort is being made by the local peace officers to enforce any of the rules and regulations ... for the protection of people upon the highway, or for the proper licensing of all motor vehicles."[71]

However, the effectiveness of the Road Patrol would be called into question just two years later. An audit of the Highway Department, which was released in 1933, criticized the Road Patrol for not following procedures, failing to collect on its fines, and poor record-keeping. The audit found that over a 10-month period in 1931 the Highway Department spent $84,678.45 in salaries and travel expenses to maintain the 24 highway patrolmen, but received just $2,027.75 in fines from traffic enforcement.[72]

In addition to the poor return on investment, the audit questioned many of the patrolmen's travel expenses, which included reimbursements for hotel rooms in Oklahoma and charges for gasoline that were deemed suspiciously regular. The patrolmen were also criticized for their failure to keep proper records, which were often prepared incorrectly and appeared contradictory.[73] Poor record-keeping was one factor in the low collection of fines. Another was the procedure established for the patrolmen to collect the fines. After writing a traffic ticket, the patrolman was personally responsible for collecting any fines awarded by the court. If the violator did not have sufficient funds to pay the fine, the patrolman was supposed to seize his car and turn it over to the Highway Department for sale. Without detailed records and close cooperation with the local courts, the patrolmen had a difficult time juggling the duties of highway patrol and fine collection. To resolve these problems, the audit recommended that the Road Patrol be transferred to the Department of Revenue where their duties would be limited to the enforcement of traffic laws and detection of revenue evaders.[74] The legislature implemented the audit's recommendations by passing Act 45 of 1933.

Over the next two years, the Road Patrol assumed a more visible role as a state highway patrol where its primary duties were to remove overloaded, improperly lighted, or unlicensed vehicles from the roads while arresting reckless drivers. According to the director of the Revenue Department, Earl Wiseman, these hazards had become "common" over the preceding years and demanded "immediate action" by the patrol. Wiseman's plan called for the initiation of patrols at night and on rural roads in addition to the constant patrolling of highways "in an effort to educate the public and put an end to such traffic violations." He qualified this policy by noting that he proceeded cautiously because "too drastic a campaign might antagonize the public and defeat its purpose." By the end of 1934, Wiseman declared his efforts a success and that the traffic laws "have been enforced with a greater degree of efficiency than ever before in the history of such legislation ... thereby making Arkansas' highways safe for the motorist and traveler."[75] Such a statement seems to overlook the rising death toll on Arkansas' highways during this period, which saw 81 more fatalities in 1934 than in 1932.

Along with the Road Patrol, the state saw additional attempts at centralizing law enforcement in Arkansas during the early 1930s. In 1931, the legislature created a Bureau of Criminal Identification and Investigation.[76] This new organization, which was endorsed by the Sheriffs' Association, acted as a clearinghouse for all fingerprints, criminal files, and mug shots for state criminals, with these records maintained in Little Rock. A Board of Directors composed of the governor, a sheriff, and a police chief would oversee the seven-person Bureau. Such an organization reflected the long-term efforts of the state's sheriffs to establish a central record-keeping entity that would assist in identifying criminals and raising the alarm for wanted fugitives. Despite its widespread support, this organization never really got off the ground and only lasted two years before the General Assembly voted for its repeal as a cost-cutting measure.[77]

The Road Patrol was not safe from attempts to end its operation either. In 1931, Representatives Virgil Butler and S. A. Turner introduced House Bill 390 to abolish the Road Patrol.[78] The bill never found sufficient support and did not come up for a vote. Still, its presence shows the continued opposition to even a limited statewide law enforcement organization like the Road Patrol.

With such a tenuous existence for the Road Patrol, Governor Futrell's hope that the General Assembly would create a powerful State Police agency in 1935 seemed questionable at best. Also, any support that might have been provided by sheriffs was probably tempered following the governor and attorney general's aggressive efforts to collect overdue taxes from them over the preceding year. Through most of 1934, the state used special collectors to audit county tax records and collect overdue auto license fees. When sheriffs would not or could not pay, the state sued the sheriffs to recover the funds. Often times, the amount due could be in the thousands of dollars, and cash-strapped counties found it difficult to set aside and forward the required funds.[79] Despite these political handicaps and the traditional weakness of a second-term governor, Futrell still possessed one very crucial means of leverage: the veto. With a controversial issue like prohibition on the table, Governor Futrell's veto threat produced a degree of leverage within the legislature and provided him significant power over how a State Police force might be organized.

In his second inaugural address, Governor Futrell related his vision for this new law enforcement agency. He stated that it must be a model of professionalism that was immune to the influences of politics and corruption and whose main duties lay in enforcing the laws of the state, providing assistance to local authorities, and maintaining order in times of unrest. The governor's high expectations for this organization were clearly reflected when he described the ideal officers as being "gentlemen, incorruptible, highly intelligent, good judge[s] of human nature, self possessed, good listener[s], not too talkative, independent by environment and nature, [have a] natural adaptation to this type of work, [with] healthy bodies."[80]

Over the next two weeks, four separate State Police bills would be introduced in the General Assembly—two in the House and two in the Senate. Only three would be of major importance, the first of which was introduced by Pope County Senator Armil Taylor and Benton County Senator Clyde Ellis on January 15. Senate Bill 20 called for the creation of the Arkansas State Rangers, which would be comprised of 29 officers charged with enforcing criminal and traffic laws throughout the state, assisting local authorities, and assuming the duties of state game wardens.[81]

The following day, January 17, Pulaski County Representative Robert Chrisp introduced the second State Police bill, House Bill 29. House Bill 29 requested that the legislature create a Department of State Police featuring 30 patrolmen who would be paid between $1,200 and $3,000 per year, and a chief who would be paid $5,000 per year.[82]

Chrisp's fellow Pulaski County representative, V. N. "Pete" Carter, introduced House Bill 150 on January 22. Representative Carter's bill would establish an Arkansas Police Department under the daily guidance of the Revenue commissioner, with oversight provided through a five-member police commission consisting of the governor, revenue commissioner, and three appointees. The police force would be comprised of a chief, holding the rank of major, three captains, four sergeants, and 32 patrolmen. The mission of this agency would be to "patrol the public highways and enforce laws relating to motor vehicles and the use of highways ... collect delinquent motor vehicle taxes, gas taxes, arrest people criminally responsible for damage to highways."[83] Carter's bill differed from both Chrisp's and Taylor-Ellis' in that the proposed agency was not focused on criminal law enforcement and was actually just a reorganization of the existing Road Patrol.

On February 5, Chrisp and Carter combined their two police bills into a single entity, House Bill 264, which incorporated what the authors believed were the best portions of their respective bills.[84] The key change was altering the mission of Carter's police force to include cooperating with local officials in the enforcement of criminal laws. This addition transformed Carter's original design of a force limited to enforcing traffic and revenue laws into a true State Police force. Even with this authority over criminal laws, the main mission of the force would be to "patrol our highways and make them safe for travel."[85] The co-authors, ever mindful of the monetary importance of their efforts, noted that the State Police's presence would reduce accidents, thereby lowering insurance rates for their constituents.

The same day that Carter and Chrisp combined their bills, Governor Futrell met with the Farm Debt Adjustment Committee. Even in this unrelated setting, the governor took the time to address the inability of the state to enforce laws like gambling and liquor without a State Police force. The governor became so agitated during his comments that he struck the table with his fist and blamed the "damned infernal roadhouses" as the scenes of this "debauchery and gambling."[86]

The governor's passion was not enough to save Senator Ellis' State Ranger bill, which was the first State Police bill introduced after the governor's inaugural address. On February 7, the Senate defeated the measure by a vote of 25 to nine after several senators derided the measure as a "further encroachment on the rights and duties of local peace officers." Taking a slightly different means of opposition, Senator Claude Holloway argued that the state already had three thousand police officers and that "29 more would not solve the crime problem."[87]

On Thursday, February 14, the Chrisp/Carter State Police bill came up for a vote in the House. In the ensuing debate, Representative Chrisp stuck to politically safe territory by arguing that the State Police would lead to improved enforcement of traffic laws and a reduction in Arkansas' "appalling" traffic fatality rate. Chrisp also relied on the examples provided by pro-state police literature to help make his case for creation of such a force in Arkansas. Unimpressed by Chrisp's arguments, Pope County Representative Dolan Burris remarked, "I have only one eye, but ... I could see flaws in this bill if I didn't have a damned eye in my head." The flaw that Burris most feared was the power a state police force might provide to a governor. He argued that "[p]olitical machines of the past would look like pikers compared to what a state police force would cause." Burris also doubted such a force could actually provide efficient enforcement of the law and predicted that the State Police officers would be more likely to "sit in their cars smoking a cigar and listening to the radio ... and maybe have a bottle of legalized liquor."[88] After a third reading, the House passed a motion to delay consideration of the Chrisp/Carter bill until February 18.

Before the bill could be brought up a second time, a washed-up professional boxer named Joe "Kid" Peck provided the State Police supporters with a tragic example of just how dangerous cars could be. On Saturday, a car, which the papers would dub the "Death Car," struck and killed a man and a woman who were attempting to cross a Little Rock street. Such a tragedy was not a particularly unusual occurrence in Little Rock. In fact, 13 pedestrians had already been killed in the first seven weeks of 1935.[89] What made the "Death Car" different was the inability of the local police to find it. In desperation, city officials encouraged Little Rock residents to be on the lookout for damaged cars with traces of blood. The car was located on February 19, and Joe Peck was identified as its driver. But for several days, the image of a "Death Car" roaming the streets of Little Rock provided ample fodder for arguments by State Police advocates.

When the House met to discuss the Chrisp/Carter bill on February 18, Representative Blair theorized that if a State Police force had existed, the driver of the "Death Car" would have been caught quickly since they were not restricted by narrow jurisdictions. Representative Wilkes lamented the high fatality rates by noting 37 people had already died in traffic accidents that might have been prevented if a State Police force had been patrolling the highways.[90] Whether it was because of the "Death Car" or not is unknown, but one representative who spoke against the Chrisp/Carter bill on Thursday had a change of heart and spoke for its passage on February 18. Not all of its opponents were similarly moved, with this debate focusing on the added cost of the State Police. As initially designed, the bill estimated an annual cost of $150,000 to $300,000, which the supporters argued would be more than repaid by the number of lives saved and property protected. With all of their arguments exhausted, the House began voting and passed the Chrisp/Carter State Police bill 67 to 30. Still, its biggest challenge lay ahead in the Senate, which already had the head of one State Police bill mounted on its wall and had indefinitely sidelined the only other attempt to appear before it.

In early March, the legislature passed a bill, known as the Thorn Liquor bill after its sponsor, House Speaker Harve Thorn, that legalized all forms of liquor in Arkansas for the first time since 1915.[91] The governor made it known that he would sign the Thorn bill only if the legislature created a State Police force to enforce its provisions. The passage of the bill had been hard fought and with only a few weeks left in the legislative session, the likelihood that an override of the governor's veto could actually be maneuvered seem doubtful.

In response, the Senate moved quickly to bring the Chrisp/Carter House bill, which had languished in the Senate Judiciary Committee for two weeks, up for debate. In a letter to the Senate Judiciary Committee, Governor Futrell strongly recommended they not "curtail their (State Police's) power" since "crime and automobile accidents are two of the greatest problems confronting our people today." Ever mindful of the budgetary restraints of the state, he noted, "in addition to regulating traffic, thereby saving lives and property ... a very slight reduction in crime in this State would more than compensate financially."[92] The governor's plea did not prove particularly effective in preventing the committee from altering the bill. Eight amendments were added that reduced salaries and personnel, prevented the use of the State Police in interfering in labor disputes, and specifically ordered all State Police personnel to refrain from getting involved in political activity.[93] Senator Roy Milum unsuccessfully attempted to introduce a number of other amendments to the bill that would have limited the authority of the State Police to enforcing traffic laws solely in rural areas and specifying that even in these rural areas the ultimate authority would still be the sheriff.[94]

Three days later, the bill cleared its subcommittee and came up for a floor debate. As expected the amended bill met with "strenuous opposition," which argued that the force was "too centralized" and "just another movement to provide more jobs and to help build a bigger political machine." Supporters countered that it would "curb the crime wave sweeping Arkansas" and "would remove the stigma of open places which are violating the laws … and which have not been closed or their operators arrested by local authorities.[95]

These arguments represented a predictable response, but possibly the most persuasive argument was the governor's promise to sign the Thorn Liquor bill if the Senate passed the State Police bill. Faced with a veto of the only liquor bill passed by the General Assembly, the senators had to decide which was more important: local control and lower expenses or legalization of liquor and a State Police force. They chose liquor and the State Police by a vote of 24 to eight.

On March 19, 1935, Governor Futrell signed the amended Chrisp/Carter bill, known as Act 120 of 1935, and created the first true State Police force in Arkansas. The Act established an independent three-member State Police Commission, appointed by the governor, which would then organize the Department of State Police and provide oversight of its operations. Initially, the State Police would consist of a superintendent, an assistant superintendent, two captains, two lieutenants, seven rangers, and a stenographer. The duties of the State Rangers were very broad and included enforcing criminal and traffic laws, collecting delinquent motor vehicle-related taxes, assisting county and city officers as necessary, acting as the state fire marshal, conducting arson investigations, establishing and maintaining a bureau of criminal identification, and enforcing motor vehicle weights and standards regulations.[96] The Act also mandated that while the State Police's authority was statewide, they were not created to undermine the authority of local officers.

With the Chrisp/Carter bill providing the organizational framework of the State Police, a means of funding this new agency needed to be established. To remedy this deficiency, the Senate Budget Committee introduced Senate Bill 534 on March 11. The bill proposed to levy a 50-cent fee on each driver's license. A portion of the proceeds from the license fee would be dedicated to fund the State Police's nearly $60,000 annual budget. With less than a week remaining in the 1935 legislative session, both the House and Senate had to consider and vote on this measure in near record time. Spurred by threats from Governor Futrell to use his veto on the Thorn Liquor Bill, the legislature pushed the bill through in two days.[97] In addition to providing funding for the State Police, the bill, known as Act 132 of 1935, added enforcement of liquor laws to the duties of the State Police. This addition was of immense importance to the governor, who considered it to be one of the most crucial responsibilities of the State Police.[98]

Though often overlooked by historians, the creation of a State Police force had fundamental implications for the future of Arkansas. First and foremost, it strengthened the state government by providing the legislature and the governor with an enforcement arm that could rigidly enforce locally unpopular and often ignored state laws like those restricting gambling or alcohol. The State Police also provided a higher authority for Arkansans of limited economic means and minimal political clout to appeal improper actions by local officers. Plus, the creation of what would become a large body of trained officers equipped with the latest in police-related equipment significantly improved the efficiency and effectiveness of law enforcement within the state.

Before any of these benefits could be realized though, State Police proponents had to overcome more than 130 years of tradition that believed the reach of power and authority should not extend beyond the county line, and whose arguments were fortified by the desperate finances of a poor state. Overcoming these arguments required the death of one progressive, state-centered program—prohibition—to see the birth of another. Considering the tremendous level of authority granted to a State Police force, it seems clear that the latter presented an equally significant change in the relationship between the state and its citizens. Thus, the success of Governor Futrell and the pro-State Police movement should be considered an important component of Arkansas' continued transition into a more modern South as defined by a stronger, more progressive state government and the decline of localism.

Chapter 2

A Burgeoning Force, 1935-1944

*"Young, but experienced, and both are eager to make a
success of the new undertaking."*
> State Police Commissioner W. V. Thompkins describing the
> department's top two officers, A. G. Albright and Bob LaFollette.

*"The one great desire of a small group was to limit the power
of the state police, in order that the governor could not order
them to certain counties to stop gambling and bookie joints."*
> State Senators W. K. Oldham and Henry Hardy on the efforts by a
> group of legislators to restrict the mission of the State Police to just
> highway patrol.

Following the passage of the Acts creating and funding the State Police,
Governor Futrell fulfilled his promise to sign the Thorn liquor bill on
March 17 and ended 20 years of a near total prohibition of alcohol within
Arkansas. The almost immediate resumption of liquor sales produced an
urgency to get the Arkansas Rangers up and running. Within a few days,
Futrell had appointed W .V. Tompkins, S. L. Cooke, and John P. Woods to
the State Police Commission and tasked them with reviewing the
applicants and selecting the members of the new force. Pursuant to Futrell's
past history of not allowing political favoritism to influence the hiring
process in state government, the commission operated fairly independently
of the governor's office. Futrell did request that the commission provide
him with a list of recommended officers and demanded that the son of an
unnamed sheriff not be hired, but otherwise he allowed the commission to
use their best judgment in hiring the 13 original Rangers.

The commission's first move was to review applicants for the position of superintendent. Since early March, the state's press had reported rumors that the governor's son-in-law and personal secretary, Grady McCall, was the frontrunner for the position. The papers were correct that McCall wanted the job, but the governor refused to use his influence to win it for him and instead steadfastly adhered to his vision of a non-political force. Another strong candidate was former Little Rock Police Chief Burl Rotenberry. Rotenberry deservedly enjoyed a good reputation from his time running the state's largest police force, and his efforts to stop mob violence and create a professional force made him an obvious and likely candidate.

One applicant who did not find a place on anyone's watch list was Jackson County's circuit clerk, A. G. "Gray" Albright. Albright had law enforcement experience following seven years as a chief deputy and two terms as sheriff in Jackson County. This was also a time in which Albright was politically active in lobbying the state legislature to increase the fees paid by the state to sheriffs. Such efforts probably did not endear him to Futrell, considering the governor's frugal nature, and it seems clear from correspondence that if Futrell had been picking the superintendent, Albright would not have been a candidate.

With the governor content to let the commission sort through the growing stack of applications that "even a state ranger couldn't jump over," it quickly became obvious they were going to earn the $7.50 per day they were allowed by the new law.[99] They also realized that the new law had created a top-heavy force with six members holding the rank of lieutenant or above and only seven rangers.[100] Reorganizing the department could wait, though, as they narrowed their search for the top two positions. For several days, the three interviewed applicants before making their decision and calling Gray Albright to their room on the evening of March 27. When Albright arrived, W. V. Tompkins, the commission chairman, opened the door and said, "Mr. Albright, I want you to meet your new assistant, Bob LaFollette."[101] Before becoming the assistant superintendent, LaFollette was the chief of police at Siloam

Springs and had earned a bit of notoriety through his involvement in a shootout with the Karpis-Barker gang. Chairman Tompkins described the two men as "young, but experienced, and both are eager to make a success of the new undertaking."[102]

With Albright and LaFollette on board, the State Police began the process of hiring the rest of the force. They borrowed two typists from the state's bonding department to prepare and mail formal applications to the almost 1,500 people who wrote or made personal inquiries about obtaining a position as a Ranger. This nearly overwhelming demand was caused in part by the tremendous interest such a force generated in the state, but another huge factor was the dire economic conditions the state found itself in during the mid 1930s. One applicant summed up the feelings of many Arkansans in a letter to the governor's secretary, writing, "God knows I need [a job]."[103]

The requirement that applicants return a rather lengthy application weeded out more than half of the initial requests, but that still left the staff and commission to choose from 600 men to fill 11 positions. Since the State Police would not have the time or resources to train the original Rangers before placing them in service, Albright and LaFollette looked for applicants who had prior police experience. Also, they tried to find suitable candidates from every region of the state so they wouldn't have to transfer anyone in order to provide suitable coverage. After spending the next month reviewing applications, the two men selected 28 of the 600 applicants to complete a written exam and oral interview.[104] The written exam was fairly lengthy and posed a number of scenarios that a Ranger might run into during his patrol.[105] From this final group, six men were chosen to become Rangers on April 30. The six offered positions were: C. T. Atkinson, Bert Frazier, Lindsay Hatchett, Gene Mooney, Ed Clark, and Louis Fishback, Jr. Atkinson joined the force as a captain and operated out of Little Rock along with Albright and LaFollette. While the others, except for Fishback, would work in their home regions. In Fishback's case, he declined the appointment and the Rangers selected John Hendricks who was an alternate from that region.[106]

Over the course of that summer, the remaining five members of the original 13 Rangers were hired. This group included Neal Shannon, G. D. Morris, J. E. Sewell, J. P. "Frip" Hill, and Earl Scroggin. Of the five, Scroggin was the one Albright refused to let get away. Scroggin headed the Little Rock police department's identification bureau and was extremely well respected for his expertise in this emerging area of police work. Scroggin did not set out to become an expert at identification when he joined the Little Rock police department in 1925 as a motorcycle patrol officer. Fate would intervene three months after he started work when he was seriously injured in a traffic accident. The severity of his injuries confined Scroggin to desk duty for the rest of his career.[107] In order to pull Scroggin away from Little Rock, Albright offered him one of the two lieutenant slots, which provided a slightly higher annual salary and more prestige.[108] Luckily for the state, Scroggin accepted the position and set out to create a statewide identification bureau from scratch. By the summer of 1936, Scroggin was well on his way with more than 55,000 criminal records on file in Little Rock from which he used fingerprint analysis to assist investigators in 64 crimes during the following year.[109]

While Lieutenant Scroggin began to put together the identification bureau during the summer and fall of 1935, the fledging State Police and its Rangers focused on enforcing the new liquor laws and rooting out moonshiners and bootleggers. By the end of June 1936, they would make nearly 1,100 arrests for violations of the liquor law, including 82 people for operating stills and 49 for possessing one.[110] By comparison, the Rangers would make a little more than 800 arrests for traffic violations with the largest charge being improper lighting on vehicles. Ranger Frip Hill, working in conjunction with local sheriff's deputies and revenue agents, made one of the largest liquor busts in the state when they found and destroyed a 100-gallon still outside El Dorado. This bust was just one of the 160 stills destroyed during the year.[111]

The Ranger's focus on liquor violations during their first year of operation earned the State Police a wealth of criticism from the state's press and civic leaders who believed they should have been concentrating on traffic enforcement. The increase in auto fatalities in Arkansas from 347 to 391 during 1935 spurred much of these complaints.[112] As a result, Albright promised to have his Rangers focus more on traffic enforcement in 1936. A promise reflected in the increase in traffic arrests to more than double the number of liquor arrests over the next two years (1936-1938).[113]

In addition to the State Police's rededication to traffic enforcement, they were involved in two high-profile investigations that produced national headlines. In late March 1936, the State Police and the Federal Bureau of Investigation (FBI) received a tip that one of America's most wanted gangsters, Alvin Karpis, was hiding out in a house on Lake Hamilton outside Hot Springs. Federal agents raided the suspected hideout, but Karpis was not inside. Believing him to be nearby, officers from the State Police and Garland County sheriff's department were called in to conduct a manhunt of the area. The manhunt did not turn up Karpis, who had been tipped off by members of the Hot Springs police department and fled to New Orleans.

A few weeks later another notorious gangster would not be so "lucky." Charles "Lucky" Luciano. Luciano had been instrumental in establishing and helping run the mafia in New York by turning it into an efficient, business-like operation that included narcotics, gambling, prostitution, liquor, guns, and murder. In 1936, the New York Attorney General issued a warrant for Luciano's arrest, and officers narrowly missed nabbing him at his New York City apartment.

Luciano promptly fled to Hot Springs, which was known as a safe haven for a number of high-profile gangsters. Shortly thereafter, a New York City police officer vacationing in Hot Springs recognized Luciano and reported the sighting back to the state's Attorney General. The New York Attorney General did not trust the local officers to guard Luciano, so the State Police were called on to transport him to

Little Rock and provide a Ranger as his constant companion until he could be extradited to New York to stand trial. While in State Police custody, Luciano was reported to have offered Ranger Captain C. T. Atkinson and Arkansas' Attorney General Carl Bailey $50,000 to allow him to escape custody.

The second high profile incident of 1936 was the rangers' involvement in the Southern Tenant Farmers' Union (STFU) strike in east Arkansas. The STFU was a union composed of black and white sharecroppers working in the cotton fields of east Arkansas who went on strike in 1935 and again in 1936 to protest the low pay planters were providing for their efforts. The planters reacted vigorously to protect their economic positions. The plantations' "riding bosses" began patrolling the roads and highways looking for union leaders and breaking up union meetings. Night riding, which often featured masked gunmen shooting into houses, was another tactic employed to terrorize striking sharecroppers. In addition to the use of vigilante-style terror tactics, the planters' influence with the local political establishment ensured local authorities would do nothing to interfere. A Marked Tree woman remembered that "the landlords have all turned to nite Riding and Mr. Dubard the sheriff was asked to stop it and he replied I cant stop it."[114] When local officers were not ignoring the problems, they were active participants. One deputy sheriff in Earle was actually convicted of peonage after 13 union members he arrested were conveniently assigned to work on his farm to pay off their fines and successfully complete their sentences.

The State Police would get involved in the STFU strike when a local union organizer, Clay East, was attacked by a mob on his way out of an east Arkansas courthouse. A witness to the attack ran to a phone and called State Police headquarters, reaching Captain C. T. Atkinson and demanded they rescue East before he was beaten to death or lynched. Fortunately for East, an unidentified man intervened and succeeded in calming the mob enough to get East taken to jail instead of the nearest tree branch with a rope around his neck. While he was in the county jail, the sheriff arrived and made sure the mob stayed away until Captain Atkinson and the rangers arrived. In short order East, Atkinson, and the sheriff shuffled out to a waiting car and sped to the relative safety of Memphis.[115]

The escalating violence between the planters and the union finally prompted Governor Futrell to call out the National Guard and dispatch the Rangers to east Arkansas to conduct regular patrols and bring order from the chaos. These patrols did act as a calming factor for the disorder that was raging in the cotton fields, but the conflict did not truly cool off until the union agreed to go back to work after the planters agreed to increase their pay to $0.75 for every 100 pounds of cotton picked.

The momentary calm dissolved in the summer of 1937 when the union again went on strike for higher wages. This time the State Police were quickly dispatched at the first sign of trouble between the planters and the union members. The sharecroppers' newspaper praised the actions of the officers, noting their presence at an open-air union meeting was the only thing that prevented violence from an anti-union mob that assembled to disrupt the proceedings. Also, the State Police were assigned to courthouse security throughout the summer thereby preventing any recurrences of mob violence against union members.[116]

The State Police force that deployed to east Arkansas in the summer of 1937 was a much different organization than the one that patrolled the roads and highways in 1936. The election of a new governor, Carl Bailey, in November 1936 and the passage of some significant State Police-related legislation by the General Assembly in early 1937 had expanded the force and modified the direction of this organization.

The first issue that confronted the State Police following Governor Bailey's election was the fate of Superintendent Albright. In a scene that would recur nearly every time a new governor was elected, the incoming chief executive began to speculate on replacing the head of the State Police. In 1937, the governor did not actually have the power to fire Albright. The State Police Commission was the only body with that authority, and it could only do so for cause, which was something Albright had not given them in the first two years. Despite the public speculation, Bailey decided not to push the issue and voiced his support for Albright.

The commissioners' positions were also protected by the original act creating the State Police. This technicality would not deter Bailey from seeking to restock the commission with his own appointees, and he requested that Superintendent Albright ask the current commissioners to "voluntarily" resign their positions so Bailey could name his own commission. Such an unpleasant task bothered Albright who had enjoyed working with the three men, but the governor felt strongly enough on the issue that he had vowed to change the legislation if he needed to replace the current commission. Albright remembered that the commission "very reluctantly submitted their resignations" in early January.[117]

With his own commission in place, Bailey felt comfortable enough to push for an expansion of the force in both size and responsibility. On January 28, Representative Wilkerson introduced House Bill 246. The bill called for the merger of the highway patrol force that the Revenue Department still operated (the Road Patrol was not actually disbanded in 1935 when the State Police was created) and the State Police's highway patrol into a new Department of State Police. Also, the new Department of State Police would oversee the highly political programs of parole and clemency. The added workload produced by these new duties necessitated an expansion of the force and for this reason the bill proposed an increase to 55 officers.[118]

Even though HB 246 enjoyed the support of the Arkansas Sheriffs' Association, numerous prosecuting attorneys, and county collectors, a significant number of foes emerged in the House. For the most part, these were the same opponents who objected to the creation of the State Police in 1935. One of the provisions the opponents were particularly upset about was the governor's ability to dispatch State

Police officers without waiting on a request by the local officials. Representative Ward pushed hard to have this power stripped from the bill by arguing it eliminated the citizens' constitutional rights.[119] The editor of the *Arkansas Democrat* agreed with Representative Ward and believed that giving the governor such power would lead to the inevitable decline of the force into a political organization.[120] A majority of representatives agreed with Ward, and the bill was amended to restrict the ability of the governor to deploy the State Police and then overwhelming passed by the House on February 11 and the Senate on February 19.

In a way, the passage of the bill represented the end of an era since the reorganized Department of State Police would no longer refer to their officers as "rangers" and instead began calling them "patrolmen."

Expanding the State Police from 13 to 55 created two immediate dilemmas for the department—where to find more than 40 qualified men and how to train them. Since jobs were still difficult to come by in Arkansas, the State Police had more than enough applicants to choose from, but with such a large number of new hires, it was unrealistic to limit the pool of applicants just to those with law enforcement experience. To overcome this restriction, the department began to plan and prepare for the State Police's first training academy. In the meantime, they narrowed the approximately 2,000 applicants down to 172 who were given written exams and from which 51 were hired.[121]

The 51 new members of the State Police, along with all of the current members of the department, quickly headed to Camp Pike to attend the first training academy in State Police history on April 19, 1937. For five weeks, the men would live in tents, rising at 6:00 a.m. to spend 11 hours working in either the classroom or in the field, learning law, geography, highway patrol, military drill, firearms, and the operation of motorcycles. When the academy concluded in mid-May, 47 officers were awarded permanent positions and four were placed on reserve status. In another first for the State Police, Patrolman L. R. Biggs became the first officer assigned to Governor's Security.[122]

A few months after completing the training academy, Sergeants Gene Mooney and Neal Shannon were on patrol in southwest Arkansas when they spotted a car matching the description of one stolen a few weeks prior and used in a July 8 bank robbery in Werner, Arkansas. Although neither officer knew it, inside the car were four armed fugitives from Texas who were dead set against going back to the penitentiary. When the fugitives saw the state patrol car following them, a chase ensued. Frustrated by their inability to shake the officers, the robbers swerved off the highway onto a narrow forest road, kicking up a cloud of dust and putting some distance between themselves and their pursuers. Shannon, who was driving, pressed on as quickly as the rough road and choking dust allowed.

Just when it seemed their visibility was improving they were faced with the gut clinching sight of the fugitives' car blocking the road and all four men targeting the officers' car with pistols and shotguns. Shannon slammed on the brakes and brought the patrol car to a quick stop as the two patrolmen struggled to throw open their doors and bring their weapons to bear. The outlaws fired first. Shotgun pellets and pistol rounds slammed into the patrol car. One of the shotgun blasts ripped into the driver's side door with several pellets striking Shannon in the chest and hand. In response, Sergeant Mooney opened fire with a Thompson submachine gun and watched as the huge .45 caliber slugs struck one of the fugitives in the head and knocked the pistol out of the hand of another. Seeing one of their partners in crime killed by Mooney's machine gun blast convinced the remaining three fugitives to make a quick exit. A move that Mooney did not contest since he was now outnumbered three to one.

For the next few days, state, county, and local officers converged in the area east of Monticello looking for the three men and even made use of an airplane to aid in the search for the first time in State Police history.[123] This time the three convicts would slip the officers' net and get out of the state before being captured.

The summer of 1937 was proving to be one full of confrontation as the State Police would be involved in another high-profile shootout in August. Alfred "Sonny" Lamb was a member of a loose-knit gang of criminals that operated throughout the Southwest. One by one the members of this group were picked up in raids around the state. Lamb, who was wanted in connection with three robberies and several murders, had been under surveillance by the State Police for two days before they decided to raid his Hot Springs home. Led by Captain Atkinson, four State Police and a number of local officers warily approached Lamb's house under the cover of darkness. As the raiding party approached, they could see Lamb sitting in a chair listening to a radio. The group split into pairs with one covering the back door and the other heading to the front, but before the officers could execute the raid, Lamb caught a glimpse of the men. Leaping to his feet, he sprinted toward the bedroom where he kept his weapons, a fact that Atkinson and the other officers were well aware of. Atkinson and the other officers raised their submachine guns and shotguns and fired bursts that tore through the thin walls and windows of Lamb's house. Atkinson's quick firing caught Lamb before he was able to reach his weapons, killing him, but luckily missing Lamb's wife, who had no idea of her new husband's criminal activity.[124]

While the entire state's attention was focused on Hot Springs due to the Lamb shootout, the *Arkansas Democrat* began running front-page stories publicizing the open gambling occurring in the resort city. This was not the first time public calls for reform in Hot Springs had sounded through the state, but it was the first time Arkansas had a statewide police force with the authority to do something about it.

This controversy was the last thing Superintendent Albright wanted to get involved in and wondered "why the responsibility of all the gambling in the state of Arkansas should be placed on my shoulders." Albright reminded everyone that they had too few men to properly conduct highway patrol and revenue enforcement, not to mention investigating charges of gambling. He did concede that the

State Police would serve any warrants that local authorities chose to swear out.[125] In this instance, the controversy proved short-lived, and gambling would continue unabated in Hot Springs, although that city's political machine, gambling, and the State Police would clash on several occasions over the next 30 years.[126]

The fall of 1937 would see the most important technological advance that the State Police would experience for nearly 50 years when the first radio system went on the air at 8:10 a.m. on October 5. The new 1,000-watt transmitter was hardly a powerhouse, and its signal could only be received within 75 miles of the tower during the day. At night though, the reception improved, and it was possible to pick up headquarters almost anywhere in the state. The difference between "possible" and "likely" were two completely different situations, however, and often the low-band AM signal degenerated into static. Two men, each one working a single shift, kept the transmitter humming from eight in the morning until midnight.[127] Also, the central location and availability of the radio operators often found them acting as a sort of press secretary for the department when big events would occur.

The first bulletin the station issued was a notice of a stolen Nash sedan in Hot Springs. The car was found two hours later just outside the spa city. Receiving the new signal were 32 patrol cars and two motorcycles, which were the only patrol units with receivers. None of the units had a transmitter and thus could not talk back to State Police headquarters. If an officer needed to speak with headquarters, he had to stop and find a phone to check in. Before the installation of radio receivers, headquarters would typically call the sheriff's office and have them track down the patrolman to pass along a message.[128] Alternatively, the officer could make regular stops on his patrol to call in to receive any bulletins or messages.

One reason for the lag in upgrading the department's technology was a lack of funding. The State Police still relied on revenue from the annual sale of drivers' licenses, but with the expansion of the department they required a certain level of sales to meet their budget.

In the fall of 1938 the sale of drivers' licenses fell far below expectations, and as a result the funds flowing into the State Police's banks account were not keeping up with expenses.

When the state legislature met in 1939, the financial difficulties of the State Police were well known, and a bill was passed in late January to increase the drivers' license fee from 35 cents to 50 cents and to authorize Albright to hire 13 new officers.[129] In mid August 1939, with Europe poised on the brink of the Second World War, Albright hired the new officers and immediately sent the men through a training academy.[130]

The addition of more officers necessitated, for the first time, creation of formal "troops," or districts, around the state to provide command and control for their officers. Five districts were created with each one commanded by a sergeant. Troop One was in Little Rock and had 11 patrolmen, Troop Two was in Newport and had nine patrolmen, Troop Three was in Fort Smith and had seven patrolmen, Troop Four was in Hope and had seven patrolmen, and Troop Five was in El Dorado and had seven patrolmen. The Uniform Division, as the Highway Patrol Division was then called, operated regular patrols in two-man cars from 2:00 p.m. until 12:00 a.m. every day.[131]

When Germany's invasion of Poland on September 1, 1939, triggered a world war, the United States began preparing for their role in the new conflict. Defense spending increased, new weapons systems were approved, and the nation began to buzz over the possibility of a peacetime draft. Still, the general mood was one that reflected America's confidence that France and Great Britain would be more than capable of handling German aggression without the United States' direct intervention. These feelings of comfort and security came crashing down in the second week of May 1940 when the Nazi blitzkrieg sliced through French and British defensive positions in northern France. Within a few weeks, the British expeditionary force was forced to flee the Continent at Dunkirk, and the French government was suing for peace to stop the German war machine.

The terrifying power of the German military sparked near hysteria in the United States over fears of saboteurs, or "fifth columnists," wreaking havoc on war-related industries and critical infrastructure. In response, Governor Bailey ordered the State Police to investigate all tips of fifth columnists and began to create a state defense board, warning that "the only thing worse than hysteria is complacency."[132] One of the first moves the state made was to ask all aliens to register with the State Police or local authorities by providing fingerprints, photos, names, addresses, and occupations. By October 1940, nearly nine hundred aliens would comply with the request.[133] Those Arkansans who were born in a country aligned with the Axis Powers were asked to turn in their firearms, radio transmitters, and cameras when the United States did finally enter the war in late 1941.[134]

Bailey also pushed for the creation of a home guard to replace the Arkansas National Guard, which had been called into active duty. Bailey's final term as governor would end before any real progress could be made in creating a home guard, and his successor, Homer Adkins, expressed little initial support for such an organization. Governor Adkins would change his mind, though, in May 1941 when he had to call on the State Police and beg the release of 400 active-duty soldiers from Camp Robinson to guard a Little Rock courthouse during the trial of a black man accused of assaulting a white girl.[135] Instead of relying on untrained citizens, Adkins' vision of a home guard was one that consisted of police officers from around the state and overseen by Superintendent Albright. Albright and the state's Defense Council divided the state into five home guard districts with each district tasked with "quelling any disturbances or disorders in defense industries." Each member of the guard would be issued a steel helmet and a red, white, and blue armband bearing the initials "H. G."[136] The plan proved popular with officers, for by the time of the Japanese attack on Pearl Harbor on December 7, the Arkansas home guard had more than 1,000 law enforcement officers enrolled and ready for duty.[137]

Arkansas' war fears also encouraged the legislature to pass four key pieces of State Police legislation in 1941. The first increased the size of the State Police. The second provided funding for a statewide radio network. The third allowed the State Police to establish a retirement system for their officers, and the last demanded that the State Police remove politics from the agency.[138] The last bill sought to improve on the perceived neutrality of the State Police by hiring officers on merit alone and forbidding patrolmen from being active in state, national, or local political races.[139]

In Albright's eyes, the expansion of the department could not occur soon enough because in August the United States Army was planning on conducting the largest peacetime maneuvers in their history in southwest Arkansas. An estimated 100,000 soldiers would conduct war games in the Hope area for two weeks, and the State Police would be in charge of traffic control and policing this huge event. One of the concerns of law enforcement agencies was the influx of prostitutes to the area. In the weeks leading up to the event, officers arrested 75 enterprising women for this charge.[140]

With this pressure driving them, the State Police hired 21 men to fill 16 vacancies and sent them through a training academy in June 1941. The average dimensions of the recruits reflected Albright's belief that "size has its psychology," with the average height and weight measured at six feet, 200 pounds. For the first time, the school was not held at Camp Robinson. That facility was filled to capacity with National Guard troops from around the country undergoing training in preparation for the coming war. Instead, the 21 men would live and train at the State Teachers' College (now the University of Central Arkansas) in Conway. Unlike past training academies, these men would not have to sleep in tents and instead slept in dorms and ate in the school cafeteria. The loss of the army base's firing range also necessitated a change in the location of target practice. All training in the proper operation of pistols and shotguns was given at the college's diary farm.[141]

Ultimately, the maneuvers went off without a hitch, although there was an embarrassing incident between State Police officers and black troops. Arkansas, like the rest of the South, supported a segregated and unequal society. For this reason black troops, who were predominately from northern states, presented an unusual sight to white southerners. In this instance, State Police officers ordered the black troops to the side of the road to allow another convoy to pass. The white officer in charge of the black troops took exception to this slight and began an argument. The argument quickly escalated into pushing and shoving between the police officers and the soldiers. As a result of the confrontation, a number of the black soldiers went AWOL and hopped trains they hoped would take them out of Arkansas. The unit's commanding general noted the next day that "the racial difficulties ...have been settled satisfactorily, but some of the northern Negroes, not understanding the attitudes of the southerner and apparently to avoid further trouble have left their command."

A similar situation would develop in Little Rock due to the presence of large numbers of black troops training at Camp Robinson. A confrontation between a Little Rock police officer and a black soldier ended violently when the officer shot and killed the man. The resulting outrage over the shooting led the army to detail military police officers to patrol "sections frequented" by the black troops when they were allowed to visit Little Rock on Wednesdays, Saturdays, and Sundays.[142] The city of Little Rock decided to hire blacks as "special policemen" to patrol along Ninth Street to prevent racial disturbances.[143]

In addition to the massive Army maneuvers, the summer of 1941 would see the first flashes of an issue that would nearly consume the State Police for the next three years and would, arguably, play a key role in the removal of the department's top two officers and a near complete organizational restructuring. On July 12, Hot Springs resident Horace Whyte made a public appeal to Governor Adkins to stop open gambling in Hot Springs. The governor was a devout Methodist and despised gambling in any form, but decided to be non-committal in his response and stated that he would "look into the matter in due time."[144]

Two months later, Adkins decided that the time had arrived to make a proper response. He demanded that all gambling in the state stop immediately and identified Phillips, Pulaski, and Garland counties as the worst offenders. He noted that recent raids by State Police officers in Forrest City were conducted at the request of a local circuit judge and warned that if other local officials did not follow suit, the state would conduct raids on their own initiative.[145]

Such threats undoubtedly concerned Albright who convincingly argued that despite the recent expansion of the force, the 60 or so officers were already greatly overworked. Not only had a recent rise in the number of auto fatalities in the state increased the pressure on the State Police to expand their highway patrol efforts, they were also expected to escort all military convoys, assist local officers, help guard defense plants, and work the numerous county fairs that occurred every fall. As a result of these demands, Albright found that they no longer had the time or personnel to enforce liquor laws, much less enforce gambling laws.[146] Instead of immediately committing officers to the task, Albright began by meeting with local officials and urging them to enforce the state's gambling laws. In Phillips County, a local citizen's committee responded and confiscated 200 slot machines whose operation over the past two years was rumored to have raised half a million dollars for their owners.[147]

Publicly, Garland County looked as though it would follow suit. Local officials claimed that the "horse parlors," or off-track betting rooms, in the six largest casinos were closing due to Governor Adkins' request. This public face was quickly shown to be a sham when the Arkansas Democrat reported that these operations had simply moved upstairs. For the rest of 1941, rumors of raids would temporarily close the bookies in Hot Springs, but when no police cruisers followed, they opened back up and continued as normal.[148]

The hands-off approach by the State Police ended abruptly on January 24, 1942, when "Adkins cracked his whip" and 12 State Police officers raided the six largest bookie joints in Hot Springs: the Southern Club, the Ohio Club, the Ozark Club, the Blue Ribbon Club, the Citizen's Club, and the White Front. Each horse parlor was assigned two officers, with one covering the front and the other the back. At exactly 1:45 p.m. the men simultaneously raided the clubs, which were full of afternoon bettors. The officers allowed the bettors to leave, but detained the employees and began tearing the telephones from the walls, smashing roulette wheels and dice tables, and confiscating loudspeakers, betting forms, and other paraphernalia. As a crowd gathered outside the clubs to gawk, a number of the spectators expressed their discontent with the situation when they realized they would not be collecting on their winning tickets.

When the raid was complete and all of the contraband loaded in the police cruisers, Superintendent Albright went to talk with each club's owner. He told them that the raid was a direct order from the governor and that all of the items seized would be destroyed, except for the telephones, which were too valuable to be destroyed and would be returned to the phone company. In the 1940s, telephones were extremely costly and had to be purchased, or more likely rented, from the phone company. With the United States embroiled in a war, telephones became even scarcer, so their confiscation represented a true blow to the casinos.[149]

The bookies did not stay out of business long, and in March the State Police raided eight locations, finding activity at three, including one betting room unknowingly leased to gamblers by the local American Legion post. Along with raids in Hot Springs, State Police coordinated with county and local officials to raid gambling establishments in Pulaski and Phillips County.[150]

Adkins' war on gambling would cool off over the summer as the governor focused more on campaigning for a second term. Shortly after the election, though, the State Police would return to Hot Springs and raid the Southern, Ohio, Citizen, Blue Ribbon, and White Front clubs. This time the officers would arrest the clubs' owners and employees in addition to confiscating gambling paraphernalia. This raid touched off a controversy over the legality of the warrants the State Police used as their authority to enter the private clubs. In the original raids in January and March, a friendly state supreme court justice, Wendell Griffin, had issued the search warrants, but a subsequent lawsuit had found such a practice to be unconstitutional. The November raids were done without the benefit of a search warrant. The leader of the raids, Assistant Superintendent Atkinson, dryly remarked that "we just happened to run across them over here and happened to walk in on all of them at the same time."[151] Predictably, the gamblers countered that the raids were a form of harassment. Also, the *Democrat* questioned the effectiveness of the raids by noting that anyone who wanted to place a wager on a horse race could do so despite the raids.[152]

The *Democrat*'s observation was undoubtedly true, but the State Police raids were hurting the gambling interests and impinging on their profits. Proof of this can be seen in the 1943 legislative session, which found the Hot Springs political machine fighting back. On January 27, long-time State Police opponents Roy Milum and W. L. Ward introduced Senate Bill 113, which sought to limit the State Police's authority to enforcing just traffic laws and forbidding them from enforcing criminal laws unless it was "the expressed request of the sheriff, prosecuting attorney, or circuit judge of the county or district in which they were called to act."[153] The Senate Judiciary Committee assigned the bill a "do not pass" recommendation, normally a sure sign the bill was destined to fail, but this bill would find support where others did not. The bill came up for a "heated debate" in February with the opponents of the bill arguing that if it passed, the state would return to counties being run by political bosses. Senators Milum and Ward countered that the State Police had been created as a highway patrol organization and that they should stick to that duty. After several hours of debate, the Senate finally began to vote, and as the roll was being taken, it was clear that it would be close. When it was complete, the State Police's flexibility and original mission had survived by just a single vote.[154]

The defeat of SB 113 did not mean the legislative challenges to the State Police were over. With the legislative session in its last weeks, the Senate began considering appropriation bills for numerous state agencies, one of which was the State Police. A so-called "economy bloc" of senators, which was led by Senator Milum, wanted the budgets of several state agencies reduced. The bloc had sufficient votes to prevent the passage of any appropriations bill, so their threats were taken seriously. After several days of negotiations between the governor's office and the bloc, the two sides failed to reach a compromise, and the closer the legislature came to the end of the session the more frantic the appeals for compromise became.

The lieutenant governor offered to act as a mediator and chaired a meeting between the two sides on March 8. After two days of negotiations punctuated by charges from the economy bloc that the Adkins' administration was the "most extravagant, most hypocritical, most political in an unsavory sense, that Arkansas has known since Civil War Reconstruction," the governor's office agreed to reduce the State Police budget by approximately 10 percent or $25,300, and the appropriations bill passed the Senate.[155] After the session had ended, two state senators expressed their belief on the true intent of the "economy bloc," when they told a reporter that

> the one great desire of a small group was to limit the power of the state police, in order that the governor could not order them to certain counties to stop gambling and bookie joints. It is common knowledge that in the very beginning the influence of the Hot Springs machine was manifest in the Senate by trying to hamper Governor Adkins in his work.[156]

This challenge to the State Police just seemed to make Adkins more resolved to end gambling in Hot Springs. In June, Assistant Superintendent Atkinson led four officers on a two-day raid in the spa town. The axe-wielding officers presented quite a formidable picture as they hacked apart gambling tables and tossed the debris into alleys. The officers also began checking employees' and bettors' draft cards to make sure all were properly registered to serve their country. On the second day of the raid, the officers, now accompanied by Superintendent Albright, merely conducted follow-up raids and found the bookies closed up tight, which prompted Albright to tell the ever-watchful press, "These bookies better take the governor's warning, because he means what he says. Whatever it takes to convince them it will be unprofitable to stay in business we will do. This time there will be no let up." The raids were impacting the gamblers, although they were still not able to completely close them down. Bookies only took bets by phone or from regulars who employed runners to deliver their wagers.[157]

In July, the governor made another aggressive move in his battle with the gamblers. When warrants issued by a state supreme court judge were ruled unconstitutional, officers were limited to raiding clubs only if they personally observed a violation. So when a justice of the peace position unexpectedly came open in Garland County, the governor quickly took advantage of his constitutional right to appoint a replacement. Adkins saw this as the perfect opportunity to install a supporter who also had the authority to issue warrants. His choice was Floyd Hurst, a local preacher who was also the father of an up and coming Hot Springs politician, Q. Bynum Hurst. Reverend Hurst did not try to hide the governor's motivations for appointing him when he told the press that "I understood I was appointed so that warrants could be obtained by State Police for search and seizure of alleged gambling … and if that is what they want, that is what they are going to get."[158]

A few weeks after his appointment the State Police conducted their first raids using warrants issued by Hurst. The *Democrat* waxed almost romantically about the efforts of the officers when it wrote, "Swinging their axes like first class timber men, Homer's boys—those husky lads from State Police headquarters—came back to town to make a shambles out of equipment at the irrepressible Hot Springs bookmaking establishments." Four clubs were raided and six arrests made, including one at the Kentucky Club whose door was locked and a "For Rent" sign hung in the window when officers arrived. Atkinson and the three other officers busted the door in with their axes and found 50 bettors inside.[159]

The men also raided a printing business whose main job was to print the daily racing forms and betting lines for 12 bookie joints. The officers seized the company's teletype machine, which was Hot Springs primary link to outside horse tracks. In an attempt to recover this valuable piece of equipment, the owner filed a lawsuit alleging that the warrants issued by Reverend Hurst were unconstitutional. The state's attorney general agreed with the complaint as did the Pulaski County circuit court, which issued a temporary restraining order against the State Police.[160]

The initial success of this lawsuit encouraged other gamblers to try their luck as well. In mid August, a group of gamblers that had been arrested in July sued the department and contended that the raids were "political spite work" that targeted them because they did not support Q. Bynum Hurst's campaign for state representative. Reverend Hurst denied these charges and said the warrants were just an attempt to stop gambling. He also made the interesting observation that the gamblers' legal counsel was the acting city attorney. The Hot Springs Municipal Judge agreed with Hurst and dismissed the gamblers' lawsuit, but the rash of legal challenges worried Adkins. He needed to make sure that if Hurst's warrants were deemed unconstitutional, the State Police could carry on the fight against gambling, and he warned that the use of undercover agents would be one way officers could observe gambling and then legally call in uniformed raiders.[161]

The Pulaski County circuit court would deal the anti-gambling drive a setback on September 17 when they ruled that Reverend Hurst's search and seizure warrants were unconstitutional. Chancellor Taylor Roberts said, "It is my opinion that the justice of the peace has not power or authority to issue a search and seizure warrant ... and it follows that the State Police have no authority to execute such a warrant."

Refusing to be deterred by the legal defeat, Atkinson took 14 men, the largest group of officers yet, and raided five bookie joints the next day where they arrested 13 people. When asked how he could do such a thing in light of the recent court ruling, Atkinson responded, "When you see them gambling, you don't need a warrant and that is what we are going to do from now on." Governor Adkins also spoke strongly telling the press that, "I shall use every power at my command to suppress gambling. Law enforcement must and shall be supreme." In one of the more interesting kernels of information the State Police released to the press was information gleaned from their review of the Tulsa Club's ledger. The Tulsa Club was one of the smaller gambling establishments, but despite its size it still reported a daily profit of $200. The rest of the week would see repeated raids and 60 more arrests, which was highlighted by officers turning the recreation room at the Citizen's Club into a "mass of kindling."[162]

The willingness of the State Police to continue raiding despite the restraining order sparked an equally aggressive response from the gamblers. In what the papers would call "The Battle of Hot Springs," the local prosecuting attorney used a grand jury made up of friends, relatives, and business partners of most of the largest casinos in Hot Springs to issue subpoenas for 14 State Police officers. The 14 were the ones who were most involved in the raids and included Assistant Superintendent Atkinson, Herman Lindsey, Carl Miller, Frank McGibbony, and R. E. Brown. The men were questioned at length about their operations, but the attempted intimidation failed to stop the raids, and October would see a repeat of September's frantic activity.[163] This included a raid at the upscale Southern Club where plainclothes officers "quietly" arrested seven men. One change was apparent, though: these latest efforts were being led by Herman Lindsey and Carl Miller instead of Atkinson.[164]

November 1943 would be another good month for Adkins and the State Police. The department had appealed the Pulaski circuit court's ruling that Reverend Hurst's warrants were unconstitutional, and the state supreme court overturned the lower court's ruling, thereby reinstating the arrests and reinvigorating the governor. His good fortune even prompted an outburst against state Senators Roy Milum and Ernest Maner who he described as "nothing more than representatives of the entrenched gambling fraternity." In Hot Springs, the news of the supreme court's verdict produced, at least publicly, an outpouring of resignation among the bookies who told the press that they would finally close their operations. Local officials lamented the loss of 15,000 dollars in annual fees the casinos paid to the city, which had been used to fully fund the road department, and civic leaders predicted 200 residents would be out of work. One bookie told the press that he was closing his horse parlor because he didn't want the "State Police to chop up the furniture."[165]

A new year showed that despite these public lamentations Hot Springs' gamblers were a stubborn group. Eight raids in January led by Sergeant Lindsey, Lieutenant Bert Frazier, and Sergeant Oliphant reflected a change in tactics. In addition to destroying equipment and seizing paraphernalia, the officers began to confiscate the casinos' bankroll. On a late January 1944 raid, officers seized nearly $3,000 from the Blue Ribbon and the Ohio Club. This new tactic emerged from discussions between Governor Adkins and Hot Springs Circuit Judge Sam Woods, who told the governor that "I believe the State Police will have to be more and more hard boiled" in their attacks on gamblers, and recommended seizing bankrolls. Adkins liked the idea and found precedent in New York where officers' seizure of bankrolls during gambling raids was upheld by the courts.[166]

More raids followed in February and March with the total number of arrests and seized bankrolls mounting, but these would represent the last attempts by Adkins and the State Police to conduct regular operations in Hot Springs. As the raids wound down, Adkins wrote to Reverend Hurst in an attempt to show his appreciation for Hursts' efforts over the past year telling him, "When you stop to think that we are fighting a group that has been entrenched for 40 years or more in this gambling racket, I think the results have been marvelous."[167]

The end of Governor Adkins' and the State Police's war against gambling was motivated by the growing demands of the campaign trail. Instead of running for an unprecedented third term, Governor Adkins chose to run for an open seat in the United States House of Representatives. With the governor's focus on the election instead of Hot Springs, raids became more and more infrequent. The end of the raids did not mean that Hot Springs and gambling ceased to impact the State Police. The issue would continue to reverberate, and when a new governor was elected in November, it would lead to major and long-lasting changes for the agency.

While the State Police's efforts to stop gambling in Hot Springs garnered front-page headlines, the raids actually occupied a fraction of the officers' time and energy. With the outbreak of a world war, the federal government lowered the national speed limit to save gasoline and reduce the wear on tires. In October 1941, the maximum speed limit was lowered from 60 miles an hour to 50, and in September 1942, they reduced it to 35 miles an hour. Such a drastic decline in speed limits did not encourage a high degree of compliance by the public. Therefore, enforcing the new law required new tactics. The first new method of speed enforcement was the use of unmarked cars. Also, officers were pulled from rural areas and assigned to high-traffic areas, particularly around major holidays when they expected traffic to be the heaviest. In another sign of the times, drivers who were convicted of speeding were often punished with the confiscation of their gasoline ration cards.

Traffic control did not simply entail arresting speeders and investigating accidents. In the 1940s, electronic traffic control devices were unheard of in Arkansas, so areas that witnessed an explosion in population due to the expansion of war-related industries created almost insurmountable traffic problems unless an officer was assigned to control and direct it. It was not just a lack of modern signals that tied up traffic. Often, the infrastructure surrounding Arkansas' defense plants proved inadequate to handle even non-wartime traffic counts with any degree of efficiency. Therefore, a State Police officer had to be assigned to many plants and military installations to direct traffic. This was especially true during a shift change when thousands of people would be entering and leaving on a single road or over a one-lane bridge.

Period	Total Arrests	Traffic Arrests	Criminal Arrests	Liquor Arrests	Total Fatalities
1935-1939	20,681	9,890	5,061	5,730	1,289
1940-1944	39,158	18,322	10,217	10,619	1,708

One of the most important changes in the State Police operations during the Second World War was the expansion of the department's radio system from a single station in Little Rock to five stations spread around the state. The new radio system represented a goal of the department and Superintendent Albright since 1936, but limited funding had hindered its realization. Just when the legislature approved the funds, the Second World War intervened to further delay the project by co-opting building materials necessary for construction of the new radio sites and restricting electronic equipment necessary to build the radios. Despite these obstacles, the department persevered and using local funds were able to complete all four stations and district headquarters by 1943.[168]

A statewide radio network was one of Albright's original dreams for the department, but he would not remain with the department long enough to fully appreciate it. The election of Ben Laney as governor in November 1944 would lead to major changes in the State Police. Three weeks after the election, Governor-elect Laney made it known that he would appoint former State Police Commissioner Jack Porter to the department's top spot. In addition to his time on the commission, Porter's past experience included a short stint overseeing the Parole Division in the State Police and working as an agent for a railroad. When Laney went public with his choice, Porter had just finished a term as the mayor of Forrest City.[169] While no conclusive evidence exists, Laney's motivation for appointing Porter hints at retaliation for the State Police's aggressive attempt to curb gambling in Hot Springs. One citizen wrote Laney complaining that "the entire department is being reorganized to get rid of one man and a very desirable man at that" and warned that any association with Leo McLaughlin, the leader of the Hot Springs machine, would only lead to "grief."[170]

Despite the criticism, Laney pressed ahead with his decision, which presented the State Police with a bit of a conundrum. According to the legislation governing the operation of the State Police, the governor could not fire the department's superintendent. The State Police Commission was the only one with the authority to remove the superintendent, and only then for cause. Even though the law did not require it, a few days before Christmas in 1944, Gray Albright, the only superintendent the State Police had ever known, submitted his resignation to the commission. Following Albright's resignation, the State Police Commission—none of which were appointed by the newly elected governor—chose to promote Assistant Superintendent Atkinson despite Laney's choice of Porter for that position.

Against a backdrop that featured Allied soldiers desperately fighting in the Battle of Bulge in central Europe, an entirely different type of combat was raging between the state's new governor and the newly elevated and defiant State Police superintendent, C. T. Atkinson. Superintendent Atkinson and the current State Police Commission of J. P. Veasey, T. J. Aycock, and E. M. Frizzel vowed to fight any attempts to remove him and argued that he was protected from arbitrary removal by civil service provisions in the State Police's enabling legislation.171 Yet just a few days later, the political pressure forced two of the three commissioners to resign so Laney could appoint his supporters in their place.[172]

Meanwhile, Porter continued as if he was already the superintendent. In early January, he submitted a State Police budget to the legislature and began working with Laney's supporters in the General Assembly to craft a bill reorganizing the department.[173] On January 16, Pine Bluff Senator Hendrix Rowell introduced Senate Bill

39, the major provision of which was a complete re-creation of the department, which authorized the governor to appoint and dismiss the head of the State Police at his leisure. The first test of the governor's influence in the legislature would occur two days later when confirmation of the governor's appointees to the commission came before the Senate. Opponents to the governor's planned reorganization had spent almost two weeks working the halls of the capitol trying to line up enough votes to stop Laney's program. These efforts failed their first test and the Senate approved the appointment of two new commissioners, Alan Patterson and Fred Coleman.[174] That same afternoon, the two new commissioners convened a meeting of the State Police Commission and named Jack Porter the department's superintendent. Atkinson remained defiant though and refused to leave his position, placing his last hope in the hands of the legislature where rumblings among Laney's opponents gave him some hope that the Senate bill reorganizing the department would be defeated.[175]

On January 24, Senate Bill 39 came up for a vote and whatever opposition existed to Laney's program decided to lay low as the bill was overwhelmingly approved, 24 to three. The magnitude of the defeat convinced Atkinson that his career with the State Police had come to an end. That afternoon he submitted his resignation to the new commission. He followed it up with a blast at the governor by publicly stating the rumors that were on everyone's lips, that the reorganization was driven by the Hot Springs political machine as revenge for Atkinson's and the State Police's gambling raids.[176] A number of other officers would also choose to leave the department when Jack Porter took over, the most notable of which was another key figure that led gambling raids in Hot Springs, Herman Lindsey. Lindsey would not be gone from the department long, and when he returned it would be in part because of his efforts in Hot Springs.[177]

When the House passed the reorganization bill in mid-February, it garnered little mention since the drama inside State Police headquarters had already played itself out by that time. With three of the department's top officers gone, a new director (the reorganization bill changed the title of the State Police's commander from superintendent to director), and an uncertain future, the department tried to return to normal. Yet, a post-war America would present a number of obstacles for Arkansas and the State Police that challenged their ability to react, and for the first time took the life of one of their own.

Chapter Three

A Recurring Change, 1945-1954

"We are through warning them."
Highway Patrol Captain Frank McGibbony
on the department's policy toward speeders.

*"Would you be willing to work ten or twelve hours a day on
a job in which risking your life is just part of the work, for
$2,400 a year and [you had to] buy your own uniform?"*
Editor of the *Arkansas Democrat*

On a hot August day in 1946, State Policeman Add Shug was on routine patrol on Highway 65 between Little Rock and Pine Bluff. As the officer neared Wrightsville, he passed a black 1940 Ford coupe driven by two young men who were heading north toward Little Rock. Something about the car struck the officer as suspicious, so Shug decided to turn around and stop the car for a license check. When he approached the vehicle, Shug asked the men for their driver's licenses, but the two nervously replied that they had lost their billfolds along with their licenses and were simply on their way to Mountain Home to visit an uncle. By now, Patrolman Shug's police instincts were on full alert. He asked the passenger, Hubert Jones, to get into his patrol car and for the driver, Jack Rheuark, to drive to State Police headquarters in Little Rock. Shug figured that if the two were wanted, the State Police's Identification Section would be able to identify them. The two agreed, and Jones got out of the coupe and into Shug's police car while Rheuark pulled back onto the road toward Little Rock.

All appeared to be in order as Shug followed Rheuark north to Little Rock, but after only a few miles, Rheuark pulled into a gas station and stopped. Shug pulled up beside him and yelled out of the window, "What's wrong?" Rheuark told him the car was overheating because the radiator was broken. The oppressive heat and humidity in central Arkansas during August made such things fairly common, so Shug got out of the car to check on the Ford's radiator without a second thought. When Rheuark and Shug met at the front of the car though, the situation would change dramatically. As Shug bent over to look at the engine, Rheuark stuck a pistol in his ribs and told him to quietly get back in his patrol car. By this time, Jones had gotten out of Shug's car brandishing a pistol as well. Frighteningly, the two had gotten the drop on Shug, and he had no choice but comply.

Once Shug and Jones got back in the patrol car, Jones covered him with his pistol and directed him to drive to a little-used side road off Highway 65 while Rheuark followed in the Ford coupe. Once the two cars were well out of sight of the main road, the two cars stopped and Shug was ordered to get out. After the men took his pistol, cartridge belt, and car keys, they shoved him toward the back of the car, opened the trunk, and told him to get in. As the sun beat down on the three men, Shug hesitated. To get in the trunk of his patrol car on such a hot day would certainly be a death sentence since it might be hours before someone passed by and even then they might not stop and open the trunk. With nothing to lose, the officer gambled and told the two that they might as well shoot him since putting him in the trunk would result in the same fate. Luckily for him, the two men were not murderers. They had robbed an Oklahoma bank a few days previously and gotten away with the rather large sum of $33,000, but they were not of a mind to kill anyone.

Instead, they decided to handcuff him to the front bumper of the patrol car, which should give them enough time to make a clean getaway before he was discovered. Shug agreed that such an arrangement sounded better, and the two bank robbers quickly cuffed him to his patrol car. Shug, though, was a quick-thinking officer, and as the two were about to leave with his gun, cartridge belt, and car keys, he asked one more favor. Would the men please take the car key off of his key ring and leave the ring and the other keys with him? When they hesitated, he explained that the other keys on the ring went to his house, and if they took them, it would cost a lot of money to get new ones made, which was an added expense that would be tough to pay for on a state policeman's salary. What he did not tell them was that on the ring was a key to the handcuffs that were currently binding him to his front bumper. Once again the two men relented, and after removing the car key and throwing the ring outside of Shug's reach, Rheuark and Jones jumped into their car and yelled, "Tell the boys not to kill us when they catch us!" With that final request, the two sped off toward Highway 65.

For a third time that day, Add Shug found luck on his side. Unable to reach the keys, the officer began yelling at the top of his lungs in hopes that someone would hear him and come to his assistance. Shortly, his efforts bore fruit when a man working in a nearby field heard the officer's cries and hurried over to unlock the handcuffs with Shug's key. Although Rheuark and Jones were able to slip the ensuing manhunt and roadblocks, they were caught two days later while they were sleeping in a Memphis motel room. Both would be convicted, and Rheuark earned a 20-year sentence in the state penitentiary for his crimes.[178]

* * *

As the experience of Patrolman Shug showed, Arkansas could be a dangerous place after the Second World War. For an overwhelming majority of the servicemen returning to America from the battlefields in Asia, Europe, and Africa, the end of the war represented a return to normalcy and a chance for a better life. In Arkansas, more than 200,000 served in the military during the Second World War and for some, adjusting to life in a civil society proved to be difficult.[179]

As a result, crime rates skyrocketed in 1946. In just the first six months of the year, the number of arrests made by State Police officers nearly doubled, totaling 7,883 compared to 4,791 during the first half of 1945.[180] The rise in criminal activity worried Governor Laney who pushed the State Police to assign two men per patrol car due to the "desperate" nature of criminals.[181] Still, in the governor's mind, the State Police's policy should be one of "stand-by" until the local authorities called them in to help.[182]

Just such a situation occurred outside Jonesboro in July 1946, when Patrolman Wyatt Patrick was called to the scene of a man barricaded inside his Greene County home. Sheriff's deputies had attempted to serve a warrant on O. O. Polk for domestic violence and terroristic threatening, but Polk refused to come out of the house and threatened the men with a shotgun. The deputies called Patrolman Patrick to assist. When the officer arrived, they realized it would be too dangerous to try to storm the house, so they decided to employ a bit of misdirection to bring Polk into custody. The plan called for the sheriff and his deputies to coax Polk out of his house, while Patrolman Patrick would sneak around the back of the house where he could approach Polk without being detected. Once Patrick was close enough, he would tackle Polk and then the deputies would come in to assist.

The plan started off well enough and the sheriff was able to convince Polk to come out of his house, but he refused to lay down his shotgun. As the sheriff kept up a dialogue with the man, Patrick crept up behind him with his sawed-off shotgun at the ready. Polk proved too perceptive and whirled around to face Patrick coming up behind him. Quickly, Polk fired his shotgun at the officer. Luckily, his aim was slightly off as pellets from the blast struck the officer's hat and grazed his skin, but did not inflict great damage. Patrick did not give the man a second chance as he fired his sawed-off shotgun, striking Polk square in the chest and killing him instantly.[183]

In the opposite corner of the state, Patrolman Glenn Minton would find himself in a similar situation that involved a call for assistance from local officers. Minton had been with the department less than a year when Bearden city marshal, Hickey Stillman, asked for his help in arresting Herbert Williams, who happened to belong to a prominent southwest Arkansas family. Williams, who was also a World War II veteran, had taken to drinking too much, which he typically followed by racing his car up and down the small town's main street. Since Bearden was such a small town, it did not have the funds to provide Marshal Stillman with a patrol car, so he was forced to perform his duties on foot. This lack of mobility prevented him from arresting Williams when he tore through the middle of town, so Stillman asked for help from his good friend in the State Police, Patrolman Minton. The next time Herbert Williams decided to race up and down Bearden's main street, Minton and Stillman were ready for him and in short order the two officers had placed him under arrest and transported him to jail.

Yet the story does not end with the arrest of a drunken reckless driver. Williams took exception to his arrest, and word got back to Patrolman Minton that Williams' was threatening to kill him and Marshal Stillman. Minton told Stillman what he had heard, but Stillman just laughed the threat off. Williams, however, was not laughing. Less than a week after Minton first heard of William's threat, Marshal Stillman was talking with friends in front of a local theater. With the officer's back turned, Williams saw his chance to get revenge. He came up behind Stillman with a 12-gauge, single-barrel shotgun and, with no warning, shot the officer in the middle of the back from 10 feet away. Stillman was killed instantly, and Williams fled the scene as a horrified crowd looked on. A call was placed to State Police headquarters, and Minton was dispatched to the scene. When he arrived, he found a crowd gathered around Stillman's devastated body. He asked them where the shooter had gone, and they quickly pointed to the railroad-switching yard across the street. Minton ran back to his patrol car, grabbed his shotgun, and headed toward the yard, which was crowded with empty boxcars waiting for cargo. Minton remembered years later,

> It was not long before I jumped him and we were running behind one boxcar and then another. A time or two he got the drop on me and could have shot me, but I couldn't figure out why he didn't. I finally ran him out of the yard and across the highway where he ran into the

mayor's house. I kicked the front door open and he had his hand on the doorknob ready to go out the back [door]. He was still carrying that old shotgun. I threw down on him with my shotgun and told him to hand over [his weapon]...I finally got the shotgun away from him and it turned out he had both front pockets full of shotgun shells. After he shot Hickey he went to reload and went into his pocket to get a shell and grabbed a [smaller] sixteen-gauge shell. He put it in the breech and it slid down in the [barrel] and he couldn't get it out. So the gun was useless.[184]

After Williams' arrest, a jury convicted him of murder and sentenced him to life in the state penitentiary. Williams would not serve much time in prison, though. Due to his family connections, he was able to gain a furlough from the governor.

The immediate post-war period in Arkansas not only saw an increase in the number of shootouts between officers and suspects, but also witnessed a rise in the frequency of burglaries and robberies. In one week in December 1945, a gang of safecrackers burglarized 20 Arkansas businesses, mostly in the northern part of the state, using nitroglycerine to blow the safe or by hammering off the safe's hinges. By December 18, the group, which consisted of two men and their girlfriends, had worked their way down to Little Rock where they had stopped for the night. As luck would have, State Police Patrolmen Bowling and Garrison drove past the gang's blue 1941 Mercury, which was parked on Fourth and Cumberland, and became suspicious of the car. Consistent with Governor Laney's request to cooperate with local authorities, the State Police officers called for assistance from two Little Rock police officers and approached the now-occupied vehicle. A subsequent search turned up nine suitcases and six bags filled with stolen merchandise. This discovery led to the arrest of the four, although they would cause more trouble for the State Police and local officers. While awaiting trial in Searcy County, the leader of the gang, Henry Mayes, pried the bars from the county jail and escaped into the night. His dash for freedom ended in Indiana where he was arrested and brought back to stand trial for his safecracking spree.[185]

A similar chance encounter led to the capture of a prison escapee from Kentucky around this same time. Patrolman Travis Ward, who had recently joined the department, was on patrol in south Arkansas and met a stolen car driven by John Esters. Esters had broken out of prison four months earlier and headed for Arkansas where he immediately returned to a life of crime by establishing a stolen car ring based out of Grant County. Esters was driving one of these stolen cars when he passed Ward. The officer recognized the vehicle and began a pursuit that degenerated into a running gun battle before ending in Sheridan when Esters lost control and wrecked. Ward arrested Ester who was returned to prison in Kentucky.[186]

Around the same time Patrolman Ward was chasing down Esters, he was also involved in the investigation of what remains today as one of the biggest murder mysteries in Arkansas' history. On February 22, 1946, Jimmy Hollis and Mary Jeanne Larey were parking on a remote dirt road outside the border city of Texarkana. All seemed to be perfect for the young lovebirds until a man wearing a white hood with crude slits cut out for the eyes and the mouth suddenly appeared at the driver's side window. After ordering the couple out of the car at gunpoint, he struck the young man repeatedly in the head with his pistol. The masked man told Mary Jeanne to run while he continued to kick her prostrate boyfriend, but this would prove to be but a momentary reprieve for the 19-year-old girl. The man would catch her and assault her as well. Both Jimmy Hollis and Mary Jeanne Larey would survive this attack, and their experience did not generate much press coverage. That would change when the masked man found his next victims.[187]

A month later, Richard Griffin and Polly Ann Moore were parking on another remote road on the Texas side of Texarkana. The two would not survive their encounter with what authorities came to assume was the same man. Early on the morning of March 24, the bodies of the young lovers were found in Griffin's Oldsmobile, both shot with a .32 caliber pistol in the head. Before being shot, the masked man raped Polly Anne. The murders produced an uproar in the border town. Texas Rangers were called in to investigate the crimes and a $500 reward was advertised for any information leading to the capture of the murderer.

By the end of March, the Rangers had exhausted all of their leads without coming any closer to identifying who killed Richard Griffin and Polly Ann Moore, and who assaulted Mary Jeanne Larey and Jimmy Hollis.[188] The situation would get even worse two weeks later when 17-year-old Paul Martin and 15-year-old Betty Jo Booker became the third and fourth victims of what the newspapers were now calling the "Phantom Murderer." Once again, the Phantom had shot both in the head with a .32 caliber pistol, but before shooting Betty Jo, the Phantom had raped her.

The second double murder in Texarkana over a two-week span prompted the Texas Rangers to send their most renowned investigator, Captain Manuel "Lone Wolf" Gonzales. In addition to the efforts of law enforcement agencies in Texas and Arkansas, citizens were taking matters into their own hands. Vigilance committees popped up on both sides of the state line, and even high school students began to set traps for the Phantom by arming themselves and then parking on remote roads in hopes the Phantom would make an appearance. Despite the best efforts of an entire community, the Phantom remained at large.

On May 3, the Phantom would strike for the first time on the Arkansas side of the state line. The murderer's fifth victim was a Miller County resident named Virgil Starks. While Starks was relaxing at his rural residence north of Texarkana listening to the radio, the calm was rent by the sounds of breaking glass and two gunshots. Starks' wife, Kate, rushed into the living room to find her husband slumped over in his chair with two gunshot wounds in the back of his head. The killer had shot Virgil through the window behind his chair with a .22 caliber rifle, and when Kate rushed toward the phone, he fired twice more, both of which struck her in the face. The small caliber of the rifle's rounds did not kill Kate, although it did knock her down, and when she heard the shooter knocking in the back door she managed to struggle out of the front door. Free from the house, Kate ran to a neighbor's house and summoned help. Kate recovered from her wounds, but help was too late to save Virgil.

Even though many questioned whether this was actually the work of the Phantom since the location of the murder and the type of weapon was different, the net effect on the community was the same. Understandably, the citizens on both sides of the state line were wracked by fear and dread over who would be the next victim. The publisher of the *Texarkana Gazette* wrote to Governor Laney arguing, "with three unsolved double murders around Texarkana, the people, particularly girls and women are greatly disturbed and frightened. [I] urgently suggest that additional State Police officers be immediately assigned to that area until these crimes are solved."[189] The governor and State Police immediately complied by dispatching additional patrolmen to the area where they coordinated with local and county officers to provide a near constant police presence around Texarkana. Even with more than 60 law enforcement officers on duty on the Arkansas side of the border, the Texas Rangers advised residents to "shoot first and ask questions later." The Rangers' questionable advice was taken to heart by at least one bar owner, who shot a man that unadvisedly looked into the window of his tavern to see if it was open.[190]

State Police Sergeant Max Tackett realized what appeared to be the first big break in the case. Before each of the Phantom's attacks, a car was reported stolen in the Texarkana region. While stolen cars in Texarkana at this time were not unheard of or even that rare, Tackett felt that this was more than just a coincidence. Working with the Miller County sheriff's department, Tackett and other officers located one of the cars stolen the night of a Phantom attack and set up surveillance. When a woman got into the car, she was arrested and questioned. She said the car was supposedly her husband's, Youell Swinney. Under further questioning, the woman also began to relate additional details about the Phantom murders that only law enforcement officers knew.

The weight of the evidence convinced the officers to arrest Swinney who remarked to officers as they put him in the patrol car, "Hell, I know what you want me for. You want me for more than stealing cars."[191] Beyond this admission, Swinney had nothing to say, so he was taken to Little Rock headquarters and clumsily administered sodium pentathol in an attempt to obtain the truth about his involvement. Unfortunately, the suspect was given too much of the drug and passed out. Without a confession and no physical evidence, all the officers had to link Swinney with the murders was his wife's previous statements, but she refused to testify in court. Just because the State Police could not link Swinney to the Phantom murders did not mean he was free to go. He was convicted for stealing the car the night before one of the Phantom murders. Due to his long history of criminal acts, Swinney was sentenced to life in the Arkansas state penitentiary for the theft, although he was released in 1973 when his conviction was overturned.[192] With no solid suspects and no further activity from the Phantom, the case slowly slipped into the background and remains unsolved.

One of the things that pushed the Phantom case onto the back burner for Sergeant Tackett was an experience that nearly cost him his life. A few months after the arrest of Youell Swinney, Tackett and a Miller County deputy sheriff were patrolling the highways around Texarkana when they initiated a pursuit of a stolen truck. After a short sprint, the truck pulled over. The two occupants were pulled out and frisked by the officers who found an ice pick in one of the men's pockets. Sergeant Tackett placed one man in the back seat and the other in the front seat of his patrol car and told the deputy to follow him back to town driving the stolen truck. What Tackett did not know was that the man riding in the front seat of his patrol car had 23 prior arrests, a pistol strapped to the inside of his right thigh, and a firm determination not to go back to jail.

Shortly after the two-car convoy began driving to Texarkana, the suspect in the front seat reached for his pistol. Tackett also reached for his gun, but proved a step slower, and the suspect shot the Patrolman in the hip. With the two men engaged in a life-and-death fight in the front seat, the patrol car ran into a ditch and overturned. When the car came to rest, Tackett had to contend with both men who were now punching and wrestling with the officer in the wreckage of the police car. The deputy driving the stolen truck had no idea what had caused the officer to run off the road, and when he got out of the truck, Tackett yelled a warning. The deputy pulled his pistol and shot the suspect that had been riding in the back seat, which convinced the front passenger to flee the vehicle instead of continuing to fight. The suspect only made it a few paces when he too was shot by the deputy. Thankfully, Tackett would recover from the gunshot to his hip, but the two suspects died as a result of the incident.[193]

The summer of 1946 would also see another high-profile crime, or at least the rumor of a high-profile crime, that re-ignited the controversy surrounding the use of State Police officers to suppress gambling. Following Governor Laney's decision to reorganize the department and end the State Police's raids on gambling in Hot Springs and around the state, many casinos and betting parlors that had been closed or at least hidden from plain sight returned to wide open gambling. One of these was the Blackfish Club in Forrest City, a town that was also the home of State Police Director Jack Porter. In June 1946, four men—two armed with submachine guns and two armed with shotguns—calmly walked into the busy gambling hall and politely informed the patrons that they were being robbed. The four men quickly grabbed the casino's cash boxes and broke into the safe, making away with a reported $80,000 of the Blackfish's bankroll.[194]

At the time, the robbery represented one of the largest in the state's history, but also one that would be clouded in controversy because no one officially reported it. Since the club was technically illegal, the owners decided not to take the matter to the local authorities, but this did not keep the patrons from talking freely about what they had seen. As a result, the state's news media splashed the story across their front pages for several days and asked Governor Laney if he was going to send the State Police in to investigate. Laney responded that he would not send them in because no one had asked for their help or even reported that a crime had taken place. Since 1946 was an election year, the robbery and the governor's refusal to dispatch the State Police became a political issue. Sam Malone, Laney's most formidable opponent in the upcoming Democratic primary, ripped into the governor saying, "It is indeed a novel idea that if a serious crime is committed in this state and local officials fail to act, that the governor of the state with his extraordinary powers shall sit back and do nothing. Organized criminals are thus on notice that they can operate in Arkansas with impunity because of the weakness of the state law enforcement department. Could it be that the governor fears to embarrass his own appointee ... whose home is in Forrest City?"[195]

Until the Democratic primary in August, Malone continued to attack Laney over the limits placed on State Police activity. He argued that if elected he would increase the department to 225 officers, not to interfere with local authorities, but to more fully enforce the laws of the state.[196] Malone fell short in his attempt to unseat Governor Laney, as Arkansas voters chose to return Laney for a traditional second term. In an interesting side note, four men robbed an illegal casino in Maryland just two weeks after the Blackfish Club was hit and used remarkably similar tactics. Just like in Arkansas, the club owners refused to cooperate with local officers, but in this case the Maryland governor chose to send in the State Police to conduct a full investigation.[197]

The verbal sparring between candidates for governor in 1946 did not compare to the ferocity of the campaigns for local offices being waged around the state. The end of the Second World War found thousands of soldiers, or "G. I.s," returning home with a new-found sense of confidence and a firm conviction of how things should be run. This new demographic naturally translated into a growing political movement that first found unified expression in the 1946 elections. Known as the "G. I. Revolt," former soldiers from around the state began to run for political office on the platform of reform.

The most effective and cohesive group of G. I. Revolt-candidates were found in Hot Springs. Sid McMath, a decorated United States Marine, led the Garland County faction of G. I.s who sought to overthrow the entrenched political machine led by Leo McLaughlin and Verne Ledgerwood. Both McLaughlin and Ledgerwood had worked hard to protect the spa city's gambling industry from State Police raids during the war and argued that the continued livelihood of the city depended upon gambling. Economic necessity or not, McMath's group vowed to end the corruption in city and county government that was fostered and funded by gambling interests. For this reason, their candidacy presented a clear and present danger not only to the local politicians but also to the casino operators.

Out of this conflict grew fears of physical violence, voter intimidation, and election fraud. In the primary elections in August, several members of opposing parties in Perry County actually armed themselves when they went to the polls to vote.[198] To prevent any escalations from marring the November elections, Governor Laney and Director Porter organized "flying squads" of State Police officers to be sent to the three most critical counties, Garland, Crittenden, and Cleveland. Even though the threat of violence in these areas was considered real, election day remained peaceful, and in Garland County the previously unthinkable had occurred. Sid McMath and his fellow G. I.s, one of which was Reverend Hurst's son Q. Bynum, ousted the McLaughlin-Ledgerwood political machine and took control of Hot Springs. The fall of the gamblers' protective umbrella spelled the end of open gambling in Hot Springs—at least for a while.

All of the special assignments, murder investigations, and assistance rendered to local officers occupied a significant portion of the State Police's time in the years following the Second World War, but the overwhelming majority of the patrolmen's time was spent on highway patrol. The post-war period saw several major problems develop that led to a huge increase in the number of traffic-related fatalities in Arkansas. The first was the return of so many soldiers whose sense of caution and restraint in the operation of a motor vehicle seemed to have been left on the battlefields. After risking their lives on a daily basis, reckless or drunken driving did not seem to pose too large of a threat. One example that typified the behavior of far too many newly returned soldiers occurred in Washington County just before Thanksgiving in 1945. The soldier and his girlfriend were traveling south on Highway 71 when State Police Officer Wallace Parnell attempted to pull the couple over for reckless driving. Instead of stopping, the driver floored his car and sped down the windy road at speeds topping 90 miles an hour. As the soldier swerved into the left-hand lane to pass a slower moving car, it met a farm truck headlight to headlight. The ensuing collision killed the driver of the truck and seriously injured both the soldier and his girlfriend.

Compounding the reckless driving of the returning soldiers was the poor condition of automobiles in Arkansas. Four years of rationing tires and mechanical parts had created a dangerous collection of worn-out cars and trucks rattling along the state's road system. The most dangerous deficiencies were improper lighting and defective brakes. As a result, the first two months of 1946 saw 71 people killed in traffic accidents compared to 41 in 1945. For the entire year of 1946, 394 people would die in traffic-related accidents versus 275 in the prior twelve months.[199]

Still, when considering the significant rise in vehicle traffic miles, the increasing fatality rate is not that great. In 1934, the year before the Rangers were created, Arkansas had a traffic fatality rate of 24 deaths per 100,000,000 vehicle miles. In 1941, when a record 503 people were killed in traffic-related accidents, the traffic fatality rate had fallen to 18 deaths per 100,000,000 vehicle miles.

In 1946, the traffic fatality rate was 12 per 100 million vehicle miles, a figure much less than at any time before 1942. Comparing these fatality rates with those experienced today shows how dangerous driving continued to be despite the falling rates. In 2001, Arkansas's 601 traffic-related fatalities equated to just over two deaths per 100 million vehicle miles.

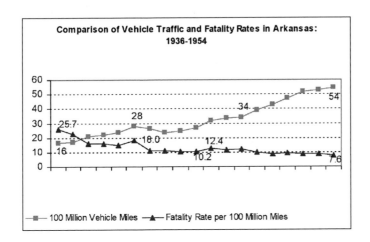

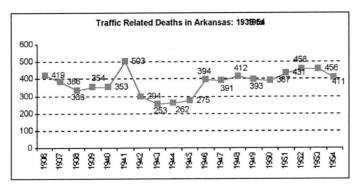

Governor Laney and the state's press cared little for a comparison of fatality rates, and in February 1946 he directed the State Police to "eliminate the needless loss of life" caused by these traffic accidents.[200] The department responded by canceling all leaves and holidays for patrolmen and assigning 50 officers to establish six roadblocks around the state where they would check the brakes and lights of every passing vehicle. The officers would also hand out safe driving pamphlets to passing motorists. The roadblocks were maintained for most of February and during its operation, nearly 25,000 cars would be given safety checks of which almost 2,000 had defective brakes and close to 5,000 had improper lighting.[201]

The high fatality rate also encouraged the state legislature to increase the size of the State Police during the 1947 session. In March, the General Assembly passed a bill adding 29 new officers and providing funds for 15 additional patrol cars, all of which would be paid for by an increase in the driver's license fee from $0.50 to $1.00. In order to win support for the bill, Director Porter had to promise the new officers would be used to establish 24-hour patrols on three of the state's busiest highways: Highway 70 between Memphis and Hot Springs, Highway 64 between Fort Smith and Conway, and Highway 61 between Blytheville and Memphis. When these new men completed the State Police training academy in July, the department fielded 84 officers and 65 cars.[202]

Even with the safety checks and additional officers, the number of Arkansans killed in traffic accidents remained distressingly high. In 1948, the State Police decided to make their patrol cars less visible by removing the distinctive white stripe from the hood and relocating the siren and red light from the top of the car to the grill on all new models. Director Porter stated that the original configuration allowed speeding motorists to easily spot the patrol cars, thus allowing them to slow down before an officer could properly pace them.[203] Director Porter also pushed for more stringent driver's testing that called for everyone to be retested every three years.[204]

Although Porter's license testing recommendations won a number of supporters from the state Safety Council and local police departments, his time with the department was drawing to a close and he would not be around long enough to see any of these recommendations to conclusion. Ben Laney had chosen to forgo an attempt at winning a third term as governor, which would have been almost unprecedented anyway. Since the reorganized Department of State Police mandated that the director serve at the pleasure of the governor, Porter did not have much hope that he would be retained. When Sid McMath won the governor's race in November 1948, it was clear Porter would soon be gone because McMath and Laney were from two different factions of the

Democratic party. McMath's G. I. Revolt, which had swept the McLaughlin/Ledgerwood political machine from Hot Springs, held no love for Laney, and all new appointees would come to Little Rock after the election, including a new State Police director.

Before any of this could come to pass, the department would suffer through a veritable trial by fire that saw three of its officers shot in confrontations with armed suspects and the first officer killed in the line of duty. The first scene of violence occurred in the backwoods of Newton County. Nestled in the rugged Ozark Mountains, Newton County long represented a haven for souls hardy enough to do without modern conveniences in exchange for privacy and independence. One person matching this description was Heywood Brown, a 60-year-old subsistence farmer who lived with his brother, Jim, and sister, Dora, in a small house near the Buffalo River. Earlier that year, Brown had reached an agreement with a retired army veteran to sell his land and even accepted payment from the buyer. In August, the buyer came to claim his property, but Brown refused to leave. Fearing for his safety and questioning Brown's sanity, the buyer went to get help from Newton County Sheriff Russell Burdine.

On August 19, Sheriff Burdine and State Police Officer Damon Wilson went to the Brown residence to serve papers committing him and his brother Jim for an examination at the state's mental hospital and seize the property for its new owner. When the officers arrived, Jim Brown was outside working in the garden, where he was placed under arrest without incident. The situation would change dramatically when the two officers went to the house to arrest Heywood. Instead of coming out of the house, Heywood began firing wildly at the officers with a rifle and shotgun. The two officers were driven away by the fusillade and hurried to nearby Harrison to put Jim Brown in jail and get additional officers to help them take Heywood into custody. Wilson and Burdine enlisted the help of Boone County Sheriff Roy Johnson and State Police Lieutenant Alan Templeton, the latter of which gathered up tear gas rounds and a tear gas gun to take to the scene.

When the group arrived back at the Brown place, they were unable to talk the suspect out of the house. The situation was complicated by the presence of Heywood's sister, Dora, who the officers thought was an invalid—a belief that Brown's neighbors would later disprove. Still, the men did not want to do anything that might harm an innocent bystander, so they decided to fire tear gas into the house to drive Heywood out. Lieutenant Templeton grabbed the tear gas gun as the four men fanned out to approach the house. Before he could fire, Heywood struck first. Without warning, a round from a high-powered rifle hit Templeton in the shoulder, knocking him down and sending the tear gas gun skittering along the ground. Wilson leaped for the gun, just reaching it when he was hit in the neck and face by a shotgun blast. Sheriffs Burdine and Johnson grabbed the two wounded officers and retreated down the steep mountainside to their patrol cars. Of the two, Wilson was the more seriously injured, and the steady stream of blood from his head convinced the sheriffs to hurry the wounded men to the hospital in Harrison.

On the way to town, the sheriffs radioed into the State Police's district headquarters in Harrison about the shootings. The district headquarters dispatched the information to State Police headquarters in Little Rock with a plea for more men. In a few hours, 20 State Police officers led by Captain McGibbony along with a handful of men from other agencies had converged on the Brown's residence while additional weapons, flashlights, and ammunition were being rushed to the scene from Little Rock via aircraft. With Brown now surrounded, a furious gun battle broke out that saw Brown alternatively firing his rifle and shotgun from the house's attic, main floor, and basement, with one of these shots grazing State Police Sergeant Clyde Grigsby's neck. Despite "several thousand" rounds fired in return by law enforcement officers, Brown continued to hold out through the night of August 19.

By the next morning, 50 officers were preparing for a "long siege" of the Brown residence. During this time, the officers were able to talk with Brown who claimed that the original land dispute occurred because he had only sold the land and not the house, so he was not moving for anyone. The standoff came to an unexpected end that afternoon. As the officers were eating their lunch, they heard a muffled report from a shotgun, then silence, then another muffled shotgun blast followed by a curl of smoke rising from the house's chimney. The officers quickly manned their positions and watched in horror as flames began to engulf the Brown's home. Evidence collected after the fire had burned itself out showed that Heywood had shot his sister, set fire to the cabin, and then turned his shotgun on himself.[205] In one of the few saving graces from the incident, State Police Officers Templeton and Wilson survived their wounds and served long, distinguished careers with the department.

Undoubtedly one of the first 20 State Police officers on the scene of Brown's residence after Wilson and Templeton were shot was Sidney Pavatt. The young trooper (the official designation of all State Police officers below sergeant was changed from patrolman to trooper on September 18, 1948) had been with the department just over a year and was assigned to north central Arkansas after he completed the State Police training school.206 Pavatt grew up outside Clinton and lived near his boyhood home with his wife and one-year-old son.

Thousands of miles away from the shootout in Newton County, a 23-year-old World War II veteran named Kenneth Speegle was running away from an Army base in Washington state, absent without leave (A.W.O.L.) and heading for his father's home in rural Marion County near Yellville. By all accounts, Speegle was a good soldier. He served with the 25th Infantry Division in the jungles of the Pacific theater where he earned a Bronze Star for heroism in battle. But by the time he arrived in northern Arkansas in early September, he exhibited no traces of a heroic soldier and almost from the moment he arrived devoted himself to a life of crime. Instead of returning to his father's home, Speegle camped out in caves and in an abandoned storm cellar that he concealed using camouflage techniques learned in the army. He occupied his time by burglarizing residents' homes taking valuables, food, and most ominously, weapons. As the nights began to grow cooler, Speegle tired of sleeping in caves and storm cellars, so he started searching for an abandoned cabin to set up his burglary operation. The search would prove successful when it uncovered a small, primitive cabin that while short on comforts at least kept him dry. After moving some of his personal items inside, including several rifles, Speegle boarded up the front windows to cut down on the draft.

The one-room cabin, located about four miles north of Yellville in the woods off Highway 14, was the retirement home of a former railroad man from Indiana named Zue E. Cook. Cook had purchased the land and cabin a short time earlier, and about the time Speegle was going A.W.O.L. in Washington state, Cook was preparing to return to the cabin from a visit to see his relatives in Indiana. This would be the last time his family would see Cook alive.

By September 25, the burglaries continued unabated, so four residents, Kenneth Arno, Bud Hampton, Mr. Rutherford, and William Pope, went to see the Marion County sheriff. Hampton had run across Speegle's camouflaged storm cellar that contained a number of recently stolen items and intended to report the find to the authorities.

In the sheriff's absence, the foursome found Trooper Pavatt and told him about the storm cellar. Pavatt asked the men to show him the cellar. After showing the trooper their find, the men also noted that an old cabin was nearby and that the burglar might be living there, a possibility Pavatt conceded, so he asked the men to show him the location of the cabin. When the five men got to the cabin, three of them, Arno, Pope, and Rutherford, circled around to the rear of the cabin while Trooper Pavatt and Bud Hampton walked toward the front door. Arno could see in the rear windows of the cabin, and he spotted a man peeking out of the cracks in the boarded-up front window as Pavatt and Hampton approached. He yelled out, "There he is, in the window!" Pavatt crouched down, drew his service revolver—a Smith and Wesson .38/44—and yelled for the man to come out of the cabin. Pavatt's order was answered by the crack of a high-powered rifle shot fired from a crack in the boarded-up window. The .38/44 round struck the officer in the chest and sent him rolling down the hill. The sight of the wounded officer sent the other four men scrambling for help, but with the nearest hospital in Harrison, medical assistance was more than 30 minutes in arriving. By the time an ambulance and other officers arrived to pull the wounded officer to safety, Pavatt had lost consciousness and would die before reaching the hospital.

The spreading news of Pavatt's murder enraged the local community from which local officers were quickly able to assemble a large posse of armed civilians and law enforcement agents to return to the cabin and arrest the killer. After firing several warning shots in the cabin, members of the posse cautiously entered only to find it abandoned. A subsequent search of the home turned up more stolen items and military paperwork for one Kenneth Speegle. With Speegle identified as the primary suspect, an intensive manhunt began. The State Police rented an airplane to fly Lieutenant Carl Miller down to Tucker Prison Farm to pick up the penitentiary's bloodhounds and transport them to north Arkansas and jumpstart the search for Speegle. The dogs did not disappoint as they quickly picked up a hot trail leading away from the cabin. Unfortunately, the trail ended when it reached Highway 14. Lieutenant Miller, who was in charge of the manhunt, ordered road blocks set up and began a grid search of the densely wooded mountains surrounding the cabin by teams made up of both officers and civilians, of which the latter numbered more than a hundred and all were armed to the teeth.

As these groups searched the area on September 26, they uncovered a shallow grave 300 yards from the cabin that contained the body of the cabin's owner, Zoe Cook. Cook had been shot through the heart. Numerous false leads were reported to the State Police, and after a week of intensive searching, Lieutenant Miller was forced to concede that Speegle had somehow slipped their cordon and fled the area. A subsequent investigation would determine that Speegle had boarded a bus at Highway 14 and ridden it into Yellville where he hopped a passing freight train to elude his pursuers.

On October 6, fate intervened in the search for Kenneth Speegle when a retired Texas sheriff named Dale Lane spotted the young man hitchhiking just west of Oklahoma City. Lane had been sheriff in Speegle's boyhood hometown and had arrested him once as a juvenile. When Sheriff Lane saw Speegle hitchhiking, he was suspicious and pulled over to call the local authorities. Speegle was arrested a short time later and his identity was verified and a call was placed to the State Police. The next day, Captain Earl Scroggin, Lieutenant Miller, and Sergeant H. R. Peterson met Oklahoma officers in Fort Smith to pick up Speegle and take him to Little Rock headquarters for interrogation. Despite the best efforts of these investigators, Speegle refused to confess and claimed that he remembered nothing since he left the Army on September 1. By the time he went to court in June 1949, enough evidence had been accumulated linking Speegle to the shooting of Trooper Pavatt that a jury sentenced him to life in prison.[207]

By the time Speegle was convicted and sent to prison, the State Police was under new management. In December 1948, Governor McMath had appointed former State Police Captain Herman Lindsey as "acting director" of the department. The temporary nature of the appointment reflected McMath's desire to appoint Garland County Sheriff and fellow G. I. Revolt candidate I. G. Brown as director. This plan would fall through when Sheriff Brown's political supporters demanded that he serve his entire term, which did not expire until December 31, 1950. Therefore, McMath made Lindsey's appointment permanent.[208]

With a new director, the State Police began to prepare for the 1949 legislative session. The first State Police bill introduced in the session contained a number of moderately controversial changes. The most hotly debated was the reduction in highway patrol officers and an increase in the Criminal Investigation Division with each State Police district being assigned a CID sergeant to work cases.[209] This lean toward criminal investigation surely worried the gamblers in Hot Springs and around the state, who had quietly reopened their operations over the past year. Governor McMath attempted to soothe some of their fears by telling the state's press that the State Police would only respond to gambling and liquor violations if they "become so flagrant as to be a state problem."[210] An attitude the gamblers took to mean that as long as their operations were not conducted brazenly, then they could continue running. This interpretation would be shattered before summer.

One of the driving factors behind the expansion of the CID was its importance to local law enforcement. Local officers rarely had the training, equipment, or experience to handle major criminal cases, and since the 1930s, they had become increasingly reliant on the State Police for assistance. The department's identification bureau had amassed over 225,000 sets of fingerprints and mug shots from criminals both within Arkansas and from surrounding states, while the crime lab grew to become an important resource for ballistics, chemical, and physical testing of evidence.[211]

Over the same period, the Criminal Investigation Division expanded from two plainclothes investigators operating out of a Division of Intelligence in 1937, to seven men in a combined Criminal Investigation and Identification Division in 1946. After the passage of the 1949 State Police bill, the Identification Division was separated from Criminal Investigation and seven CID officers were assigned around the state, with Lieutenant H. R. Peterson placed in overall command of the unit.[212]

The first big operation by the CID and Highway Patrol after McMath became governor destroyed whatever hope gamblers had that they could operate unopposed. In February, Garland County Sheriff— and almost State Police Director—I. G. Brown led a raid consisting of county and city officers along with 10 State Police officers commanded by Lieutenant Glenn Garnett on five gambling joints the night before the horse races started at Oaklawn Park. Forty gamblers were arrested, and a clear message was sent that they had no friends in Sheriff Brown or Governor McMath.[213]

The State Police followed the Hot Springs raid with one surely intended as a jab at former Governor Laney. On March 15, troopers raided the Blackfish Club in Forrest City where they arrested seven people, including the club owner Henry Mallory, and confiscated four slot machines, roulette tables, bookie paraphernalia, and a machine gun. Following the raid, Governor McMath laid down the gauntlet to gamblers around the state by telling the State Police Commission that, "situations where local officers ignore law violations will be handled by the State Police just like the Blackfish Lake Club raid." The best way to catch these lawbreakers, he argued, was the aforementioned expansion of the Criminal Division.[214]

The more aggressive deployment of CID officers also created controversy. During the race for governor in 1950, Ben Laney decided to attempt a comeback and ran against McMath for the Democratic Party's nomination. During the campaign, Laney criticized McMath's use of the State Police and CID as a "private Gestapo" and a "private investigating company" meant to further entrench his political machine.[215] McMath dismissed such charges and reiterated his previous assertion that "if any gambling problems became so large and so flagrant to become a state problem then it is the duty of the state to take over."[216] Laney's criticism of McMath on the operation of the State Police and several other state agencies failed to sway enough of Arkansas' voters to his side, and McMath crushed Laney in the primary elections in August to win a second term.

Once McMath was elected to a second term in 1950, the State Police renewed their efforts to curb gambling. The CID sent officers undercover to investigate complaints of gambling around the state and identified 13 establishments in four counties (Garland, St. Francis, Phillips, and Ouachita) that conducted open gambling. Director Lindsey and Governor McMath held a joint press conference to publicly warn the 13 clubs that they were being watched, and unless they ceased operations, the State Police would begin raiding them. Many clubs, like the Southern in Hot Springs, made a public show of closing their operations while others continued without pause, certain that they would be protected by local authorities.

During April and May 1951, the State Police followed through on their warnings and raided clubs that allowed gambling and sold liquor without a license. In Camden, the hometown of former Governor Ben Laney, the department raided three clubs, including the renowned Plantation Club where they arrested the owners and confiscated liquor. These raids infuriated the town's mayor, who claimed that the State Police had not shown the city police the proper respect because they did not tell them about the raids beforehand and also that they conducted their operations without a search warrant. The mayor told the *Arkansas Democrat* that the State Police meant to "embarrass our local officers ... [and] we've cooperated enthusiastically with State Police in the past. But I'm tired of fooling around with irresponsible leadership. As far as I'm concerned, we are through with the State Police."[217]

In Hot Springs, the local politicians and businessmen were even more upfront in their support of gambling. A caravan of 50 cars transported 350 businessmen, civic leaders, and prominent residents from the spa city to Little Rock to meet with Governor McMath. The leader of the caravan was a former member of McMath's G. I. Revolt, Q. Bynum Hurst. Hurst's political allegiance had swung in-line with the gamblers after he was elected to municipal office in 1946, and his motivation for arranging the caravan was to convince Governor McMath to keep his "hands off" of gambling in Hot Springs.[218] The request would be ignored, and until 1952 when McMath left office, State Police and Revenue Agents would continue to periodically raid gambling joints in Hot Springs and around the state.

While gambling investigations were a headline grabbing operation for the CID investigators, they actually worked a wide range of cases during this period. For example, in May 1949, Sergeant Wyatt Patrick solved a string of safe-cracking burglaries in east Arkansas. Later that year, officers would investigate charges of physical abuse at the girl's reformatory school and at the state mental hospital after high-ranking members of its staff were involved in a violent fight at a café. Also, in May 1950, the CID established a "sex crimes file" that compiled descriptions of sex offenders, their criminal history, and detailed crime data to "assist all officers of the state in the prevention and solution of sex crimes."[219]

All of the press coverage heaped on the CID in 1949 and 1950 tended to obscure the myriad of duties being performed by Highway Patrol officers. The clearest example of this occurred in Van Buren County. In April 1949, Clinton City Marshal, and later a member of the State Police's Weight and Standards Division, Haskell Sitton, was relaxing at his home when three armed men approached his house. Marshal Sitton had arrested one of the men, Wes Hunt, a few days previously, and now Hunt was determined to have his revenge. Marshal Sitton's son, Leroy, who would grow up to become a state trooper, remembered what happened next:

> The first shot came in through the window and hit the headboard [of my parent's bed], which kept it from hitting my mom, Mattie. Dad kind of pulled the curtain back [then] Dad got hit. They then started shooting around the windows. The next window they would have shot into would have been mine, but Dad started shooting through the front door and knocked one of them down.[220]

With one of the suspects shot, the other two fled the scene. Sitton would recover from his wounds, but while he was recuperating, Van Buren County was essentially without reliable law enforcement. As a result, the sheriff admitted that "conditions had been growing worse" and made a plea to Director Lindsey to send in additional State Police officers. A request he readily granted, and until another city marshal could be hired, the State Police provided extra troopers to police the county and local communities.[221]

Haskell Sitton would not be the only law enforcement officer involved in a life and death situation, as the summer of 1949 would prove to be a dangerous one for State Police officers, too. In one week in August, two troopers were shot. The first, Guy Downing, was struck in the shoulder by shotgun pellets while responding to a disturbing-the-peace call outside Little Rock.[222] Downing would recover fairly quickly, but another trooper would not be so lucky. Trooper Bill Gordon was on patrol outside West Memphis with a Crittenden County deputy sheriff when he spotted a car with a broken taillight. The trooper pulled the car over and was talking with the driver when the passenger, W. A. Price, walked behind Gordon, pulled a pistol, and fired six shots at the officer's back. One of the rounds found its mark, striking the trooper's spinal column. The wound would paralyze Gordon from the waist down, but he remained with the department as an ordinance officer working out of the Little Rock headquarters.[223]

Even with all of the special assignments, like those in Van Buren County, the Highway Patrol's focus remained traffic control, speed enforcement, and working to reduce the state's unacceptably high number of traffic fatalities. In late 1949, the first official Safety Council was established in Arkansas. Consisting of several hundred prominent businessmen, lawyers, judges, and politicians, the Safety Council's goal was to reduce traffic accidents and lower the fatality rate. The council presented a number of good suggestions to the governor and legislators as a way to accomplish these goals. The first was to increase the State Police to 215 officers of which 180 would be dedicated to highway patrol.[224] Also, the Safety Council recommended that the State Police be solely responsible for drivers' licensing and that the officers administer tougher tests. Through the rest of 1949 and 1950, local chapters of the Arkansas Safety Council were organized and began agitating for increased enforcement and tougher standards necessary to operate a motor vehicle in Arkansas.[225]

Governor McMath supported all of the Safety Council's recommendations, but he could not guarantee their implementation because of deteriorating state finances. As the 1940s were ending, state revenue had begun to decline from its peaks during the Second World War. Plus, Arkansas' finances were sapped by the net loss in population suffered during the 1940s as more and more people left the state for higher paying jobs in war-related industries in the north. This situation forced McMath to order all state agencies to reduce their budgets by five percent in 1950-1951.[226]

While many state agencies could reduce their budgets by cutting back on services, the State Police found that it did not have that luxury. If an emergency necessitated the presence of troopers or investigators, the State Police was honor-bound to respond and had to worry about the budgetary consequences later. This applied in the case of an emergency like the deadly tornado that ripped through Warren and killed 53 people in 1949 or an extended manhunt like the one the occurred in January 1950.

One of the objects of this particular manhunt was a name familiar to the State Police, Jack Rheuark, the bank robber who in 1946 kidnapped Trooper Add Shug and handcuffed him to the bumper of his patrol car. On New Year's Eve, Rheuark and three other prisoners assaulted a Tucker Prison Farm trusty guard and murdered him with his own shotgun before fleeing into the cold night. The next day, State Police, county officers, and prison trusties began an exhaustive manhunt. Trooper Ray Shipp, who was also a pilot, took controls of a small plane and flew with Assistant Director Carl Miller in the area around Tucker searching for the four armed fugitives while the head of the CID, H. R. Peterson, oversaw operations on the ground. The dangerous nature of the fugitives prompted Peterson to warn his fellow officers that "it's going to be rough for anyone who encounters them."[227]

The first solid sighting of the men occurred the next day when three of the convicts kidnapped an England man and stole his car. They did not make it far before they ran into a roadblock manned by a Lonoke night constable. Certain they would be recognized, the fugitives ran the roadblock in a hail of gunfire, which wounded the officer. Nearby, Troopers Shipp and Leo Wilcox heard the constable radio for help and rushed to the scene where they initiated a pursuit of the stolen car that reached speeds of more than 90 miles an hour. The chase ended in North Little Rock when the fugitives wrecked their car just before hitting a roadblock set up by North Little Rock officers. Despite the presence of State Police and North Little Rock officers, the three escapees managed to slip their pursuers in a swampy area.

On January 3, a difficult search became a miserable duty for the officers manning 24-hour roadblocks and attempting to track the escapees when sleet and snow began to fall from the skies and the temperature refused to rise above freezing during the day. Still, January third did bring some good news. Lieutenant Peterson and a prison trusty located the missing fourth escapee who was hiding in an abandoned cabin near the prison farm. The frigid weather also drove the three remaining fugitives to seek shelter, and when a house in Protho Junction was broken into, State Police identification experts Captain Scroggin and Leon Gershner were called in to investigate. The pair quickly determined from a fingerprint analysis that the three convicts had been there earlier in the day.

The search would end on January 5 when a North Little Rock police captain saw three men attempting to break into a car. The captain called for help before chasing the would-be thieves into a shack. Wisely, the captain chose to wait for backup and once they arrived, a flurry of shots were fired into the small, ramshackle building. As a result, the three men, two of which were now wounded, surrendered to police and ended the manhunt after five days of frantic activity.[228]

With the fugitives back in jail, State Police Director Lindsey tallied up the cost of the operation and determined that the State Police spent nearly $4,000 over and above their normal operating cost to assist in the manhunt. Expenses, the director reminded the governor, the State Police did not have in its budget.[229]

Governor McMath sympathized with the pressure Director Lindsey and the State Police were under and agreed with the state Safety Council's request for additional officers. When the General Assembly convened in January 1951, McMath told them that he wanted to add 135 troopers to the department, despite the clear revenue shortage the state was experiencing. The legislators responded half-heartedly to the governor's request and instead introduced a bill that authorized 25 additional men—22 were to be troopers, two were to be lieutenants, and one was a clerical position. These new positions would be funded by increasing the percentage of drivers' license fees dedicated to the State Police from 50 to 100 percent and also tacking on fees to all court cases that resulted from State Police arrests. The McMath administration realized that this bill, even though it was a shadow of what the governor requested, was a more realistic proposition considering the nature of the state's finances and agreed to support it. By February, the bill passed the Senate and was signed into law by the governor.

The addition of these new positions authorized a State Police force of 130 men and women (females only held clerical positions at this time) of which 104 were commissioned officers. Still, it took considerable effort for the department to find enough qualified applicants to fill the 22 trooper positions. As the editor of the *Arkansas Democrat* so accurately described the department's dilemma, "Would you be willing to work 10 or 12 hours a day on a job in which risking your life is just part of the work, for $2,400 a year and [you had to] buy your own uniform?"[230] The State Police did provide a $10-a-month clothing allowance, but with a single uniform costing roughly $250, it was not much help.

The poor pay, long hours, and difficult working conditions naturally led to high turnover among the troopers. As a result, in the late 1940s and early 1950s the State Police saw an average turnover of 25 percent each year.[231] One way the legislature tried to assist the agency in retaining officers was by approving and funding the first pension program in 1951. Officers were able to make contributions to a retirement account, which was then matched by the state.

The previous year—1950—saw Arkansas become one of only two southern states to experience a decline in the number of traffic fatalities. The following year would not be so kind, and by summer 1951 it was clear that traffic-related fatalities would be well above the previous year's totals. The state Safety Council returned to prominence, and a daily reminder of the number of auto fatalities in the state returned to the front page of the *Arkansas Democrat*. Pressure began to mount on Director Lindsey to do something to lower the rising death toll. After all, many thought, the legislature *had* increased their personnel. Lindsey told his troopers to have zero tolerance for speeders, announced a return of unmarked cars to the Highway Patrol, and ordered officers to establish roadblocks around the state to conduct safety checks.[232]

One of the troopers given a solid blue unmarked car was Melvin Delong. Trooper Delong patrolled Pulaski County south of the Arkansas River in his new car where he stuck primarily to highway 67 and highway 65 and was surprised by the success he was having in arresting violators. Motorists' lack of familiarity with the unmarked police car allowed the officer to easily pace speeding motorists and observe reckless drivers. In what would be an oft-repeated performance, Trooper Delong issued six citations over a two-hour period on a road that had rarely provided him with a comparable number of violators while he was driving a marked car.[233]

The results achieved by Trooper Delong and others convinced the department to expand their unmarked fleet from five to 28 by repainting 20 cars currently in use and buying eight new vehicles.[234] For the rest of 1951, the results did look positive as traffic fatalities in December fell below those experienced for the same month in 1950.[235]

Despite these efforts, 1952 produced even more traffic-related fatalities than 1951 with 458 compared to 431. Undoubtedly, the increase in traffic deaths reflected the tragic frequency of multi-fatality auto accidents that repeatedly ripped apart families and emotionally devastated survivors. Accidents like the one outside of Camden in which eight people were killed, including three teenagers, and another that took the life of seven people in east Arkansas were all too common in 1952.

The way to reduce traffic-related deaths, according to the State Police, was three-fold. First, the state needed to empower the department to test, issue, and revoke drivers' licenses, a responsibility that included maintenance of a central database containing the driving records of all drivers in the state. Second, the department needed to increase its salary scale to improve retention and attract qualified applicants. Finally, the director should be appointed by and answerable only to a non-political State Police Commission instead of the governor. Such an arrangement would remove the pressure of politics from the agency thereby improving morale and the effectiveness of the officers.[236]

Throughout the summer and fall of 1952, ranking officers from the department took this message to the people by speaking at civic clubs and issuing press releases reiterating their arguments. The department's Safety Division, headed by Lieutenant Jack Rhea and Sergeant Mack Thompson, also worked diligently to promote a new program they hoped would improve the residents' driving habits by encouraging a more considerate motorist. The program's tagline, "courtesy is contagious," was printed on bumper stickers and pamphlets, and the state's professional bus and truck drivers were enlisted to spread the message, as well.[237]

The Safety Division also pushed the state's newspapers to run front-page articles on proper driving techniques and common mistakes. Whether it was from these publicity efforts or simply a coincidence, accident rates did fall after the campaign was initiated, but for real change to occur, the department continued to argue that additional legislation was needed.

Before any legislation could be enacted to address these requests, the state had to pass through another election cycle. The most important race culminated in August following a heated runoff for the Democratic nominee for governor. Sid McMath had decided to challenge the traditional two-term limit for governors in Arkansas and had drawn several challengers. The most formidable opponent proved to be Francis Cherry, a judge from Jonesboro.

Aside from the weight of tradition pushing against McMath's reelection, the governor had a much bigger factor working against him. In 1951 and 1952, the Arkansas Highway Department and the Highway Commission came under serious criticism that alleged corruption, mismanagement, and rampant cronyism existed within the organization. In an attempt to determine the validity of the charges, the General Assembly authorized an audit of the Highway Department and the Highway Commission. With the governor's race winding down to its conclusion in August, preliminary results from the audit showed that most of the rumors and accusations were all too true. The findings provided more than enough firepower for Cherry to discredit McMath and erode his support around the state. As a result, when the votes of the runoff election were counted in August, Francis Cherry routed Sid McMath, and change was again in the air for the state and its State Police.

Governor-elect Cherry was well aware of the changes the State Police had been lobbying for over the past year and, in many aspects, agreed with them. He stated that he wanted an "independent State Police director" that was "removed from the domination of the governor." Also, he supported a larger force that was more focused on highway patrol instead of CID.[238] Whatever changes were in store for the State Police, its commander, Herman Lindsey, would not be around to see them happen.

On November 28, Governor-elect Cherry appointed former State Police Captain Lindsey Hatchett to the department's top spot. The 43-year-old former officer had left the State Police to work for the federal government during the Second World War and was most recently employed in private business in Little Rock when Cherry tapped him for the director's position.[239] In what must have been a surprising statement, Hatchett told the state's press that he wanted to actually reduce the number of officers employed by the State Police from 162 to 144 of which 84 would be assigned to Highway Patrol. The reduction in force would allow for higher salaries, which did fulfill one long-standing request by the department, but few had previously considered a reduction in officers as a means to that end. The bulk of these reductions would be taken out of the department's Investigation Division, which was essentially abolished during Hatchett's tenure as director. Now, all investigators would wear uniforms and only assist local officers if it was a major case.[240]

With such a lead-in to the 1953 edition of the General Assembly, the session promised to be a full one for the State Police and it did not disappoint. First, legislation was passed creating a new seven-member State Police Commission, a move that was intended to reduce the influence of politics in the operation of the department. By expanding the commission and appointing each member for a seven-year term, the perception was that a single governor would never be able to pack it with his own appointees. Also, the commission was expressly forbidden to install police equipment in their personal cars.[241] The General Assembly also acquiesced to Governor Cherry and Director Hatchett's desire to reduce the department to roughly 140 total employees and 84 troopers.

The biggest change resulted from the same audit of the Highway Department and Highway Commission that had such a negative impact on the political fortunes of former Governor McMath. One of the areas the audit criticized were the state's efforts in enforcing truck weight laws. The Highway Department had 13 weigh stations spread around the state to weigh trucks, assess gasoline taxes, and ensure proper licenses, but the officers at these facilities and those operating roving patrols actually belonged to the Revenue and State Police Departments.

This division of duties between three very different agencies undermined the efficiency of the operation and prevented any of the departments from placing too much concern on their performance. The net effect of these factors was a miniscule rate of detection. The audit determined that in the first three months of 1951 (the only time period from which the Highway Department even had any data), just over 107,000 trucks were weighed, but only 1.4% were deemed overloaded. A percentage far below those experienced in other states. Also, the audit found that "uniform diligence is not applied" at every weigh station.[242] Therefore, the audit stated, "We believe a more vigorous administration of the functions of the weighing stations would increase the revenues from that source and, more importantly, would diminish the number of trucks that are overloading the highways."[243]

The General Assembly saw the State Police as the natural agency to oversee all aspects of this operation and passed legislation creating the Weights and Standards Division. All of the current employees from the Highway and Revenue Departments would be transferred to the State Police and 30 new officers would be hired to improve enforcement.[244]

Giving the State Police full authority over weights and standards also led to a virtual reunion of original state rangers. The department asked its first commander, Gray Albright, to return to the agency as commander of its newest division. Albright agreed, and in July 1953 he once again became a member of the Arkansas State Police. Also joining Albright was Bob Lafollette, Albright's original assistant commander, as the assistant commander of the Weights and Standards Division, and Gene Mooney and Frip Hill as district supervisors.[245]

By July, the new division had been set up and its men trained, but the 89 newest members of the State Police still lacked uniforms and official vehicles. Albright did not allow such trivial concerns to hold up his men, and in its first month of operation, the division had weighed more than 56,000 trucks and collected over $50,000 in fines, gasoline taxes, and license fees. This collection rate was roughly 50 percent higher than what had been achieved using the three-way division of responsibility. Still, Albright felt his men would "do better when we get to working a bit more smoothly."[246]

The apparent improvements made in the Weights and Standards Division were quickly overshadowed by the growing number of traffic fatalities. It was clear by mid-summer that the state would threaten the record death toll set in 1941, and the State Police's Safety Division and Highway Patrol redoubled their efforts to stop the slaughter. In September, the Highway Patrol created "flying squads" composed of eight officers working out of four unmarked cars who would be dispatched to "hot spots" around the state to crack down on reckless driving and speeding. Clearly frustrated, Highway Patrol Commander McGibbony told the press, "We are through warning them."[247]

The department also sought help in enforcing speed laws with a brand new technology that was just beginning to make appearances in police departments around the country: radar. The first radar employed by the State Police was borrowed from the Highway Department, which had been using it to conduct a study estimating traffic speed—a study that determined, on average, 15 percent of Arkansans drove in excess of the speed limit. This new radar was a stationary tool that had to be transported in a suitcase and was quite cumbersome due to its heavy weight (45 pounds) and demanding power requirements, which needed to be hooked to a car battery to operate. Still the promise of such a tool led the Arkansas Democrat to declare that the game of "hide and seek between police and speed violators" was over.[248]

Such promise proved premature as November and December 1953 very nearly set a record for the number of Arkansans killed in traffic accidents. In November alone, 61 people died, and by the end of the year fatalities remained over 450. Captain McGibbony was at a loss to explain the high fatality rate, which persisted despite all of the efforts made over the previous 12 months by the State Police, the local Safety Councils, and the state's news media.[249] With nothing left to do but try even harder, the State Police Safety Division formed a partnership with the Democrat to focus the entire state's attention on traffic safety. For the entire year of 1954, the paper ran weekly articles on traffic safety that included driving quizzes, tips, and a daily death toll. Also, the paper sponsored a safety slogan contest that drew 5,000 entries before the editors selected "Safety makes sense—sense makes safety" as the best entry and awarded the winner a $50 savings bond.[250] Meanwhile, Safety Division head Jack Rhea continued to talk to civic groups, schools, and anyone else who would listen to a lecture on the safe operation of motor vehicles.

The goal of these efforts was a reduction of traffic fatalities below 400, which was a figure that would bring the state's fatality rate more in line with the national average of seven deaths per 100 million vehicle miles.[251] Even though this was an aggressive goal, they very nearly achieved it. Efforts like the one the department gave over Labor Day weekend, which saw every commissioned officer working traffic, undoubtedly helped reduce fatalities by discouraging motorists from speeding or driving recklessly. Still, accidents like the multi-vehicle one in mid-September on the Arkansas River bridge in Little Rock, highlights the uphill battle facing the state. One truck, whose flat bed was loaded with men heading out to pick cotton for the day, sideswiped another truck that had jackknifed in the middle of the bridge. The unprotected cotton pickers were thrown off the truck bed, killing four. By the time the chain reaction of crashing cars and trucks had stopped, more than 20 people, all of whom were driving or riding without the benefit of modern day safety features like seat belts and air bags, would be seriously injured. Also, Trooper Les Caldwell wrecked his patrol car and broke his leg while he was hurrying six injured men to the hospital.

Trooper Caldwell was not the only State Police officer injured in the line of duty in 1954, which turned out to be a particularly dangerous year. In February, Trooper Bill Struebing was called out to investigate a suspicious man who had been sitting in a parked car for two hours at the intersection of highways 62 and 65 eight miles north of Harrison. What Struebing did not know as he approached the lonely car parked on the side of the road was that its occupant, a 51-year-old Tulsa man named Marvin Huff, had murdered his wife and was the subject of an intensive manhunt in Oklahoma. Trooper Struebing asked the man for some identification only to be told by Huff that he did not have any with him. Struebing told him that meant he would have to ride with him to the district headquarters in Harrison to be identified. Calmly, the man agreed and as he got out of his car, drew a pistol and opened fire. Struebing was hit in the thigh as he retreated behind his car door. Once there, Struebing returned fire, squeezing off three rounds that knocked Huff to the ground. Struebing yelled out for the man to drop his weapon, but instead, Huff decided to take his own life and placed his pistol to his chest and pulled the trigger. With a gunshot wound to the thigh, Struebing would be out of service for a time, but would fully recover.[252]

The other deadly incident involving State Police officers in 1954 would occur just a county away from the scene of Struebing's confrontation. Two days before Christmas, Searcy County Sheriff Billy Jo Holder was talking with some friends outside of the Longhorn café in Pindall when three men with a glint of trouble in their eyes approached him. The seeming leader of the trio was Junior Brewer, who along with his father-in-law, Sam Hillis, and friend Otis Buckner began cussing at Sheriff Holder. The verbal confrontation quickly turned physical as the men began to scuffle, and Hillis grabbed for the sheriff's gun. Fearing a deadly resolution, the sheriff extricated himself from the scene and went for help.

The sheriff returned with Troopers Tommy Goodwin and Joe Bodenhamer and State Police Sergeant Otto Griffin. As the four officers approached the café, they could see Brewer, Hillis, and Buckner inside, so they yelled for them to come out with their hands up. Hillis and Buckner froze, but Brewer took off toward the back door of the café. Not wanting to lose their man, Sergeant Griffin and Trooper Bodenhamer went to the right and Trooper Goodwin went to the left of the café. Griffin and Bodenhamer arrived at the back just as Brewer busted out of the door. Griffin startled the man by shining his flashlight in his face and ordering him to freeze. Instead of stopping, Brewer hastily aimed a pistol and fired. The bullet struck Griffin in the leg and delayed the officers long enough for Brewer to sprint around the corner of the café, right into the arms of Trooper Goodwin. Brewer refused to go down without a fight and fired two shots at Trooper Goodwin, both hitting the officer, one in the chest and the other creasing his forehead as he fell to the ground. By this time, Griffin and Bodenhamer had rounded the corner and emptied their pistols into Brewer, killing him.

The officers rushed the seriously wounded Goodwin and the less seriously hurt Griffin to the hospital in Harrison, which was the same hospital that had seen so many State Police officers over the past six years. In 1948, Damon Wilson and Alan Templeton had been taken there after they were shot in Newton County, and Sidney Pavatt had died in route to that facility. Once again, three State Police officers were rushed to the Boone County hospital over the course of a single year, although this time all would survive to enjoy long, distinguished careers with the department.[253]

Despite all of the carnage the State Police witnessed on the highways, the deadly confrontations they faced, and the pressure they felt to reduce traffic fatalities, there were still instances of levity that helped lighten the burden. One such example occurred in December 1953 when Trooper Maurice Gately was pacing a speeder on highway 67 south of Little Rock at 3:30 in the morning. Satisfied that he had locked in the violator's speed, Trooper Gately moved in to pull the subject over. As he approached, he noticed something sticking out of the man's trunk, but in the early morning darkness he could not make out exactly what it was. Gately pressed the accelerator down and began rapidly closing the distance. When the officer turned on his siren and red light, the suspect refused to stop and a short pursuit followed, which was brought to an end when Trooper Gately forced the suspect's car off the road. Once the driver was in custody, the trooper was finally able to determine the massive object sticking out of the car's trunk. It was a 700-pound safe that turned out to have been stolen from a Hot Springs car lot. When Trooper Gately asked the 21-year-old driver what he was doing with a safe in the car, the man professed his ignorance of the safe's origin or how it came to be in the car's trunk since, he argued unconvincingly, when he stole the car it was already in the back.[254]

As Trooper Goodwin lay recovering in his Boone County hospital bed, the State Police was preparing to go through yet another change in leadership. In August, a relatively unknown politician, publisher, and postmaster from Madison County, Orval Faubus, had surprisingly bested incumbent Governor Francis Cherry in the Democratic Party primary. With no real opposition put forth by the state's Republican Party, Faubus was guaranteed election in November, and if tradition held, a new director of the State Police would be quickly appointed. Thus the mood at Little Rock headquarters and in the district headquarters around the state was one of expectation, intense interest, and concern over the direction the department would take under the guide of this new, unknown governor.

Chapter Four

Faubus and a Trooper in Every County, 1955-1966

"It was a terrible time."

Highway Patrol Captain Mack Thompson
describing the Little Rock Central Crisis.

In November 1959, a 23-year-old felon serving time at the hell that was Tucker prison farm talked his way into a three-day furlough to see his ailing father. The young convict's name was Joe Hilderbrand and his manhunt would forever occupy a place in the history of the State Police.

Joe was an interesting character. He was born and raised near the small community of Dover in west-central Arkansas where he spent most of his time in the dense forests and steep hills that defined that rugged region. He married early, which was not unusual, but his choice of a woman twice his age surely raised a few eyebrows. Joe's trouble with the law started after a young couple from out of state were robbed and then tied to a tree after they stopped at a rest area on highway 7. The couple identified Joe as their assailant, and he was tried, convicted, and sentenced to a three-year stretch at Tucker in 1958.

When Joe failed to return to Tucker after his furlough expired, officers from the Pope County sheriff's office and the State Police raided Joe's parents' house. The officers had the house under observation and believed him to be inside. They decided to take no chances since the last time they had come there to arrest Joe for robbing the two tourists, he had forced an armed stand-off with the officers. The men ordered the occupants of the house out, and when Joe did not emerge, they fired tear gas shells inside. After waiting for the fumes to subside, officers searched the cabin but found no one inside. In actuality, Joe had hidden in a pit under the house and used a wet feed sack to protect his eyes and nose from the tear gas. After the officers left, Joe emerged, eyes red and skin stinging from the gas, and hit the woods. When officers asked nearby residents, no one seemed to know where Joe was, and with no leads the officers assumed they would cross paths with the young fugitive sooner or later and simply let the matter drop.

For the next 10 months, Joe Hilderbrand lived in the woods around Dover where he could find food or shelter at his parents' or his wife's house or even an empty cabin when the weather got too bad or his food supply too low. It seemed that everyone knew Joe was there and that he was a wanted fugitive, but no one wanted to see him captured, and everyone refused to help officers find him. Even people whose cabins Joe broke into seemed to understand and sympathize with the young man. They told officers that Joe only took what he needed to survive and tried to minimize damage to their houses by repairing the locks he had broken. Some people even left canned goods on their porch with a note asking him not to break the windows. One lady summed it up quite nicely when she wrote a letter to Governor Faubus on Joe's behalf explaining, "We love our mountain boys."[255]

The sheriff's office would not hear from Joe again until August 1960 when a man matching his description stole a car in Russellville. State Police and local officers from Harrison to Russellville set up roadblocks attempting to catch the thief, but their efforts came to naught. Even with this near brush with the law, it is possible that officers might never have caught Joe if he had not decided to run off with his wife's 17-year-old niece, Frances, on September 5. The inclusion of the young girl in Joe's life on the run angered many of his former supporters who stopped giving him the food and shelter he had been living off for the previous 10 months. Without this support, Joe had to rob grocery stores and filling stations to get food and also had to steal cars to dodge the growing police presence.

The spate of robberies and car thefts forced local officers and State Police to begin "a determined effort" to catch Joe in October. State

Police Lieutenant Paul McDonald oversaw the manhunt and tried to coordinate the 17 State Police officers, bloodhounds, airplanes, sheriff's deputies, game wardens, and city officers in a search of the vast Ozark National Forest. McDonald vowed, "We'll keep him on the run and not give him any rest until he's caught."

For a time it appeared that Joe would never stop running. On October 3, a trooper passed Joe and Frances on a country road, but by the time he got turned around, the two had ditched the car and fled into the woods. On the fourth, the pair stole another car and robbed a store north of Dover. Officers found the car abandoned with an empty gas tank the next day. On the fifth, Joe and Frances stole a car from a farmer near the Newton County community of Boxely. The farmer shot at the two with a shotgun, which shattered the back glass of the car, but left Joe and Frances uninjured and slightly ahead of their pursuers. Later that afternoon, a trooper spotted the stolen car and turned to give chase. Joe swerved off the main highway onto a deeply rutted log road. The ruts were too deep to allow the patrol car to pass, which forced the officer to abandon the pursuit. When other officers arrived, they walked down the narrow path and found that Joe's car had also gotten stuck and been abandoned. Joe and Frances fled in such a hurry that they left their coats and extra food in the car.

For another week, state, county, and local officers diligently searched the area for any signs of Joe and Frances. The State Police operated from a command post they set up at a deer camp 13 miles north of Dover. The camp had cabins where their officers could eat, sleep, and plan their strategy, but it was so hot, most chose to sleep outside on cots.[256] Even Joe's father, Lytle Hilderbrand, began to help the police search for his son in hopes of finding him before Joe fulfilled his vow to "keep running until they kill me."

The Hilderbrand manhunt would finally come to an end on the evening of October 12. That morning Joe and Frances, nearly overwhelmed by hunger and worn down by the elements, wandered into an isolated farmhouse in Pope County. The two fugitives explained to their gracious hosts that they had gotten lost in the woods and had to spend the night and needed some food and a ride. The farm family obliged, but when they dropped the pair off at a country store, a passerby recognized them and called police. Twenty State Police officers along with men from the Pope County sheriff's office and the Clarksville police department converged on an area 20 miles north of Dover. Lieutenant McDonald ordered officers to set up stakeouts on three nearby houses, expecting Joe and Frances to break into one of them that night searching for food or shelter. Just as the sun was beginning to go down, Troopers Pete Tracy and Howard "Bear" Chandler arrived at Elmer Page's home near the community of Treat. Around 9:00 p.m., the officers heard someone approaching the house and then open the gate. The men switched on their flashlights and surprised Joe and Frances as they were walking toward the front porch. Tracy yelled, "Stop or I will blow your heads off!" The pair wisely dropped their weapons—Joe was carrying a .30-30 caliber rifle and Frances had a .22 caliber rifle and a .32 caliber pistol—and Bear Chandler handcuffed them, bringing to a successful close a manhunt that had lasted over a month.[257]

The story of Joe Hilderbrand does not end there, though. Joe was tried and convicted for escaping and for the crimes he committed while he was on the run, but due to his folk hero status, he was given a suspended sentence and sent back to Cummins to serve the remainder of his original term. He did not stay at Cummins long. In December 1960, prison officials ordered Joe to undergo mental tests at the State Hospital in Little Rock. The doctors judged that Joe was mentally unstable and remanded him to their care. By July 1961, the same doctors decided that Joe was fit enough to go back to Cummins. The night before he was to return, Joe unscrewed the bars on his cell window, fashioned a rope out of sheets from his bed, and slipped out the window to freedom.

Just over a year later, Joe remained at large and largely forgotten by everyone but State Police Sergeant O. E. "Blondie" Bowden who continued to ask around about Joe. That is until a 15-year-old girl lodged a complaint that he had assaulted her. Apparently, other people with the governor's ear had complained as well because Governor Orval Faubus claimed to have been the spark that re-ignited the State Police's manhunt of Joe Hilderbrand. Whatever the source, on October 1, 1962, Captain Paul McDonald, Lieutenant Buck Halsell, and Sergeant Bowden met to plan a strategy for capturing Joe. The three decided that a "maximum effort by a minimum amount of personnel disguised as hunters very possibly could work."[258]

The group selected six men, Lieutenant Milton "Scrub" Mosier, Sergeant Tommy Goodwin, Sergeant W. A. Tudor, Investigator Ervin Young, and Trooper Charles Tackett, to accompany Captain McDonald on the operation. The men loaded their camping and hunting gear into two borrowed jeeps and Investigator Young's van, which boasted a butane stove. Also accompanying the officers was a trusty from Cummins Prison Farm who was the designated cook. On October 2, the men quietly set off for a campsite at Harris Ford on the Big Piney River about a dozen miles north of Dover and nine miles overland from the Hilderbrand residence. The seven "hunters" arrived that afternoon, set up their tent, ate a hearty meal, and planned their strategy.

They decided to split into three groups. Sergeant Goodwin and Investigator Young were ordered to get as close to the Hilderbrand residence as possible without being seen and watch for Joe to appear. The other groups would "hunt" in the woods north and south of the residence where they hoped to catch sight of the young fugitive. One of the locals who they trusted to keep their real identity a secret offered to drive the three groups to their jumping off points since his truck would not arouse Joe's suspicions if he spotted it. The men readily agreed since the prospect of hiking overland through the dense Ozark National Forest did not seem particularly inviting.

The men shook themselves awake the next morning at 4:00 a.m. and met up with their transportation. The local man dropped the three teams off without incident, and the manhunt was on once again. While

Sergeant Tudor and Lieutenant Mosier walked the woods near the
Treat community, Captain McDonald, Lieutenant Halsell, and Trooper
Tackett trudged around south of Joe's house. Meanwhile, Goodwin and
Young warily crept toward the Hilderbrands' ramshackle house. They
successfully gained a well-hidden position that offered a good view of
the front of the house and quickly spotted a man matching Joe's general
description working on a car in the front yard. Over the course of the
morning, the two became convinced that the man working on the car
was indeed Joe Hilderbrand. The actions of Joe's in-laws proved to be
the real clincher. The two would take positions near the road and yell a
warning whenever a car appeared after which Joe would run inside the
house. Convinced, Goodwin and Young backed their way out of the
position and headed back to camp.

It was decided that the officers would raid Joe's house the next
morning. Once again, the officers got an early start and a lift from their
local ally to their jumping off point several miles from the Hilderbrand
residence. The plan called for Goodwin and Young to go to the front of
the house and the other four to go to the back. Once everyone was in
position, they would give the signal via walkie-talkies to move in and
order Joe out of the house. At 10:00 a.m., the two groups had split up
and were approaching the house. Goodwin and Young arrived in
position first and saw Joe once again in the front yard working on a car.
Apparently, Joe's skill as a mechanic paid off because in a short time he
slammed the hood down and hopped in the car. Goodwin and Young
were startled. If Joe got the car started and moving, they might have to
start their search all over again, and no one wanted a repeat of the epic
1960 manhunt. Goodwin and Young jumped up and charged down the
hill with their guns drawn, yelling at Joe, "Don't move—you're
covered!" Joe saw the wisdom of the request, and the two officers
quietly took him into custody.

That night, the seven men retired back to their campsite where
they decided to enjoy a final night eating charcoaled steaks delivered by
Trooper Kenneth Brown and Lieutenant Boone Bartlett, and a bath in

the frigid Big Piney River to wash off the ticks and chiggers picked up after two days of hiking. Once again the state convicted Joe, but after receiving a record number of petitions for pardon, the parole board released him in 1964.[259]

* * *

The election of a relative unknown like Orval Faubus as governor in 1954 might have surprised some in the state, but Governor Faubus's choice for State Police director was anything but an unknown to the department. On January 15, 1955, Faubus selected Herman Lindsey, the former officer and director under Governor McMath. Although McMath and Faubus would have a falling out, initially the political ties between McMath and Faubus were strong. This link undoubtedly played a role in the reappointment of Lindsey to the department's top spot.

With the director in place, the department anxiously awaited the outcome of their appropriation bill in the recently convened 1955 session of the General Assembly. As usual, the state faced serious budget problems, and the reluctance of legislators to increase taxes placed every state agency and department's budget in the line of fire. While these monetary restrictions prevented the addition of officers to the State Police's roster, at least they were able to maintain the status quo. Also, with the ouster of Director Lindsey Hatchett and Governor Cherry, the department re-established the Criminal Investigation Division in February and staffed it with 10 investigators.[260]

One important, though numerically small, change was the transfer of the state's fire marshal duties from the Insurance Department to the State Police. Previously, the state fire marshal did little investigative work and thus provided few benefits to the state's law enforcement officers. Instead, local officers, fire department officials, and State Police troopers conducted all arson investigations. Now, the State Police would oversee its operation by assigning a lieutenant and a sergeant whose sole responsibility was to review blueprints, inspect buildings, teach fire safety, and investigate cases of arson throughout the state.

The first commander of the Fire Marshal's Section was Ben Kent, but Lieutenant Kent only remained at this position a few weeks before choosing to enter the private sector. His replacement was Mack Thompson, who had transferred over from the Public Safety Division when the Fire Marshal's Section was created in July 1955.[261] Lieutenant Thompson did not have long to wait for his first high-profile arson investigation. On July 17, a prominent Little Rock lawyer's home exploded and burned to the ground.[262] Thompson and Little Rock fire department officials sifted through the ashes for several days and finally determined the explosion and subsequent fire were accidental.

The summer of 1955 was proving to be an explosive one for more than just Lieutenant Thompson. The city of Little Rock saw a violent strike by public transit drivers. Physical confrontations between the non-union drivers hired to replace the union workers grew from an exchange of fists to an exchange of gunshots. The level of violence grew so great that the mayor of Little Rock sent a request to Director Lindsey asking for the State Police to intervene and provide protection for the buses and non-union drivers. Director Lindsey declined to intervene due to a restriction placed in the State Police's enabling legislation that specifically forbade their involvement in labor disputes.[263] The origin of this particular caveat dated back to the original bill creating the State Police and reflected one of the most common criticisms expressed against the creation of State Police forces during the 1930s when several states misused them as strikebreakers. Therefore, when the Arkansas State Police was created in 1935, special restrictions were included to ensure similar abuses did not occur. For several months, it appeared that the Little Rock police officers and private security would be able to contain the violence and the strike would be settled at the negotiating table, but then in November, masked men tossed a bundle of dynamite into a moving bus. The driver was able to escape unharmed, but the subsequent explosion totaled the bus and convinced the mayor and the bus company that things were far from under control. This time the State Police agreed to increase their presence in the city and to assist local officers in patrolling bus routes and investigating the bombings. The brazenness of the last bombing created an avalanche of criticism for the unions even though they denied any knowledge of the act. Either way, the two sides finally began to make some progress at the bargaining, and a resolution was reached without further sabotage.[264]

At the same time the city's public transit corporation experienced a war between labor and management, a local dairy also ran into serious labor problems. Like the union bus drivers, the dairy's union workers walked out on strike in the summer of 1955. When non-union workers were hired as replacements, tensions quickly mounted. On a steamy July night, two explosions ripped through the dairy, destroying equipment, but luckily not resulting in any injuries since the facility was closed.

Little Rock police, State Police, and fire department officials rushed to the scene and began a search of the facility. The officers located a third, unexploded charge containing 20 sticks of dynamite inside a boiler. Trooper Floyd Weaver went into the boiler and safely removed the explosives. The State Police took the lead in the investigation with Assistant Director Carl Miller, CID Commander Alan Templeton, and Investigator Paul McDonald chasing down leads on the case. Naturally, suspicion fell on union workers, but by the end of the week the investigation was at a standstill. CID investigators gave two prime suspects polygraph tests—the polygraph machine was a tool that Assistant Director Carl Miller held in high regard and even credited it with solving 18 cases over the previous five years—but the results of the tests were not conclusive enough to charge either men. Ultimately, the dairy bombing cases were never solved despite the hard work and intense effort expended by the officers.

A case that would have a different outcome occurred as 1955 was drawing to a close. Over a three-week period in November and December, three people were murdered and one person robbed along highway 67 in the state. The last of these murders occurred just north of Hope. A 30-year-old woman from Texas was found in the ditch beside the highway with a small caliber bullet wound in her head. Trooper Jim Rowell was the first officer on the scene and after securing the body and waiting for CID Sergeants Milton Mosier and Buck Halsell to arrive, Trooper Rowell began to canvas the area. While he was driving north along highway 67, a man with a dog flagged him down and directed him to a bloodstained floor mat and towel lying in the ditch a few miles north of the body. The man's dog had alerted him to this key bit of evidence, which Trooper Rowell quickly took into custody.

It would take almost a week to identify the body, but little additional clues were provided that explained how the woman ended up being murdered. After the woman's picture was run on the front pages of the state's newspapers, a handful of tips were called into the CID's investigative team, which was headed by Captain Alan Templeton and Sergeant Paul McDonald out of Little Rock and Sergeants Mosier and Halsell operating locally. Luckily, someone saw the woman hitchhiking in Texas and remembered her being picked up by a northbound truck driver. The investigators retraced the murdered woman's steps from her hometown to the place where she was picked up and finally to the place where her body was dumped. Then they began researching what trucks would have been northbound on highway 67 at that particular time and place. The search quickly narrowed down to a truck operating out of South Carolina and driven by 30-year-old David Geiger.[265]

Certain they had found the right man, the officers asked local officers in South Carolina to arrest Geiger and hold him until Sergeants Mosier and Halsell could go and pick him up. A week later—January 4, 1956—Geiger was back in Arkansas and at State Police Headquarters in Little Rock. Geiger's version of events was that the woman had found his .38 caliber pistol in the glove box of his truck and then, inexplicably, placed it to her head and committed suicide. The suicide so unnerved the man that he dumped her body instead of reporting it to the police. The investigators did not buy Geiger's story, and he was charged with murder on January 5.

While the CID was nearly being overrun with cases, the Highway Patrol could feel the collective stare of an entire state looking to them to reduce the frustratingly resilient traffic fatality rate. The previous year, 1954, had seen a drastic reduction in motor vehicle fatalities, but in 1955 traffic fatalities were occurring more frequently not only in Arkansas, but also throughout the country. The national outcry led to numerous state and national campaigns, like a special "safe driving day" and a media campaign entitled "slow down and live." These programs kept Safety Section head Jack Rhea running around the state conducting safety training and holding press conferences, but drivers seemed to refuse to heed his warnings, so the department chose to act more aggressively. On holiday weekends like Memorial Day and Labor Day, Director Lindsey ordered every officer—even CID investigators— in uniform and pulling double shifts to increase their presence on the highways.[266] While these intensive enforcement efforts did help reduce traffic fatalities while they were ongoing, overall they did not prevent deaths from rising toward 400 once again.

October 1955 proved to be one of the deadliest in the state's history when sixty-three people were killed in traffic-related accidents. One reason for such a record month was an accident that occurred in southeast Arkansas on October 3. At 5:00 a.m., rookie Trooper Buren Jackson was awakened by a call from the chief of police at Eudora who told him, "We have got a bad accident down here and it looks like there may be some fatalities. Can you come down here and help us with it?" Jackson told him he could and headed off into the early morning darkness to work what was at that time the worst traffic accident in Arkansas history.

When he arrived, he found the bodies of seven black men lined along the side of the road and more than a dozen injured people awaiting medical attention. The cause of such carnage was a head-on collision involving a Nash automobile and a school bus just outside the small town of Eudora. The Nash, from which all seven fatalities were pulled, had taken a curve too wide and struck the bus, which contained

members of the Philander Smith College football team returning from
a game in New Orleans. Jackson remembered that:

> I started trying to get people identified. You could hardly get in on the
> radio from down there. The lieutenant had sent a trooper in to man
> the radio since it was normally off the air that early in the morning.
> Little Rock [headquarters] and the press were calling about the
> wreck. We couldn't get the bodies moved because it was during
> segregation days. They would not haul dead or injured blacks in white
> ambulances. You had to haul them in black ambulances, of which
> there weren't many … however you could get them to the hospital
> that was the way you sent them.[267]

As it turned out, the day was just getting started for Trooper
Jackson. Before the officer could finish working the bus accident, he
received an emergency call to respond to a wreck near the Cummins
prison farm involving a circus convoy. A truck carrying the circus' tigers
had overturned, and the overheated and scared tigers were attempting
to escape. Luckily, they were able to get the truck turned upright and
the tigers cooled off by throwing water from the roadside ditch on them.

November would see more of the same when a truck hauling 80
Mexican cotton pickers ran off an embankment outside of Prescott.
Fortunately, only one person was killed, but with more than 80 injuries
ranging from minor to life threatening, the few small hospitals in the
area were quickly overwhelmed. As a result, the seriously injured had
to be crammed into every available room and hallway for treatment.[268]
Following a final flurry of fatal accidents on New Year's eve, the number
of traffic fatalities in Arkansas that year settled at 416, just above 1954's
total of 411 and the State Police's goal of 400.[269]

Although the number of traffic fatalities disappointed the Highway
Patrol, they still had a number of high-profile successes during the year.
In June, the State Police received a tip from the Federal Bureau of
Narcotics to be on the lookout for a 1953 Mercury with a Texas
license. As fortune would have it, Trooper Gerald Harris spotted a
Mercury with Texas tags on highway 67 outside Beebe and pulled the

car over. Once Trooper Harris approached the car he knew this was the one the federal agents had warned him about. The odor of marijuana "overwhelmed" the officer, who quickly took the men into custody and searched the car. The search did not have to be all that intensive since the two Mexican nationals had packed the entire trunk and half of the backseat with burlap sacks stuffed with bricks of processed marijuana. The traffic stop netted 190 pounds of marijuana, the largest in the state's history, and a deserved thank you from the Federal Bureau of Narcotics.[270]

In November, troopers made another important stop. Early that month, an 18-year-old Arkansas man shot and killed a police officer in Kentucky. Officers in Kentucky speculated that the man would flee back to his home state, so word was passed to the State Police to be on the lookout. Once again, luck would be on the State Police's side as Trooper Bill Miller spotted the suspect's car three miles north of Jonesboro on highway 63. Ed Vanderhook, Walnut Ridge's chief of police was riding with Trooper Miller that day, and the two officers gave chase. The pursuit ended with both the suspect and the trooper wrecking their cars. In fact, Chief Vanderhook was thrown from the vehicle, but was uninjured. In a smart move for a cop-killer, the suspect quickly emerged from his wrecked car with his hands up. Trooper Miller took him into custody without incident, and the man was extradited back to Kentucky to stand trial.[271]

The next year, 1956, would get started with a bit of an uproar at State Police headquarters. On January 14, troopers picked up a 20-year-old hitchhiker named Guy Jones and transported him to Little Rock to verify his identification. After officers obtained the man's fingerprints, he asked to use the restroom to clean up. No one saw the harm in such a request, so they pointed the facilities out to him without a second thought.

The officers began to get worried when Jones did not return in a timely manner, so they decided to go looking for him. During the search, one of the troopers noticed that his patrol car was missing and another found that the outside window in the bathroom had been left open. Then it dawned on the men that Jones had climbed out of the window and stolen a patrol car. The State Police radio operators issued an alert to all Pulaski County officers to be on the lookout for a State Police patrol car. The search did not take long, and the car was found abandoned a few blocks away.

A search of the neighborhood did not turn up Jones, so officers figured he had fled the area. Actually, Jones had circled back to State Police headquarters and was watching all of the commotion from an apparently well-hidden vantage point. As soon as night fell, Jones decided to try again. He boldly walked up the hill to the headquarters, got into CID Sergeant Paul McDonald's unmarked police car, and drove off into the night. A short time later, the theft was discovered, and another alert was sent out to officers in the immediate area to be on the lookout for an unmarked State Police car. Jones undoubtedly heard the bulletin since the unmarked car also contained a State Police radio. Convinced that he would be caught driving the police car, he ditched it near a cemetery in Little Rock, walked to a car dealership, and stole his third vehicle for the day. Jones was able to slip his pursuers in the new car, which was not reported stolen until the next day, and evade capture for another week until officers in Roswell, New Mexico, arrested him.[272]

With the State Police still a bit red-faced after two of their patrol cars were stolen in a single day, they began to receive criticism for their lack of activity in enforcing gambling laws in Hot Springs. The state's attorney general, Tom Gentry, was the governor's most vocal critic, and he seized upon Faubus's 1954 campaign promise to enforce gambling laws throughout the state.[273] It was clear to even the most ardent Faubus supporter that the governor's campaign rhetoric had not reflected his actual governance, since casinos in Hot Springs were in fact up and running "wide open." These gambling joints had been open for quite sometime since the previous governor, Francis Cherry, did not care to run afoul of the Hot Springs politicians, either, and sidestepped any arguments for enforcement by saying whatever happened in Hot Springs was the responsibility of local authorities and not the State Police.

When the state's Baptists passed an anti-gambling resolution at their annual convention in November 1955, Attorney General Gentry knew he had a heavy political stick to swing at Faubus, and he vowed to "stay after him until something is done to stop [gambling in Hot Springs]."[274] The first method Gentry chose was to file suit in Hot Springs chancery court seeking to padlock one of the most brazen casinos, the Tower Club. In the court case, Gentry subpoenaed State Police Director Lindsey to explain why his officers were not enforcing the law in the spa city.[275] The case was dismissed before Lindsey had to testify, and the two men had a public reconciliation a week later when a joint press conference was called. Lindsey told Gentry and the state's media that the State Police were at the attorney general's disposal if he wanted to "clean up the gambling mess in Hot Springs." Gentry thanked Lindsey and told him that he had already obtained "search and burn" warrants from a Hot Springs municipal judge, but had decided to hold off on serving them since it appeared that the casinos were beginning to close up their operations.[276]

In fact, the gambling clubs were just practicing the time-honored tradition of laying low until the attention of the state's press and/or whichever crusading politician had targeted them moved on to easier targets. By the end of February, Oaklawn's racing season was in full swing, and the accompanying crush of visitors to the spa city proved too tempting for the casinos to stay closed no matter who was watching. Therefore, clubs like the Southern, Belvedere, and Reno were packed every night with gamblers. Attorney General Gentry saw his chance and took Lindsey up on his offer. State troopers raided the Southern and Reno Clubs on February 29, arrested 17 people, and confiscated a substantial amount of gambling equipment.[277] Over the next week, three additional raids would follow, although they yielded less and less each time.

The declining arrests and seizures did not reflect a decrease in gambling in the city, but instead reflected the ability of the casino owners to be forewarned anytime a raid was imminent. One such example occurred on March 7. Attorney General Gentry had dispatched undercover agents to Hot Springs where they found the Southern Club packed with 500 patrons playing slots and table games. Gentry called the State Police at 11:00 p.m. to assemble a raiding party at their Little Rock headquarters. At 12:20 a.m., the raiding party rolled out of Little Rock, but by the time they arrived in Hot Springs at 1:30 a.m., the Southern Club's door was closed and its lights were dark.

By the end of March, Gentry had given up trying to close down the casinos in Hot Springs. With "gambling and drinking running as free as water over Niagara Falls" and a thousand people a night cramming into the Belvedere casino, Gentry knew his efforts had been for naught and laid the blame squarely at the feet of Governor Faubus.[278] He told the state's press that he had been "blocked at every turn by the powers that be," and if anyone wants the gambling to stop, they needed to take it up with the governor.[279] When the media asked Governor Faubus to respond to the challenge, he laughed, took out a copy of the State Police's enabling legislation and read from section 42, which stated that they were not intended to usurp the authority of local officers. The implications were clear. If the gambling in Hot Springs was going to be stopped, it was going to have to be done from within the community and not by state officers.

With the gambling raids at an end, the State Police could focus on what seemed to be an unfortunately consistent problem, the state's traffic fatalities. By March, fatalities were 200 percent higher than the same period in 1955, causing the *Arkansas Democrat* to remark that, "Arkansans are killing themselves with reckless abandon."[280] Safety Section chief Lieutenant Rhea noted that they did not have enough troopers to completely enforce the traffic laws, so the drivers of the state had to be safety conscious and it was imperative that the Safety Section successfully impart such a mindset on Arkansans.[281]

In June, another high-ranking State Police officer, Captain Frank McGibbony, was spreading the message of safe driving in a speech to a civic club in Blytheville, but he ranged a bit off of the standard safety line by recommending the State Police become an independent state agency.[282] Director Lindsey had first offered this proposal several years previously when the McMath administration was in office, but it had generated little support among legislators or the governor's office. The general idea was that the State Police would become an agency like the Highway Department, which was answerable only to a highway commission and whose director could only be fired for cause. Reducing the power and authority of the governor was not a reform that Faubus could get behind, and he responded that "any public service cannot be taken entirely out of politics," therefore it would make no difference how the State Police was organized.

Faubus was willing to support one of the department's primary goals, though. In a meeting with the Legislative Council in the fall, the governor voiced his support for a major expansion of the agency's personnel. The huge increase in traffic fatalities in 1956 to 486 deaths and the accompanying outcry from the state's press created an environment that supported such an expansion even if it would require new taxes to pay for it. When the legislators began to gather in Little Rock in January 1957, Director Lindsey laid out the design for the new force by requesting more than 90 new troopers, an addition that would more than double the number of road officers and for the first time in the state's history provide a trooper in every county.[283]

To pay for the new officers, cars, and equipment that accompanied the expansion, the legislature passed a bill that doubled the driver's license fee from one to two dollars. As one state representative noted, the more than 700,000 additional dollars raised by this increased fee was meant to stop the "slaughter" on the state's highways.[284] The bill also provided a long overdue pay raise of $100 a month for the officers and was designed to attract more qualified applicants and improve retention.

Even though the need for more officers appeared urgent, the new law would not go into effect until the state's next fiscal year, which started on July 1, 1957. The entry of the new troopers would also be delayed by the presence of national guard troops at Camp Robinson— the location of the State Police training academy—until mid August. Once the soldiers were done, the State Police would move in and conduct two concurrent six-week training academies for all of the new officers and also for officers who were already working but had not yet been through the training school. By 1957, the latter group had grown quite large since the State Police had not had a training academy in a number of years.[285]

The delay did allow the department plenty of time to sort through the "several hundred" new applications that came pouring in after the new law was passed. The minimum qualifications remained essentially the same as those used to select the original 13 Rangers. For example, applicants must have a high school diploma, a clean background, be familiar with firearms, stand at least five feet 10 inches, and weigh 175 pounds. If an applicant met the minimum qualifications, he had to pass a written exam and sit through an oral interview with Director Lindsey, Captain Scroggin, or another top-ranking officer.[286] One long-standing factor in the hiring process that was not publicly mentioned, but was generally understood, was the need for a successful applicant to have someone speaking for him. Most often, that someone was the applicant's local state senator or representative who could call the governor or Director Lindsey and provide a testament of the applicant's suitability for the position. As one trooper recalled, "Back then, you didn't just sign on and get hired. You had to have somebody pretty stout in politics to get the job."[287]

When the first training school began on August 18, 72 men donned khaki recruit uniforms and prepared to embark upon six weeks of intensive instruction in firearms, criminal law, traffic law, accident investigation, and physical training. The training cadre took great pains to meticulously plan the recruits' day to maximize the amount of training completed, but before the first training academy could be completed, outside events would interrupt and demand a change of plans.

Commonly known as the Central High crisis, the fight to integrate Little Rock's Central High School in September 1957 represented, for the first time since the Civil War, a state's open defiance of federal authority and foreshadowed just how difficult it would be to end racial discrimination in the former Confederate states. At the time, Faubus's active campaign to prevent the integration of Central High created worldwide criticism of the United States and demonized Arkansas as a backward, prejudiced state. Still today, the events of September 1957 resonate and influence people's perceptions of Arkansas and the South.

The path to the Central High crisis began in May 1954 when the United States Supreme Court ruled in *Brown vs. the Board of Education* that separate schools for blacks and whites were inherently unequal and thus unconstitutional. The following year, the Supreme Court issued an implementation decree that mandated all segregated schools become integrated in a reasonable amount of time. The implementation decree created an uproar in southern states where many politicians argued that such an order encroached upon their state sovereignty.[288]

While many southern leaders and politicians spoke openly about their willingness to defy such an order, Arkansas Governor Orval Faubus was not one of them. During his gubernatorial campaign in 1956, Faubus took a moderate position on integration and told the state that integration was inevitable and that he would not defy federal laws. Early efforts at integrating Arkansas schools had seen mixed reactions from the white citizens. In Fayetteville, integration of the high school occurred with few disruptions, while in the small east Arkansas town of Hoxie, strong opposition from local citizens developed, but ultimately failed to prevent successful integration. Outside of Arkansas, other southern schools suffered through civil unrest, with the clearest example occurring in 1956 in Clinton, Tennessee, where local whites rioted for several days after their high school was integrated. With the situation so clearly out of control,

Tennessee's governor had to call out the State Police and national guard to bring the situation under control and protect the black students.[289] Even with these examples of civil unrest, Governor Faubus seemed resigned to the inevitability of integration in Little Rock's school system and gave no indication that he expected a similar situation to develop in Little Rock. His public stance would change dramatically after two interrelated issues convinced Faubus that opposing the inevitable could yield tremendous benefits.

The first factor that arose from the proposed integration of Central High School was a bitter class conflict between the city's white residents. Virgil Blossom, the superintendent of the Little Rock School District, had developed a plan for gradual integration of the city's school system that would begin at Central High in 1957, move to junior highs in 1960, and finally elementary schools in 1963.[290] Blossom and the school board had decided to delay integration until 1957 by which time the city's third high school, Hall High, was to be completed. Hall High was located on the west side of Little Rock, where most of the city's most prominent citizens lived. In addition to Hall High on the west side of town and Central High in the middle, the city had recently opened Horace Mann High School in the city's east side, which served predominately black neighborhoods.

This delay seemed to confirm white working-class families' belief that the school system was only forcing them to integrate while protecting the more affluent neighborhoods in west Little Rock, which would be served by the overwhelmingly white Hall High. This perception was only encouraged by the fact that all of the school board members lived in west Little Rock. As one historian has written, this perception "added class conflict to the racial controversy and allowed segregation spokesmen to charge that integrationists were sacrificing the common citizen while protecting the wealthy."[291] Another student of the crisis argued that it was "more about class than race" and that for the white working class it seemed that "the people in power, the better class, somehow always figured out how to come out on top."[292]

The second factor influencing Faubus's change in strategy was his overriding desire to win an almost unprecedented third term as governor. For most of his predecessors, even running for a third term was unthinkable, since Arkansans so rarely awarded it to their chief executive. Yet, Faubus saw the potential political support that could be won if he tapped into this wave of bitterness over integration.[293] Simply speaking out against integration would not be sufficient to forge the type of support necessary to win a third term, especially after Georgia Governor Marvin Griffin came to Little Rock in August and spoke at a fundraiser for the local chapter of a southern segregation group called the Citizens' Council.[294] Amid a raucous atmosphere, Governor Griffin argued that southern states had to use every available resource to prevent integration, even if it meant calling out the national guard to stop black students from entering white schools.[295]

With the first day of school less than a week away, Faubus had to do something to prove his allegiance to Little Rock's alienated white working class, but he hesitated to take the unquestionably extreme step of using the national guard to forcibly deny federal authority. Faubus first attempted to use the court system to stop or at least delay integration. In August, several Central High students' mothers formed the Mothers' League as a vehicle to stop integration. Faubus exercised more than a little influence over this group and directed them to file a lawsuit requesting that all attempts at integration be delayed due to the level of violence that would undoubtedly occur.[296]

On Friday, August 29, Governor Faubus appeared as a witness in the suit's court hearing and warned that "violence, bloodshed, and riots" would occur if black students enrolled at Central.[297] In actuality, Faubus had little evidence that such extreme unrest would result. Still, Faubus's testimony convinced the chancery judge to grant a temporary injunction before sending the case to federal court for final resolution. In an unusual Saturday session, the federal judge, Richard Davies, would not be so easily swayed, and he ordered integration to proceed as planned on Tuesday morning.

With his only hope of legally stopping integration squashed by Judge Davies, Governor Faubus made his most critical decision as governor. On Sunday night, Faubus made a televised address where he gravely informed the state that he intended to call out members of the Arkansas National Guard and assign them to Central High where they "will not act as segregationists or integrationists." Instead, he said they would be tasked with preserving "law and order."[298] This public pronouncement raised more questions than it answered since no one knew if Faubus really intended the use the guard simply to stop violence or if this was a pretense chosen to explain their call-up and deployment to Central where they would then forcibly stop integration.

The 270 citizen soldiers were not the only men being hurried to Central High. A much smaller detachment of State Police officers were assigned to 12 posts near the school and five roving units that would patrol the immediate area. These officers had four stated objectives: 1) "to regulate, direct, and expedite … vehicle traffic in the vicinity of Little Rock Central High," 2) to add "protection for the personal property and safety of the residents in the Little Rock Central High School area," 3) "to seek, identify, search, seize, and detain, if the occasion demands, all persons and equipment of a suspicious nature attempting to enter the area of Little Rock Central High," and 4) "to assist the Arkansas National Guard in their function of maintaining peace and order in the area of Little Rock Central High School." More specific guidance was given for objective three. Officers were directed to stop any vehicle that made more than three passes or was occupied by three or more males.[299]

Working beside the troopers and investigators were officers from the Little Rock police department. While these two police agencies had a good history of cooperation, a growing conflict between Little Rock Mayor Woodrow Mann and Governor Faubus over his placement of soldiers and troopers around Central injected some tension between the two departments. Mayor Mann harshly criticized Faubus, saying his prediction of violence was just a "political hoax" and that the Little Rock police department could control any situation that arose.[300] In the first week of September, this tension did not appear to adversely affect the officers' interaction or deployment, but it would promise to return with a vengeance just when the situation appeared the most critical.

Amidst all of this turmoil and promise of impending civil unrest, the State Police family was suffering through an unexpected tragedy. In mid-August, Highway Patrol Commander Frank McGibbony was seriously injured when he slipped while helping his son push a car up a grassy hill, and the car rolled backward over the prone officer. McGibbony was rushed to the hospital in critical condition, but sadly, Captain McGibbony would not recover from his injuries and died on August 29. The death of the State Police's long-time Highway Patrol commander was a huge blow to the department, especially considering they were on the eve of the most important operation in its 23-year history. The tragedy unexpectedly thrust a young lieutenant named Mack Thompson into a position of tremendous responsibility where his decisions, along with those of Director Lindsey and CID Captain Alan Templeton, would be watched and judged not only by people in Arkansas, but also around the country and the world as the crisis in Little Rock quickly become an international news event.

Lieutenant Thompson had been with the State Police less than a decade when Captain McGibbony died. In addition to his time as a trooper in northeast Arkansas, Thompson had spent time in the safety section, headed the small fire marshal's section, and had most recently been acting as assistant Highway Patrol commander, a job he later downplayed as a sort of an "errand-boy" position.[301] With only a few days to prepare for the start of school, Thompson, Captain Templeton, and Director Lindsey swung into action. First, all recruits who had previous law enforcement experience were pulled out of the department's ongoing recruit school at Camp Robinson. Next, each State Police district dispatched a portion of their troopers to Little Rock where they were each assigned a post and instructed to keep the traffic moving and clamp down on any signs of trouble. At that point, the only thing the officers could do was wait and hope for the best.

As the skies began to brighten on September 3, an early morning crowd had already begun to congregate outside Central High. By the time students started arriving for their first day of classes, the crowd had swelled to more than 300 anxious spectators, all of whom eagerly watched the steady stream of wide-eyed teenagers to see if the nine black students enrolled in Central High would arrive. None would arrive on the first day. The school board's fear of violence had prompted them to ask the nine black students to stay away, and when it became apparent that none would be arriving, the crowd quickly melted away.

After federal judge Davies again ordered integration to proceed regardless of potential unrest, the nine black teenagers once again prepared to face a screaming, jeering crowd and enter Central High. At 8:10 a.m. on September 4, the Little Rock nine began arriving in front of Central High, which was ringed with national guard soldiers. By this time the crowd numbered more than a thousand, and at the first appearance of the black children, they unleashed a storm of taunts and jeers. Shouts of "Go home, nigger, you will never get into this school," and "two, four, six, eight, we ain't gonna integrate," bombarded the children. One of the nine, Melba Pattillo—whose younger brother Conrad would go on to become the first black captain in the State Police—recalled later that the crowd screamed and threatened to kill her and her mother as they tried to approach Central.[302] When the first black child reached the cordon of guardsmen surrounding Central, the soldiers refused to step aside and instead remained motionless and silent. The soldiers' commander, Lieutenant Colonel Marion Johnson, approached the young girls' escort, a local black activist named Harry Bass. Bass asked him if the guard intended to prevent their entrance, to which Colonel Johnson replied, "That's right." When Bass asked the colonel who had given him these orders, Johnson told him that they came directly from Governor Faubus.[303] The governor had lied about the guard's mission. He had expressly defied the federal government and in the process stained the image of the state and jeopardized the well-being of the nine black students now caught between soldiers and a sea of angry white faces. With a bit of luck and even more courage, the black children and their parents escaped the mob scene surrounding the school, but as Melba Pattillo remembered, they left something behind during the integration of Central High, their "innocence."[304]

For the rest of the week, the crowds continued to arrive early and stay until it became obvious that the black students were not going to be coming back. With the national guard still surrounding Central, the school system petitioned Judge Davies to delay integration, but once again Davies denied the request. Still, the school system could not very well tell the children to come back as long as Faubus continued to order the soldiers to prevent integration. Over the next two weeks— September 9 through 20—the Little Rock nine stayed away, and the crowds got smaller and smaller. By the 20th, the receding threat of violence outside the school meant only 15 guardsmen and four troopers remained around Central High.[305]

Instead, all of the action was taking place in the courtrooms and around the negotiating tables where Governor Faubus and his representatives attempted to stave off federal intervention in the Central High crisis, but by the 20th, all of Eisenhower's patience had been used up. An injunction was filed in federal court that overturned Faubus's use of the national guard to prevent integration. As a result, on Saturday, September 21, Faubus removed the national guard from Central High and essentially washed his hands of any responsibility for what might happen when the nine black students arrived to start classes on Monday.

With no soldiers to "preserve law and order," as Faubus initially described the guard's role, the responsibility fell almost entirely on the Little Rock police department. This was a responsibility that Mayor Mann had been pushing for since August. He told the state's press that, "the maintenance of law and order will be where it belongs—in the hands of local law enforcement authorities and the citizens of this community."[306] But, the mayor's police chief, Marvin Potts, was not as certain of that fact as he was. At 10:00 a.m. on Sunday, Chief Potts called Director Lindsey at home to tell him he disagreed with the mayor's decision to place the onus of law enforcement entirely on his police department. Lindsey sympathized with him, but reminded him that the State Police could not intervene unless they were sent by the governor or requested by local authorities, so unless Mayor Mann had a change of heart, no troopers would be available on Monday when the Little Rock nine would finally be able to come back to Central High. Chief Potts had been the city's police chief since 1947 and had spent even more years working the city as a uniformed officer, so he knew what the police department could and could not handle. With this in mind, he promised to call the mayor and get back with Lindsey.

An hour later, Chief Potts called back to say that he had convinced the mayor to write a letter requesting help from the State Police and that he would hand-deliver it at 4:30 p.m. The two agreed, incorrectly as it turned out, that 50 State Police officers acting on a stand-by basis should be enough to control the crowd and prevent a riot. Lindsey immediately got on the phone to his newly elevated Highway Patrol commander, Lieutenant Thompson, and the head of the CID, Alan Templeton, and ordered them to report immediately to Little Rock headquarters.[307]

The three men decided to assemble 54 State Police officers—40 from the Highway Patrol and 14 from CID—as a "ready reserve" to assist Little Rock officers if needed. Also, it was made clear that State Police personnel would not be under the command of the Little Rock police department and would only deploy following a request from either Chief Potts or Assistant Chief Gene Smith whose officers would be manning barricades outside Central.[308]

At 5:00 a.m. on September 23, Thompson, Templeton, and Lindsey arrived at headquarters for a final discussion of their plans as 54 officers from around the state began to converge on Little Rock. By 7:30 a.m., the State Police's "ready reserve" had assembled on Central High's football field where they would wait to see if the Little Rock police department could handle the already growing crowd on Battery and 15th Street outside Central.[309] Meanwhile, two CID investigators were sent into the crowd to "measure as accurately as possible, the attitude of the persons gathered near Little Rock Central High School."[310] Also, a number of troopers were pulled from the "ready reserve" and inserted into the police line that surrounded Central.

By 8:30 a.m., the crowd had grown to more than a thousand restless people who grew more and more agitated every time the Little Rock police shifted their positions or even remotely appeared to be preparing for the arrival of the nine black teenagers. Around 9:20 a.m., the Little Rock nine arrived at the back entrance to the school where they hurried inside, hoping to avoid most of the crowd. While the maneuver helped avoided an immediate confrontation, when word spread that the nine children were inside the school, the crowd erupted. A writer for the *Arkansas Democrat* reported that "wails of hysterical women and fearful threats of men charged the tense air."[311] Shouts of "keep the Niggers out!" exploded into the air and the crowd surged forward, pressing on the police barricades, and scuffling with officers. The State Police's remaining "ready reserve" was called in to bolster the thin line of officers holding off the crowd.

The teeming mob, now pressed tight into the barricades, turned their attention on the only things standing between them and their goal of ejecting the Little Rock nine from Central, the police officers. In particular, the crowd focused their anger on the city officers who they associated with the pro-integration stance of Little Rock Mayor Woodrow Mann. To them, the troopers were symbolic of Faubus and segregation and thus escaped much of the initial verbal abuse.[312] The crowd yelled for the officers to switch sides and actually convinced one Little Rock officer to take off his gun and badge and cross the barricades. Fortunately, this was the only such incident of officers walking off the barricades.

For the next two hours, city and state officers held off the crowd, which had also spread out from the school to attack people of color wherever they found them. Three black men made the mistake of pulling into a filling station near the school to have their car serviced and were set upon by members of the crowd. A barrage of bottles convinced the three men to flee, but several members of the crowd decided to seek retribution against the service station owner and pushed a car off the hydraulic lift. At 11:00 a.m. a Hispanic man walking near Central was surrounded by members of the crowd who thought he was black even though the man pleaded with them that he was not. Trooper Glenn Minton and several members of the Little Rock police department rushed in and successfully extricated him before the confrontation turned physical.[313] One of the most publicized instances of mob violence occurred when a black reporter was struck and kicked several times by members of the crowd, an act that was captured by a news photographer and remains one of the symbolic photographs of the Central High crisis. State and city police officers once again pushed through the crowd to pull the man to safety before he was seriously injured.[314] A similar incident occurred when a black man driving a truck full of landscaping tools passed near Central on 15th Street. Members of the crowd blocked the truck's path and started rocking it back and forth. Trooper W. D. Davidson, who was assigned nearby, witnessed the incident and recalled:

> A man from the crowd jumped onto the rear bumper and speared a shovel through the rear glass and then ran back in the crowd. Trooper Floyd Weaver broke from the ranks and ran into that crowd and caught the man. A struggle was occurring and myself and another trooper ran in to help Weaver. Weaver had one arm, the other trooper had the man's other arm, and I was pushing ahead opening a path back to the sidewalk. By this time other officers had come to our assistance. Some guy in the crowd who was blocking our path told me, 'If you hit that man you are dead.' So I shoved him to the side and all hell broke loose. It felt as if I did not touch the ground for several feet as the crowd surged forward."[315]

The three officers would make it safely back to the barricades, and the man was hustled off in a city police car. This would be one of the first of 45 integration-related arrests that officers made in Little Rock over the next 24 hours.[316]

The increasing level of unrest outside Central raised concerns within the Little Rock police department that they might not be able to contain it much longer. Around 11:30 a.m., the police department chose to remove the nine black students hoping to diffuse the situation outside. Just after noon, a Little Rock officer got on a bullhorn and informed the crowd that the nine teenagers were no longer in school, to which the crowd began chanting, "We don't believe you!"[317] To convince them, the officers allowed two female crowd members to inspect the school and report back on the validity of the officers' claims. When the two women confirmed that the black students were not inside the school, the crowd began to disperse, but the day was just beginning for city and state officers.

Reports of fighting between groups of whites and blacks, vandalism, and bomb threats began pouring in, each requiring the attention of an already stressed police force. One rumor called into State Police headquarters was that 500 Ku Klux Klan members from Louisiana had formed a caravan and were heading north to join in the fight for segregation. The State Police ordered Trooper Ingram to observe highways 81 and 65 for the caravan and report in if they actually made the trip—they never appeared. For the rest of the night, 28 troopers doubled up in 14 police cars to patrol inside the city limits and around Central High where they backed up city officers and responded to calls for assistance.

The experiences of September 23 convinced Lieutenant Thompson and Captain Templeton that if they were going to help ensure the security of the Little Rock nine the next day, they would need more men. Thompson called in 25 additional troopers, which left each State Police district with just a single officer to work accidents and assist local officers. Meanwhile, Templeton ordered all 16 CID investigators in the State Police to report to Central High. These decisions increased the total number of State Police personnel assigned to Central on

September 24 to 81.[318] Also, Director Lindsey dispatched officers to investigate gun sales at five businesses in Little Rock that sold firearms. This task most likely reflected Faubus's desire to unearth evidence that the current unrest would escalate and become the "bloodshed, violence, and riots" he had predicted in August unless integration was stopped. The probe determined that 72 guns had been sold by the five businesses through the first 19 days of September. This sales volume was comparable to the same period in the previous year.

Tuesday, September 24, would prove to be anti-climatic when compared with the previous day's turmoil. The threat of violence outside the school kept the Little Rock nine away from Central, thus deflating the passions of the more than 400 protestors who had assembled. With nothing to protest, the crowd dispersed, and a relative calm returned to the city, but the national repercussions from the events of September 23 were just beginning to appear. In the eyes of the federal courts and President Eisenhower, integration of Central High had to proceed and the defiance of Governor Faubus needed to be reined in. Eisenhower's first step was to federalize the Arkansas national guard. His second was to call in the renowned 101st Airborne Division from Kentucky, explaining, "Mob rule cannot be allowed to override the decisions of the court."[319]

That night, almost 3,000 soldiers from the 101st flew into Little Rock Air Force Base where they were escorted by State Police officers to their bivouac site just outside the city in Camp Robinson. Along the way, a number of the trucks and jeeps were targets for rocks thrown by Little Rock residents upset by the presence of the federal troops, but such incidents were minor.[320] A more troublesome issue facing the 101st was what to do about the black soldiers in the unit. Despite protests from within the unit, the 101st commander decided to exempt his black soldiers—which represented almost 20 percent of the total force—from duty at Central High. Instead of deploying to the school every day, the men remained in Camp Robinson or at the Little Rock armory.[321]

When the soldiers from the 101st took positions around Central High on September 25, they quickly showed the crowd that they would not be as gentle or as accommodating as the national guard and police officers had been. Any time groups of people began to assemble outside the school, squads of soldiers would advance with bayonet-tipped M-1 rifles extended to hurry them along. In the eyes of Captain Templeton, such a commanding presence meant that "the duties of the Little Rock police and the Department of Arkansas State Police were virtually eliminated." Within a day, the 81 State Police personnel assigned to Central fell to just 10 troopers and five investigators.[322]

The number of officers assigned to Central continued to fall as protestors stayed away from what Governor Faubus referred to as the "occupation" troops stationed around Central. Troopers could return to highway patrol, and the department could go ahead with the second training school planned for October. Unlike the large training class in August, the October class contained both new recruits and veteran officers who had not yet been through a training school. One such veteran officer was Trooper Wayland Speer. Trooper Speer had been hired by the Weights and Standards Division in 1953 before transferring over to Highway Patrol in 1954, meaning that by 1957 he had been working for four years without the benefit of a training school. Speer was so experienced that he actually took and passed the sergeant's exam while he was in the training academy, undoubtedly a feat never to be repeated in State Police history.

One unexpected and controversial outgrowth of the Central High crisis was the use of CID officers to investigate civil rights groups in Arkansas. This practice started in 1958 when the state's Legislative Council ordered the State Police to investigate what role civil rights groups like the National Association for the Advancement of Colored People (NAACP) had played in the integration of Central High. Even after this initial investigation was concluded, Governor Faubus and his aides continued to direct the CID to keep tabs on civil rights groups that began to organize in Arkansas in the late 1950s and early 1960s. Typically, these investigations consisted of CID officers observing meetings and writing down the license plate numbers of those attending. Then, the automobiles' owners would be identified and their names passed on to the governor with a detailing of any criminal record the owners might have had.[323]

Surveillance of civil rights organizations was not unique to Arkansas. In June 1961, officers from around the South attended a conference in Atlanta to discuss and exchange information on what they considered subversive groups, which included the NAACP, the Congress of Race Equality (CORE), and the Student Nonviolent Coordinating Committee (SNCC).[324] Officers in Arkansas feared that these groups would spread dissension among the state's black residents, which would greatly increase the likelihood of racial conflict. Also, these groups were regarded as communist controlled, which during the height of the Cold War's hysteria was a label that would almost certainly earn the recipient a little extra attention by federal or state authorities. Facing such a "grave threat" as the spread of communism, Faubus undoubtedly felt justified in having the State Police monitor these supposedly communist groups.[325] To CID Lieutenant Howard Chandler, "We just had a job to do. There was a mandate from the governor and the legislative council to check on this and so we supplied this (information)."[326]

The CID kept tabs on segregationist groups, as well. Investigators regularly monitored and recorded the license plate numbers of people attending the Ku Klux Klan's monthly meeting in south Little Rock during the late 1950s and the early 1960s.[327]

The most visible face of the State Police remained the Highway Patrol, and as the tumultuous fall of 1957 began to slip into the background, the demand for experienced officers and new troopers alike to get back to patrolling the highways began to build. Traffic deaths were running well ahead of the previous year with 450 fatalities by December versus 436. While the issue frequently graced the front-pages of the state's newspapers, it gained renewed focus after Governor Faubus attended a governor's conference in which the main topic of discussion was highway safety. When he returned to Arkansas, Faubus proclaimed that he was "shocked" by the number of people killed in auto accidents in the state.[328] Arkansas and 17 other states had increased the size of their highway patrols in an effort to reduce traffic deaths, and Governor Faubus called a meeting with Director Lindsey to discuss what the State Police needed to do to be successful. Lindsey told the governor that the new troopers would not be working on their own until early 1958 since the department was still waiting on enough cars for each of them. Also, it would take time for benefits of the new driver's license section of the State Police to be felt. These 15 troopers were supervised by Sergeant Bill Miller and were charged with administering the state's first mandatory driver's license exam.[329] Plus, the license section began compiling a central database that held the driving records for all the state's drivers. Previously, if a driver had his license revoked in one county, he or she could simply go to the adjoining county's revenue office and buy another one.

With the most dangerous time of year traffic-wise yet to come, newly promoted Captain Mack Thompson decided to make an all-out effort at traffic enforcement over the Christmas and New Year's Day holiday. Through December, the department cancelled all leaves, reassigned all of their CID investigators and license examiners to highway patrol, and re-instituted the use of unmarked cars. In mid-December the department received 50 new cars, so for the first time the full weight of the expanded agency would be felt around the state. To improve the officers' safety, especially with so many new men, Thompson assigned members of the state's civil defense network to ride with troopers over the holidays.[330] These extra efforts resulted in a slightly lower number of traffic deaths than initially predicted, but the state still ended the year with 488 traffic-related fatalities—two more than 1956.

The increase in deaths during 1957 placed a bit of pressure on the State Police to show some tangible benefits from having a trooper in every county.[331] Early results proved to be very encouraging. By Memorial Day, traffic deaths were running almost 50 percent below 1957 levels, but this holiday would be the first big travel weekend of the year. So, Captain Thompson decided to employ the most aggressive traffic enforcement program in State Police history. A few weeks prior to Memorial Day, Thompson began hinting to the media that the department would be conducting a surprise enforcement program. When Memorial Day weekend arrived, the public learned just how extensive it would be. First, all members of the State Police, whether they belonged to CID, fire marshal, or identification sections, were assigned to highway patrol duty. Second, troopers were placed in private planes flown by pilots from the state's civil defense network where they would observe traffic and then radio the location of violators to patrol units on the ground. The effort proved to be a tremendous success, and the state recorded just a single fatality over the three-day holiday.

Emboldened by their success over Memorial Day, Captain Thompson planned for an even bigger enforcement effort during the July Fourth holiday. This time the department would have the benefit of a "secret weapon." Over the past year, Sergeant Melvin Delong had been testing and researching various types of in-car radars for use by the State Police. As a result, the Fourth of July holiday would be the public debut for the preferred unit, an Electrofab Radar Meter. This was not the first time officers had used a radar to enforce the speed limit, but it was the first time in-car radars were available and the first time they actually belonged to the department. Previous radar efforts required the State Police to borrow the Highway Department's stationary radar unit. The benefits of an in-car radar were mobility and stealth. It took quite a bit of effort to set up and move a stationary radar, not to mention the fact that it is readily visible by approaching motorists. This "secret weapon" would then be used in conjunction with the successful practice of placing every man on the highways, deploying unmarked cars, and flying airplanes to catch violators. "We are going to be rough," Captain Thompson warned, "on all drivers who violate the law, with no exceptions."[332]

Over the three-day Fourth of July holiday, 170 officers worked the highways providing 24-hour coverage. Despite this unprecedented show of force and a display of cutting-edge traffic enforcement tools, a shockingly high 10 Arkansans died in traffic accidents. Looking back years later, Captain Thompson remembered thinking he had the problem of reducing traffic fatalities "whipped" after their success over Memorial Day weekend. Thompson continued,

> So the Fourth of July came around and we were going to have another [surprise enforcement program] ... [w]e had two radar sets, but we didn't tell the press we had only two. They played that up big. [But] good God Almighty they killed them faster than we could count them. So I figured those special programs don't help too much.[333]

Although Captain Thompson was discouraged by the results of the Fourth of July special enforcement effort, the State Police continued to roll them out on holiday weekends. But before they could try again, one of their own would fall in the line of duty.

On August 17, Trooper Ermon Cox pulled his car into a filling station in Osceola. Cox was one of the 92 new officers hired the previous year, which he had joined after owning a small country store in east Arkansas. Riding along with the off-duty trooper was his nine-year-old son Bennie. At the same time that Ermon and Bennie pulled into the station, a 30-year-old man named William Young walked out. To Cox, Young clearly looked inebriated, and when the man got behind the wheel of his car, the officer felt compelled to stop him. Cox followed Young to his house near the Mississippi River and watched the man enter while he sat in his car in the driveway. Cox began to back out of the man's driveway when Young came out of the front door, aimed a high-powered rifle at the officer and fired. Cox was struck and killed as his young son looked on. Bennie gave officers a description of the man and a posse composed of 40 police officers and 40 volunteers quickly spread out to find Young. A short time later, members of the posse captured Young on a small island in the Mississippi River that was 15 miles from his house.[334] Young was tried, convicted, and sentenced to death for the murder of Trooper Cox, a sentence that was carried out the following year.

The summer of 1958 would also see another important State Police-related event, although it was certainly less tragic. In the Democratic primary for governor, Orval Faubus handily defeated his opponents by winning every single county in the state. Clearly, his opposition to integration at Central High had delivered the long hoped for, but extremely rare, third term. While not guaranteed, it seemed very likely that a third-term governor would mean that the State Police would finally keep a director for longer than four years.

Another bit of good news for 1958 was a reduction in traffic-related deaths to 441 from 488 in 1957. Also, traffic-related arrests jumped 50 percent in the 12 months after the troopers were added, with more than 35,000 arrests. The most common arrests were for speeding (10,636) and driving while intoxicated (4,629).[335] Finally, it seemed, the expansion was paying off in a tangible way.

One benefit from the placement of a trooper in every county that did not show up in the monthly fatality statistics or arrest reports was the relationship that often developed between communities and their trooper. For the first time, dozens of small communities and lightly populated counties whose only law enforcement might be a sheriff or a city marshal would be able to call on "our trooper" to investigate crimes, respond to an emergency, or even settle personal disputes and marital problems. The "our trooper" phenomenon existed before the late 1950s, but with the expansion, it became even more widespread and so common that most officers could relate some example of it. One trooper remembered invitations to eat dinner with area families being posted everyday on a community bulletin board.[336] Also, during holiday seasons it was not unusual for a trooper to go out to his car and find a ham or turkey left inside for his family.

Offsetting the benefits of this familiarity was the officers' political vulnerability. If the trooper ran afoul of the sheriff or local politicians, he ran the risk that they would call the governor or director and have the man moved or worse. One north Arkansas county proved to be so rife with political turmoil that the department went through four troopers in a two-year span, causing Captain Thompson to lament, "I think it is impossible for one to get along."[337] In another county, a trooper proved "too good" at enforcing liquor laws after arresting a number of apparently well-connected citizens buying and transporting liquor from a wet to a dry county. As a result, an angry state representative called the governor, and the governor called Director Lindsey who transferred the trooper to another post.[338] Such conflicts were not all that common, though, since State Police and local officers typically worked well together and relied heavily on one another.

State Police officers working in more populated areas like Pulaski County often did not experience the same sense of community as those in rural areas. There were just too many people for them to develop a close relationship. Plus, the size and expertise of the Little Rock police department and the Pulaski County sheriff's department did not necessitate State Police assistance to investigate crimes or patrol the streets nearly as often.

While Little Rock was in the midst of yet another year of unrest over integration of the city's schools in 1959, the State Police focused on highway patrol and rural law enforcement. Traffic-related deaths would rise in 1959 to 457, but considering the number of multiple-fatality accidents during the year, they were just lucky it was not much higher. In July, for example, a car-versus-train collision killed seven people, and Halloween weekend saw 21 people killed and more than 15 injured.[339] What most people did not consider, though, was that the fatality rate for 1959 was 6.5 deaths per 100 million miles traveled, which was well below the rates experienced through the rest of the 1950s. This rate was higher than the national average of 5.4 deaths per 100 million miles traveled. This difference prompted the National Safety Council to argue, "Despite increases in personnel, Arkansas still lacks enough traffic officers at the state level."[340] With 148 troopers, the State Police could field one officer per 54 miles of paved roads. The Safety Council believed that the proper ratio was one officer per 23 miles. If the state had followed this recommendation, they would need to add almost 250 more officers, which was an expense the state and its taxpayers could not afford.

The poor finances of the state and the limited funding it provided to the State Police became evident in 1960 as the governor's office publicly criticized the department and hinted that "all is not well" inside the agency.[341] Ever since the 1957 expansion, the State Police had struggled to meet their expenses. As it turned out, the increased driver's license fee had not been sufficient to meet their annual budgets. This necessitated that the agency leave some positions unfilled and, in the spring of 1960, reduce every officers' monthly expense account to $35.[342] Another complicating factor was the seasonal nature of driver's license fees. Most Arkansans renewed their licenses annually during January, so all of the State Police's revenue came in during February. Since the 1957 expansion took effect in July of that year, the department had to borrow money from other state funds to pay for operations until their revenue came in and they could repay the loan. This recurring practice of borrowing and repaying budgets proved confusing and could result in the curtailment of activities as cash ran tight. Colonel Lindsey—the State Police had changed the designation of their ranking officers to a more military style in 1961—remarked that "We stay in trouble financially."[343] By 1962, the department found that their current level of revenue would be $300,000 below their budgeted appropriation.

The 1963 session of the General Assembly provided the department with their best hope for increasing the amount of revenue dedicated to the department and preventing them from making drastic cuts in both personnel and service. To this end, three different State Police funding bills were introduced in the legislature. The first asked for an increase in the annual driver's license fee from two to three dollars. This increase would provide an additional $800,000, cover their projected shortfall, and even provide funds for 12 additional officers. The Senate passed the bill, but it met such overwhelming opposition in the house that its sponsors pulled it before it was even voted on. Still, they were not totally devoid of hope for additional revenue. A second State Police-related bill was introduced requesting $300,000 from the Highway Department, but this bill also met defeat in the house. A third bill was also introduced that allowed drivers to buy a license every two years and increased the two-year driver's license fee to $5, but this never found support in the Senate and quietly died. A few weeks later, the 1963 session of the General Assembly came to an end, and the State Police had no new revenue to show for it. What it did have was a full-fledged financial crisis on its hands.[344]

No other option remained for the State Police to pay for their budgeted expenses and thus keep the department operating unless massive cuts in expenses were made. First to go was the Criminal Investigation and Fire Marshal Divisions. Their 19 investigators were reassigned to Highway Patrol and paired with other troopers so their cars could be removed from service. Also, the traffic safety section reduced their presentations, driver's tests were delayed, long distance phone calls were reduced, and none of the 14 vacancies within the department would be filled. A few days later, Colonel Lindsey and the State Police Commission ordered cars removed from service in nine cities and their officers paired with other troopers. In some posts, up to three officers shared a single car.

An even more serious cost cutting measure resulted from the department's order that officers severely limit their mileage. Trooper Jim Bray, who was posted at Mena, recalled, "Our orders were to drive to the city limits and park our car and sit there. The only traffic violation we would move for was a DWI. I lived about three blocks from the city limits, and for a few weeks, I wouldn't put seven miles on my car."[345]

These "economy measures," as Colonel Lindsey called them, came as a huge shock to the people of Arkansas and to the legislature, as well. It seems that no one realized that the State Police budget passed by the legislature was really meaningless unless there was enough revenue to pay for all of the approved expenditures. Criticism began to roll in from every corner as citizens criticized the legislature, and the legislature and the news media criticized the governor and State Police.

Some people argued that the legislature's decision to return the men, equipment, and responsibility for weights and standards back to the Highway Department should have reduced the expense of operating the State Police. Actually, the Highway Department had always paid the expenses of the Weights and Standards Division of the State Police, so their transfer had no effect on the State Police's finances. The real motivation to move the weights and standards back to the Highway Department was the seeming disinterest the State Police showed in the division and its operation.[346] This combined with the Highway Department's feelings that since they "paid the bills they should control it."[347]

As long as State Police cars were idled on the side of the highway, the controversy refused to die. After a few weeks, it began to focus almost solely on Governor Faubus as people began to question if the financial crisis was real or just a political gimmick Faubus had concocted to wring additional taxes from Arkansans without risking his reelection hopes in 1964. These doubts spurred calls by the Legislative Audit Committee, headed by Garland County Senator Q. Bynum Hurst, for a full audit of the department's budget and operations. Faubus knew that the situation was real and serious, but he did not feel it was his fault that the State Police did not receive additional funding in the last session. Faubus placed a heavy share of the blame on Colonel Lindsey and even publicly hinted that he had considered changing leadership as a result.[348] Even though Faubus chose to retain Lindsey, this episode would severely strain relations between the two men for the rest of the governor's time in office.[349]

At the State Police Commission's April 20 meeting, a visibly angry Governor Faubus severely criticized the department and its top commanders, pointing to a breakdown in the chain of command and other indiscretions that had embarrassed him and the department. He ordered all Highway Patrol officers back on the streets with no mileage restrictions and a return of all CID and fire marshal investigators to their original duties. Accordingly, the State Police began operating normally and would address their lack of funding at some undetermined time in the future.[350] While this move did return the State Police to normal operations, it also confused many in the state's press who wrote, "the course of ... the controversy has been so erratic the people will have to be forgiven if they cannot decide whether there is or is not a bona fide crisis and whether there is or is not wrong doing in the State Police."[351]

The press hoped that the forthcoming State Police audit would shed some light on the situation. When it was released in June, the auditors confirmed that the driver's license fees, which represented the sole source of income for the department, were more than $300,000 below the level required to fully fund the department's annual budget. The audit also exposed complaints that low-grade tires, fear of transfers, long hours, low pay, poor equipment, and the absence of air conditioning in cars combined to lower morale within the department.

A more fundamental and damaging issue highlighted by the audit was that the "department is run by cliques and clans," which naturally introduced political favoritism into the promotion process. The growth of factionalism in the State Police appears to be an offshoot of both the necessity for political support to be hired and the lack of job security for the department's director. Since 1935, each governor had exercised a substantial amount of influence over who was hired by the State Police, but once hired, officers were generally protected from being fired for political reasons. Still, men hired by opposing governors might find themselves shut out of promotions when their political faction did not occupy the director's position. By the early 1960s, these factors allowed two separate groups to develop, with one side led by Colonel Lindsey and the other by Lieutenant Colonel Carl Miller. Just before the audit became public, Colonel Lindsey tried to "resolve the friction between Chief Miller and myself" by calling a meeting of all ranking officers in the State Police.[352] The two made a public attempt at resolving their differences that resulted in Miller assuming a more visible role in the department's operation.

Probably not entirely coincidental, at the same time that the State Police were stumbling through their financial crisis, they were also the center of another political controversy. Like so many times before, the source of the controversy originated in Hot Springs. During his first gubernatorial campaign in 1954, Orval Faubus promised to shut down wide-open gambling in Hot Springs, which had reopened during the Cherry Administration, by saying, "I would have them [State Police] prohibit any violations that come to my attention—and the Hot Springs situation is big enough that it would come to my attention."[353] After becoming governor, Faubus changed his tune by arguing, "If Hot Springs has a problem they have plenty of authority to solve it. If I did something about it, they would call me a dictator."[354]

The implicit approval of gambling in Hot Springs encouraged dozens of casinos to open in the spa town, which even saw some that rivaled Las Vegas in their opulence and betting volume. Chief among these casinos was the Vapors. With thick carpets and chandelier lighting, it provided the perfect environment for the hundreds of gamblers who came in most nights to play the nearly 40 slots, three craps tables, roulette wheel, and numerous blackjack tables. During racing season at Oaklawn, the crowd could number close to a thousand, especially on nights when a nationally renowned singer like Patti Page ("How Much is that Doggie in the Window?") performed in its showroom.[355] The throngs of people flocking to casinos in Hot Springs wagered an estimated $50 million each year, of which the city of Hot Springs collected $140,000 as an "amusement tax." The Hot Springs City Council spelled out the monthly fees charged to casino operators in an ordinance passed in 1958 that imposed $50 on each cocktail lounge, race wire operator, and bingo game, as well as $200 on bookmaking establishments and $500 on "large" gambling casinos.[356] Rumors also abounded that the casinos funneled a significant amount of under-the-table money to people in positions of authority at both local and state levels.

Such wide-open gambling provided fodder for Faubus's political opponents. The election year of 1962 saw its emergence as a recurring news story when *Sports Illustrated* ran an article on the upcoming racing season in Oaklawn, which it described as "one of the hottest in history—unless the FBI intervenes." Coming from such an unlikely source, the state's news media, in particular the *Arkansas Gazette*, pushed the issue to the front pages. As a result, during the 1962 Democratic primary for governor, candidate Ken Coffelt made gambling in Hot Springs one of the main planks in his platform. Like other failed gubernatorial candidates who railed on gambling in Hot Springs, Coffelt failed to ride the issue to the governor's office when Faubus easily won the primary and, by default, the election.

After the 1962 election, the gambling controversy appeared destined for obscurity until a bomb blast rocked the Vapors casino in early January 1963. Since it exploded at noon, the casino was relatively empty and no one was killed, but more than a dozen people were injured and $125,000 in damage was done. Investigators from the State Police's Fire Marshal Section, Hot Springs police department, and FBI rushed to investigate and determined that the bomb had been placed in the front men's restroom. The local rumor mill argued that the bomb signaled an attempt by organized crime to force their way into the lucrative gambling operations that were run by locals in Hot Springs.[357] True or not, the bombing was never solved, but it did renew calls for Faubus to use the State Police to crack down on illegal gambling. The editors of the *Gazette* surmised that, "In all realism there is no reason to anticipate a clean-up at Hot Springs until reform is embodied in the platform of a governor who will fulfill his promises."[358]

The *Gazette* expanded its criticism of the continued practice of gambling in Hot Springs by focusing on the State Police's non-enforcement as well. Part of their displeasure resulted from the findings of the department's 1963 legislative audit, which identified political favoritism in the promotion process as another problem within the State Police. Calling it "the most disturbing aspect of the auditor's report," the editors argued that "Mr. Faubus had made the State Police a political arm of his administration [and] Hot Springs offers the most notorious example of selective enforcement." The only way to "remedy" such a relationship according to the *Gazette* was to vote Faubus out of office.[359]

Many within the state legislature agreed with the *Gazette*, including Ashley County Representative Nap Murphy. Representative Murphy decided that the only way the State Police would enforce state gambling laws in Hot Springs over the objections of Governor Faubus was if they were specifically ordered to do so by the legislature. During the 1963 session of the General Assembly, Murphy introduced House Bill 116, which called for the creation of a new division within the State Police whose only task was to investigate violations of the state's gambling laws and "cause the immediate arrest of the person or persons found to be violating such laws."[360] Q. Bynum Hurst, Garland County's powerful state senator, criticized the bill stating, "When the state constitution was framed, counties and judicial districts were set in that framework because people like to have law enforcement at home."[361] The *Gazette* countered that "Murphy's bill ... has such obvious merit that not many of the bill's opponents in the General Assembly would care to be caught voting against it."[362] One representative that did not mind was Garland County's Nathan Schoenfield who repeatedly tied the bill up through filibusters.

With time to plan an effective method of killing the bill without incurring the political cost, the *Gazette* found that Garland County representatives "offered a classic study in how to destroy a piece of legislation without meeting the issue head-on." In late February, the House added two amendments that destroyed any chance that the bill might pass. The first broadened the scope of the new division to include investigations into liquor, prostitution, narcotics, and rioting. On the surface such an amendment seems legitimate enough, but with each additional task the division would lose more and more supporters who might have a financial or personal stake in some of the targeted vices. Plus, it seems arguable that by including riot investigations as a responsibility, the division might ensnare some fairly prominent people involved in civil unrest surrounding the continued efforts to integrate Arkansas' schools. The second amendment removed the State Police from the governor's purview and placed it under the state's Attorney General, a move Faubus's supporters in the legislature would never approve.[363] One representative who voted for the amendments expressed a common argument against the bill, saying, "if we are not enforcing the laws we have now, I can't believe we would enforce a new one any better."[364] With the bill dead in the water, the continued existence of open gambling in Hot Springs seemed secure.

The state legislature was not the only government body interested in the activities in the spa city. The brazen actions of the Hot Springs casinos also prompted the federal government to conduct two investigations in the city. Unlike Representative Murphy, the federal government was not interested in stopping illegal gambling in Arkansas. They saw this as a state issue and refused to get involved. Instead, the federal agents tried to determine if the gamblers in Hot Springs were violating federal anti-gambling laws passed in 1961 that forbid interstate gambling in any form. More specifically, the 1961 statutes outlawed the interstate transportation of gambling paraphernalia into a state where gambling was illegal.

The most serious investigation began a few days after Representative Murphy's anti-gambling bill was amended into obscurity. In late February 1963, United States Attorney General Robert F. Kennedy ordered agents from the Justice Department's Organized Crime and Racketeering Section and the Federal Bureau of Investigation to look into gambling in Hot Springs after receiving a petition from the Arkansas Christian Civic Foundation.[365] During the next year, the presence of an estimated 30 FBI agents in Hot Springs raised the pressure on Faubus to do something to distance himself from the gamblers.[366]

In mid February 1964, Kennedy's chief investigator, William Hundley, called a press conference that refocused attention on

Hot Springs' casinos. Hundley described the city as "quite a gathering place" for mobsters from New York and Chicago, and promised a complete investigation. This announcement probably encouraged the state legislature to pass a resolution in March requesting that Garland County authorities end open gambling or else state officers should be sent to finish the task.[367] The resolution actually gave Governor Faubus an opening to make a show of compliance with their wishes. The day after the legislature passed the resolution by a vote of 91 to 3, Faubus ordered the casinos to close. If they did not comply, he promised to send in the State Police to do it by force. Still, Faubus left the time frame for the casinos to close vague, asking them to do so within a reasonable time.

In addition to the federal gambling investigations, part of the motivation for Faubus's changing stance stemmed from the entry of a new kind of opponent in the governor's race, a Republican who might actually win. Winthrop Rockefeller had moved to Arkansas after the Second World War and built a large ranch on top of Petit Jean Mountain near Morrilton. Rockefeller first entered public service when Governor Faubus appointed him to head the fledgling Arkansas Industrial Development Commission (AIDC) whose mission was to entice Northern industry to Arkansas where they would build new industrial plants and create high-paying jobs. By 1964, Rockefeller's famous name, his charitable activities, and his praise-worthy actions as director of the AIDC earned him enough statewide recognition to become a legitimate candidate for governor. His entry in the 1964 race ensured that the election would not be decided until November, which was an extremely rare occurrence in a state dominated by Democratic candidates since the end of Reconstruction in 1874.

Throughout the campaign, Rockefeller promised to use the State Police to close down gambling in Hot Springs.[368] This vow garnered support from a number of church groups who had been frequent critics of Faubus's blind eye to activities there. In an effort to defuse some of the charges, Faubus finally decided to make at least a show of fulfilling his vow to use the State Police. With just three weeks until Election

Day—and long after the peak gambling season during races at Oaklawn—Faubus ordered a raid on a small supper club outside of Hot Springs called Judd's Steakhouse. Two officers, Jack Hinson and Otho Pace, donned civilian clothes and entered the club. After ordering dinner and playing the three slot machines that were lined up at the end of the bar, the two walked out and summoned State Police Captain Paul McDonald, Lieutenant Bob Ward, Sergeant W. A. Tudor, and Trooper Glenn Minton to raid the club. The officers arrested the owner and confiscated the three slots along with more than two hundred bottles of alcohol. Meanwhile, large casinos like the Vapors remained unscathed.[369]

The intense interest generated by the Faubus-Rockefeller match-up helped propel a record number of Arkansans to the polls in 1964.[370] Although, Faubus won the election with 56% of the vote, Rockefeller's ability to garner more than 40% of the vote hinted that political change was not far off.

Faubus's victory did not mean the press let the continued gambling in Hot Springs slide by without mention. In March 1965, the *Democrat* once again took pains to point out that wide open gambling still occurred on a regular basis.[371] Unbeknownst to the *Democrat's* reporters, CID officers were already in the spa city conducting their own investigation into off-track bookmaking and attempting to measure the magnitude of casino-style gambling. Faubus and Lieutenant Colonel Miller charged one of the department's most trusted officers, Lieutenant Howard Chandler, to take his special squad of CID investigators to Hot Springs in early March. In addition to Chandler, this group included Sergeant Ollie Andrews and Trooper H. H. Atkinson.

For the most part, the investigators did not have a hard time getting into casinos in the city and observing gambling, but the casino owners had recently instituted a small roadblock for the officers by turning their operations into private, members-only clubs. As a result, everyone who entered had to produce a membership card, thus adding a degree of difficulty for the officers who risked discovery if they were forced to apply for membership. One way the officers used to skirt this impediment was to recruit confidential informants who could obtain membership cards and then escort their "guest" inside. This method was successful in getting Trooper Atkinson inside the Southern, Belvedere, Vapors, Turf Club, and Citizens casinos on March 5 where he observed an abundance of slots and table games.[372]

Another method used by Chandler's men to get around the membership card requirement was by checking into one of Hot Springs' more upscale hotels or motels, which provided their guests with temporary membership cards. In May, Chandler pulled a highway patrol trooper, Charles Winn, off the road, gave him $40 in expense money, and sent him to the Royale Vista Inn where he was instructed to obtain a temporary membership card and visit the Vapors and Southern casinos. The undercover operation went off without a hitch, and the next morning Trooper Winn provided Lieutenant Chandler and Sergeant Andrews with a handwritten sketch of the two casinos' floor plans showing the location of 35 slots at the Vapors and 51 slots at the Southern, along with a handful of table games.

The officers believed they had enough hard evidence to approach Hot Springs Circuit Judge Dobbs to ask for a search-and-seizure warrant. After calling in four additional officers in preparation for a raid of the two clubs, the three went to see Judge Dobbs. At first, Dobbs refused to issue a search warrant, arguing that, "I am not going to allow the State Police to come over here and take over." He even threatened to issue a warrant for Winn's arrest if he had played any of the slots while he was undercover, a charge that Trooper Winn quickly denied. After an extended negotiation period, Judge Dobbs relented, but on the condition that the warrant was issued to the Garland County sheriff's office and not the State Police. Chandler and his team agreed to the condition and went to meet the sheriff.

When all was finally in place, the State Police officers split into two groups and accompanied the Garland County sheriff on a raid of the

Southern and Vapors casinos. By this time, though, the casinos had received plenty of advance warning, and all of the slots so meticulously noted in Trooper Winn's sketch were gone. The casinos had used white tablecloths and ashtrays in a half-hearted attempt to cover the slot machine holders still clearly present throughout the clubs.[373] For the rest of Faubus's time as governor, the State Police made a few more attempts at reining in wide-open gambling, but their focus was never strong enough to actually stop or even seriously impede gambling in Hot Springs.

As might be expected, the department exhibited a much more committed effort toward reducing traffic accidents and traffic-related fatalities. In 1961, the state experienced its fifth consecutive year with traffic fatalities measuring below 460. In spite of the ever-rising number of vehicle miles traveled in Arkansas, the fatality rate had fallen to a record low of six fatalities for every 100 million vehicle miles traveled in 1961. The good times were not destined to last, though, as the next five years witnessed a stunning 47% increase in fatalities, which peaked at 674 in 1966.

In part, this dramatic increase in fatalities resulted from the absence of modern-day safety equipment in automobiles like seat belts, anti-lock brakes, and air bags. Yet these important safety advances were not available before 1962, either, so another catalyst must have developed in the interim. One possible culprit was the completion of Arkansas's three "super highways," which had began construction in the latter half of the 1950s and were 50% complete by 1966. The interstate system in Arkansas consisted of I-40 cutting across the middle of the state, I-55 slicing through the northeast corner, and I-30 running from the southwest corner of the state and intersecting with I-40 in North Little Rock.

Traffic Fatalities in Arkansas, 1955-1966

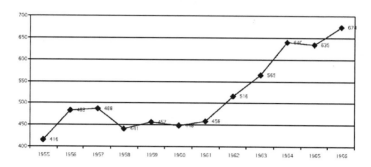

Traffic Fatality Rate in Arkansas, 1955-1966

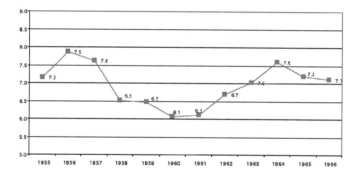

These new roads were intended to make driving safer, but at the same time they presented a number of new problems for the state's drivers. First and foremost was the inexperience Arkansans had in driving on controlled access, multi-lane divided highways. Traveling the wrong way, stopping on the highway, and abrupt lane changes were just a few of the more common errors created by the new highways. Also, the interstates featured more fixed objects that people could hit, including overpasses, signs, and bridge abutments.

The new roads prompted a number of changes in the State
Police, the first being Colonel Lindsey's notification to the State Police
Commission in October 1962 that the department would need to add
almost 50 troopers to adequately patrol the interstates.[374] A short time
later, Lindsey followed with a request for new, more powerful police cars
since it had become more and more common for violators to outrun the
department's aging, economy-minded fleet.[375]

In May 1963, the commission approved a plan to create a separate
accident division within the Highway Patrol that would focus only on
working wrecks on the new interstates. The State Highway Department
wholeheartedly approved of the creation of a dedicated interstate patrol
so they could receive more detailed accident reports, thus allowing
them to better determine the safety of their new highway designs.[376]
With the department at the apex of its funding crisis in 1963, only five
officers could be assigned to this new Accident Investigation Division,
which was commanded by Melvin Delong who had attained the rank of
captain by this time.[377]

A determination to stop the jump in traffic-related fatalities finally
engendered enough support during the 1965 session of the General
Assembly to resolve the State Police' on-going funding crisis. After the
brief freeze of highway patrol operations in March and April 1963 due
to a lack of revenue, the department had returned to its full schedule,
but in order to meet its expenses it had to rely on loans and infusions of
cash from Governor Faubus's emergency fund. Colonel Lindsey and
other State Police officers lobbied strenuously for additional sources of
revenue. When legislators read of the mounting death toll on the
highways, few argued against additional State Police funding. As a
result, the legislature assessed a one-percent fee to admission at the dog
races in West Memphis and the horse races in Hot Springs, instituted a
five-dollar-per-year chauffeur's driver's license, and obligated general
revenue funding to support the CID. These new revenue sources
combined with the continued assessment of the two-dollar annual
driver's license fee allowed the department to fully fund current

operations and approve the addition of 100 more troopers, bringing the total number of troopers to 260.[378] While the additional revenue was still not enough to fully fund every new position authorized, the department was able to add 73 new troopers.

One of the first moves the department made was to enlarge the interstate patrol. This would have unintended consequences, though. As more officers were assigned to the interstate patrol, it began to create a backlash among other Highway Patrol troopers who sarcastically referred to the patrol as the "Green Berets" since they were set apart from the rest of the division and only worked accidents and traffic enforcement on the interstate. In one illustrative example, a young trooper remembered, "we were getting off of patrol and were coming down the ramp to the blacktop, and there was an accident right at the end of the ramp. My training officer called a Highway Patrol officer and told him he had a wreck. We stayed until he got there and then we left. That was how bad it had gotten."[379] Due to the hard feelings such actions created, the interstate patrol did not last long as a separate force.

The 1965 General Assembly also tasked the State Police with improving driver education in the state. The main effort revolved around electronic driving simulators that had become a popular method of teaching defensive driving techniques to new drivers. The legislature provided $500,000 to the State Police to purchase 16 trailers, each containing 12 driving simulators. The intent was to tow these trailers to schools and colleges around the state and conduct safe-driving seminars. Captain Bill Miller transferred from command of the driver's license section to the safety section to oversee this program, which proved wildly popular and kept the officers assigned to the safety section quite busy.

Even though the impetus behind the additional officers and new revenue streams was traffic enforcement, local and county law enforcement agencies still relied on troopers and investigators to provide assistance and expertise, and at times to take over all phases of law enforcement in a community. More often, the State Police were called in to handle situations or provide assistance to local officers who were just as undermanned and alone as the troopers. Therefore, whenever a trooper heard a dangerous situation develop on the radio, he was quick to respond. These situations always contained the ingredients for violence, and even though the State Police commanded their fair share of respect, they were not immune to its outbursts. The department was reminded of this early in the 1960s.

On Christmas Eve night 1960, Trooper Elton Brown was dispatched to a bar fight in Altus. Riding with the trooper that night was Franklin County Sheriff Robert Pritchard. When the two men arrived at the bar, they saw the instigator of the fight, Jack Quail, standing outside. Quail also saw the two officers, and when they got out of the car, he turned to run only to stop, pull a pistol from his waistband, and fire at Trooper Brown. The bullet struck the officer in the stomach and lodged in his hip. Seriously wounded, Brown was able to return fire before Quail disappeared into the darkness. Trooper Brown was rushed to the hospital in Ozark where the doctors told the press that he had a "50-50" chance of surviving. Luckily, Brown survived, although it would be six months before he could return to duty. The shooter, Jack Quail, was arrested a few hours after the incident and earned a rather lengthy sentence in the state prison.[380] The same night that Elton Brown was shot, Trooper Carroll Turner was slightly wounded while serving a Malvern man commitment papers to the state mental hospital. Officers killed the man in the subsequent gun battle.[381]

In 1965, three other State Police officers would be seriously injured in the line of duty, one of which would prove fatal. The first involved Sergeant Freddie McKinley who was working interstate patrol one spring night near Benton when he pulled over a drunk driver. While McKinley struggled to remove the man from the car, another drunk driver careened into him and threw him into a ditch. Despite the pain from two broken legs and numerous other injuries, he told a civilian that came to help him, "Get my flashlight and direct traffic. Somebody else may hit those cars."[382] The severity of his injuries prevented McKinley from returning to Highway Patrol, so after an extensive recuperation period, he returned to the department and worked in the central records and administration sections until he retired in 1980.[383]

The second incident occurred in north Arkansas in June and involved Trooper Ken Hendrix. At 8:30 p.m. on June 22, three armed men pushed into the home of a Mountain View bank manager demanding the keys to the bank. The manager gave the men the keys, but warned them that the bank vault was on a timer and could not be opened until the next morning. While two of the men watched the bank manager and his wife, the third went to try to open the vault. After several hours, the would-be robber returned empty-handed and confirmed the truth of the manager's statement. The three men then decided to take the manager and his wife to the bank to see if they could force him into opening the vault. After arriving there near midnight, the manager convinced them there was nothing he could do until morning, but the robbers did not feel safe in delaying their flight. Instead, they bound and gagged the couple and grabbed a bag of silver coins valued at $2,500 that had been left outside the vault and fled into the night. After 45 minutes, the banker's wife managed to squirm free and called police with a description of the men and their car.

Twenty-five miles to the west, Trooper Ken Hendrix was on his regular, late-night patrol when he heard the bulletin on his radio. Just as the weary trooper pulled into a service station outside Marshall to get a soft drink, an older model Pontiac matching the description of the bank robbers' car passed by. Hendrix turned around and pulled the suspects' car over. The officer approached the car and asked for each of the three occupants' driver's licenses. In doing so, he noticed the moneybag from the bank containing the silver coins. He hurried back to his patrol car, grabbed his shotgun, and ordered everyone out of the car. With the assistance of Searcy County Sheriff Sutterfield, who had just arrived, Hendrix told the three men to lie on the ground. Sensing their last opportunity to escape a jail sentence, one of the men pulled out a pistol and fired at the officers. One round struck Hendrix in the left arm, knocking the shotgun from his hands. A second robber leaped for Hendrix's shotgun at the same time the trooper was scrambling to pick it up. The two men wrestled over the weapon while the sheriff emptied his pistol in the direction of the other two robbers. The sheriff's fusillade convinced the two men to flee in opposite directions, but the struggle between a wounded Trooper Hendrix and the third robber was not going as well. Apparently deciding that the trooper was not going to give up his shotgun, the bank robber let go and grabbed the officer's service revolver. The man quickly pointed it at the two men, who were at a distinct disadvantage since the sheriff's gun was empty and Trooper Hendrix was wounded. The robber then ordered Hendrix to drive him out of the area. Hendrix replied, "Okay, go ahead and shoot me. I am not going with you." Convinced of Hendrix's sincerity, the bank robber grabbed the officer's shotgun, and upon finding the keys to the robbers' Pontiac missing—Trooper Hendrix had taken them when he pulled the car over—he walked off into the woods. With the three robbers once again on the run, Trooper Hendrix picked up the bag of silver coins from the robbers' car, radioed an alert, and drove himself to the hospital. Two of the three bank robbers would be caught within a few days by the ensuing manhunt, but the third actually made it out of the country before being brought to justice. Meanwhile, Trooper Hendrix fully recovered from his wound and for his actions received one of the first "Trooper of the Year" awards in department history.[384]

The next year, 1966, the department would be struck by the death of the third officer to die while on duty. Trooper Harry Locke was on patrol early one morning in September on U.S. Highway 79 between Clarendon and Marianna. J. B. Shaw, a night policeman from a nearby community, rode with Locke that night. It is believed that Locke and Shaw were in pursuit of a fleeing vehicle when they lost control of the patrol car in a tight turn and slammed into a concrete culvert. The impact ejected Locke from the car and fatally injured the officer. Officer Shaw was also seriously injured in the accident.[385]

While the department grieved for their fellow officer and his family, they were becoming enmeshed in an issue that became a recurring scene of scandal and unrest in the state for the next five years. The state's prison system had never been a source of pride for the state, but since most of its problems remained unspoken and well hidden from the view of most Arkansans, no one seemed to pay too much attention.

This out-of-sight, out-of-mind attitude began to change in August 1966 when CID commander Major Bill Struebing dispatched investigator H. H. Atkinson to the Tucker Prison Farm. Initially, Atkinson was asked to investigate a claim that prisoners had been leaving the prison farm to buy alcohol at a nearby liquor store. At the time, the state's penitentiaries worked on the trusty system whereby prisoners judged to be reliable and trustworthy were given weapons and used as guards. While such an arrangement was definitely cost-effective, it did not create a particularly secure facility, and as a result, escapes occurred on a fairly regular basis.

When Investigator Atkinson arrived, he found that the claims of alcohol smuggling were all too true, but they paled in comparison to the other problems going on inside the prison farm. Every building proved to be filthy and unsanitary. In the kitchen, "flies were very thick" and rotting food and dirty dishes lay piled on the counters. The prisoners' barracks were just as bad. Mattresses were rotten, and the toilets were broken. The prisoners suffered greatly from these conditions, and to Atkinson they appeared to be seriously underweight and in poor health.

Atkinson first moved to strengthen security. He reassigned the worst trustees back into the prison population, ordered additional guard towers constructed, and conducted a sweep of the prison where he confiscated 82 homemade weapons, including 61 knives. Next, he attempted to address the living conditions of the prisoners. The kitchen and barracks were cleaned, and the prisoners' food ration was increased to a more sustaining level.

Clearly, the conditions at Tucker were a symptom of a much bigger problem than prisoners sneaking out to buy alcohol. So Atkinson began to interview prisoners, trustees, and wardens at the facility. Very quickly, the officer uncovered serious instances of physical abuse, the most infamous of which was the "Tucker telephone." The telephone consisted of an electric generator from a ring-type telephone that was placed in sequence with two dry cell batteries. Then wires were attached from the batteries to a prisoner's toe and groin. The trustee or warden would then turn the crank on the generator sending a painful electric charge to the prisoner who was said to be receiving a "long distance call."[386] Another feared means of punishment was the strap. This was a five-foot long piece of leather attached to a wooden handle and used to administer lashes to a prisoner's bare back.

After a few days of interviews, Atkinson called in help from fellow CID Officers James Beach and Billy Skipper. For three days, these officers interviewed everyone associated with Tucker Prison Farm and unmasked a depth of corruption and abuse never before imagined. In addition to the verified instances of physical abuse with the Tucker Telephone, wardens were being paid off, skimming money from government contracts, and entering into lucrative contracts for the farms' produce. As a result of their findings, Governor Faubus fired all three of Tucker's wardens and placed Atkinson in charge of the prison. Also, three troopers and three investigators were dispatched to beef up security on August 30.[387]

Governor Faubus's firing of the wardens at Tucker and the news media's outrage over the use of the Tucker telephone and the strap as tools of punishment proved confusing to prisoners in the state's other large penitentiary, Cummins. At Cummins, trustees still relied on the strap, and living conditions were not that much better than those at Tucker, so the inmates wondered why there was no outcry over their living conditions. On September 2, 146 of Cummins' 1,500 prisoners went on a sit-down strike. In response, Major Struebing led 30 troopers to Cummins where they convinced all but eight of the convicts to return to work. Still, the prisoners were not satisfied, and on September 6, the same 146 prisoners again refused to come out of their barracks to work in the fields. State troopers, trustees, and the wardens decided to send two trustees into the black barracks where 104 of the striking convicts were housed to try to talk them into going back to work. The convicts were in no mood to listen to the trustees and began to punch and kick the two men. Troopers fired tear gas into the barracks and shotguns over the convicts' heads before rushing in and pulling the two trustees out. Once the two were safe, ventilation fans were turned on to clear out the tear gas, and 10 convicts were ordered out. These 10 men were each given 10 lashes with the strap as an example to the rest of the inmates who then quietly filed out to work. In the nearby barracks for white prisoners, wardens called out the suspected ringleader and administered 10 lashes with the strap, which convinced the remaining 41 inmates to also return to work.[388]

Normally, such incidents would be a political nightmare for a sitting governor during an election year, which 1966 was. But this year would be the first in more than a decade that did not feature Orval Faubus as a candidate for governor. Faubus had decided relatively early in his sixth term that it would be his last, which left the political landscape ripe for change. Winthrop Rockefeller, the man who emerged from this battle-scarred arena, would be an important part in the transition of the State Police from past to present. The foundation for this critical change though was created during the Faubus years. Between 1954 and 1966, the State Police nearly tripled in size, starting pay for troopers had grown, and new technologies and improved equipment were beginning to appear. More importantly, by the 1960s, the Arkansas State Police was no longer a new organization. All of its commanding officers had decades of time working for the department, and most of its troopers had years of experience working traffic, responding to emergencies, and investigating crimes. Such attributes proved critical, since the next 14 years would be some of the most tumultuous in the state's and the department's history.

Photographs

The original Rangers

The Arkansas State Police in 1937

A technician works on a patrol car's radio in the 1950s.

A. G. "Gray" Albright.
(courtesy of Jim Albright)

The State Police's first splitting of Arkansas into Districts.

Mr. Pickens on duty as a State Police dispatcher in the 1940s.

Arkansas State Police Headquarters. The State Police moved into the old state penitentiary in 1937. (Courtesy W. D. Davidson)

The State Police's First Radio Transmitter. (Source: ASP Biennial Report, 1938-1940)

Kelly Pique   Allen Bufford

The entire Department of Arkansas State Police in 1945. Standing in front are Governor Ben Laney and Director Jack Porter. (Courtesy of Travis Ward)

The original members of the State Police's Motor Vehicle Inspection section. Front row, left to right, W. A. Tudor, Don Denton, W. A. Wren, Garland Hughes, Glen Bailey, Doug Harp, Dale Miller, Dean Friend. Back row, left to right, Gerald Garrett, Elton Brown, Bill Ingram, Robert Jones, Bill Killabrew, John Eggers, Robert Hill, Neil Rowe, Bill Miles, William (Red) Swindle, William Mason, Bill Mullenax, James Morgan, and Bob Reynolds. (Courtesy of Dale Miller)

*The Arkansas State Police's October 1957 Training School Class. Many of these officers had already been working as troopers for the State Police—one as long as four years—before they attended the academy. From left to right, **first row:** Eugene Harris, Joe Ashcraft, Charles Oliphant, George Fullerton, Bobby Gunn, Daryle Rose, Sid Riley, Fount Allen, Ermon Cox, J. L. Fleeman, Jerry Maynard, Carroll Turner. **Second row:** James Morgan, Bill Morganstern, Willie Neighbors, Jay Allen, W. D. Davidson, Willie Hopper, Jack Henson, Allie Landreth, John Westmoreland, Tom Newby, Buren Jackson, Barney Pfoff. **Third row:** Pete Tracy, Harold Titsworth, John Hicks, Jack Ditmars, Roy Ross, Wayland Speer, Billy Bob Davis, Willie Ingraham, and Hugh Kane. (Picture courtesy of W. D. Davidson)*

Trooper Sidney Pavatt. (Source: ASP Annual 1978)

Ken Hendrix. (Source: ASP Annual 1978)

Trooper Louis Bryant. (Source: ASP Annual 1978)

Trooper Ermon Cox (Source: ASP Annual 1978)

Bear Chandler

Early radar

A trooper stands next to his 1950s Pontiac Police Special.

Interstate opening

State Police Director Bill Miller. (Courtesy of Bill Miller)

Lynn Davis. (Source: ASP Annual 1978)

Colonel Tommy Goodwin. (Source: ASP Annual 1978)

Herman Lindsey

Hansel Bradford (left) and Joe Brewer sporting the short lived western style hats in 1969. (Courtesy of Hansel Bradford)

Barbara Cart

Colonel Doug Harp. (Source: ASP Annual 1978)

The State Police's first black trooper, Marion Taylor, seen here delivering a speech on driving safety. (Source: ASP)

Gambling equipment destruction. (Courtesy of Bill Dever)

Burning gambling equipment. (Courtesy of Bill Dever)

Gambling liquor seizure

Interstate opening

Troopers W. A. Wren (left) and Mel Hensley stand beside their patrol cars. Wren's unit still has the pre-1978 markings and color while Hensley's represents the new white-with-blue-striping design. (Courtesy of Mel Hensley)

The State Police reintroduced motorcycles for a brief period in 1976.

The State Police respond to a hostage situation in Jasper involving Keith and Kate Haigler (pictured in bottom photo) and a commercial bus.

Trooper Robert Meek (left) and Sergeant Hansel Bradford investigate a bus wreck outside Jasper that killed 20 people in 1980. (Courtesy Hansel Bradford)

Fortified firing position at the CSA compound. (Courtesy: Bill Young)

Troop A S.W.A.T. team members, (from left) Tommy Hill, J. M. Scarberough, and Phillip Valez. (Courtesy: Bill Young)

Some of the weapons seized at the CSA compound. (Courtesy Bill Young)

Troop L's S.W.A.T. Team during their deployment to the CSA siege. From left to right, Bill Burnett, Les Braunns, Keith Ferguson, Charlie Brooks, Rocky Baker, Robin Casey, Joe Hutchins, Dennis Johnston. (Courtesy Win Phillips)

A flyer for a survival training seminar at the CSA. (Courtesy Buddy Acoach)

Chapter Five

A Time of Troubles, 1967-1980

"This is the end of an era."
>—Arkansas State Police Colonel Lynn Davis regarding
>the crackdown on wide open gambling in Hot Springs.

*"Had it not been for the State Police, local law enforcement,
and the National Guard, I am convinced that tragic violence
would have engulfed the area."*
>—Arkansas Governor Bill Clinton on the actions of the
>State Police and others during the Cuban Refugee Crisis in 1980.

*"What happened in [Fort Chaffee] was the Army's business.
What happened beyond the gates was our business. We took
care of our business."*
>—Trooper Tom Morrow regarding the riot
>of Cuban Refugees in 1980.

A high-speed chase often represents the most dangerous incident in a state trooper's career, and almost every officer can recount at least one that stands out as especially hazardous. Arguably, the wildest chase in State Police history occurred in October 1977 when four prison inmates stole a bus and led officers on a 50-mile chase. In the late afternoon on October 19, inmates from Cummins State Prison boarded a prison bus after a day spent working on the new diagnostic center in Pine Bluff. Riding in the bus were 40 inmates, the bus driver, and a prison employee named Ronald Armstrong. Four of the inmates had concealed screwdrivers and a hatchet they had stolen from the work site. After getting outside the city limits, the four inmates rushed to the front of the bus wielding their screwdrivers and hatchet. Since the bus did not have a protective cage that separated the driver and guard from the prisoners, there was nothing to stop the inmates from taking control of the bus. Also, the four prisoners were the only ones who carried weapons, so neither the driver nor the guard had a chance to stop them.

The inmates ordered the driver to turn south off Highway 65 onto Highway 81. This change in direction warned the prison guards following them that something was seriously wrong inside the bus. They radioed the State Police for assistance. Before additional officers could arrive, the inmates succeeded in putting some distance between themselves and the prison guards. This allowed them to stop and let the 36 inmates who did not want to participate in the jailbreak off on the side of the road. They also released the driver, but decided to keep the one remaining prison employee, Ronald Armstrong.

Fortunately for the State Police, an ambulance driven by a reserve sheriff's deputy passed the bus on Highway 81 and decided to turn around and shadow the escapees while radioing in their position to fellow officers. Because of the deputy, officers knew the inmates had turned off Highway 81 onto State Highway 199. Apparently, the escapees thought better of their choice and turned around. By this time, State Police officers had closed the gap. The first officer to arrive was Sergeant David Rosegrant who remembered,

> I set up a roadblock on [Highway 199] just before you get to 81. At the time I was driving a little old 1976 Chevrolet Nova. I am catty-corner across the road. Keep in mind, it is in the evening in September and I have a school bus coming towards me. I wasn't completely sure if this was a school bus full of kids or inmates. They came around this long curve and I see the ambulance, so I know who it is. Also, when they got on a straight stretch coming towards me you could hear him gas it. He hits me and knocks me out of the road. I shoot at the bus a couple of times with a shotgun. He heads across the highway onto a county road, which just makes a semi-circle and comes back to the main highway. I jump in my car, which is dragging its bumper and take off.[389]

Instead of heading back out on Highway 81, the inmates drove the bus onto a narrow country road that merely circled around a large hill before intersecting once again with the main highway. The bus drove to the top of the hill where it stopped and let off two of the four inmates before once again barreling down the road and heading southbound on Highway 81 at speeds nearing 100 miles an hour. Newly arrived troopers would catch the two inmates on the ground a short time later.

The inmates' wrong turn and brief stop had allowed additional officers to catch up so that now 14 state and deputy sheriff's cars trailed the bus. The officers did not want to shoot at the bus or try to force it off the road since Armstrong was still inside. The inmates made sure of this by forcing the guard to stand at the backdoor where following officers could clearly see him. Once they reached Starr City, the inmates did the unthinkable—they pushed Armstrong out of the back of the bus while it was still moving. Armstrong was then struck by a Lincoln County deputy sheriff who was following hard on the heels of the bus and did not have enough time to avoid him. Luckily, Armstrong's injuries were not severe and he would fully recover. While the inmates' decision to throw Armstrong from the bus had temporarily slowed the pursuing officers, it proved to be a huge mistake since they no longer had a shield that prevented the officers from engaging the bus with gunfire—a tactic the officers selected with gusto. As Sergeant Rosegrant recalled, "The bus [was] being shot at by individual cars as they neared the bus. One car would approach and shoot, then back off, and another would take its place.... There were over 400-and-something bullet holes in the bus, and not one individual was hit until after the bus was stopped."

While the bus and its long tail of pursuers were heading south toward Starr City, Trooper John Poindexter sped northward on Highway 81 from Monticello. Outside of Starr City, he pulled his car across the highway to set up a roadblock. For several minutes, Trooper Poindexter thought he would be the only one standing in the bus' path, but in short order additional deputies and troopers began to arrive where they created a more formidable, but less-than-certain barrier to the speeding bus. As the officers waited on the bus, a southbound tractor-trailer pulled up. Trooper Poindexter told the driver to pull off the road to the right and get out of the cab. A few minutes later, the waiting officers saw the speeding bus round a corner with a trooper driving beside it in an attempt to force it off the road. Seeing the roadblock, the pursuing officers slowed. As the bus got nearer, the officers at the roadblock opened fire. The gunfire forced the bus to swerve where it struck the tractor-trailer and abruptly ended the chase. Officers swarmed the bus and arrested the two escapees who were wounded in the closing melee after a Corrections officer fired a shotgun at them.[390]

* * *

Winthrop Rockefeller's ascension to the governorship of Arkansas in January 1967 promised huge changes for the Arkansas State Police. His public pronouncement that he wanted "the agency taken out of politics" and to increase "professionalism" mirrored quite closely statements made by previous politicians, but Rockefeller represented a unique entity in Arkansas politics.[391] He was a true outsider who did not owe his capital, either private or public, to a political faction or group within the state. Therefore, when he said he wanted change in the State Police, there was no reason to doubt his sincerity or ability to achieve it.

The most logical place to begin making changes in the State Police would be at the director's position. As tradition dictated, a change in governors normally meant a change in the department's commander, and early rumors appeared to confirm that such a move was in the making. The leading candidate appeared to be Major Mack Thompson, who was the former Highway Patrol commander and current commander of the department's General Services Division. But after 20 years with the department, which included eight years as Highway Patrol commander, Thompson felt worn down by the tremendous stress of the job, and he was ready for a change. His decision to spurn Rockefeller's offer reflected this, along with his desire to be closer to his aging parents and to raise his children in his hometown of Paragould.[392] Major Thompson did agree to stay on for a time as commander of the General Services Division, which oversaw all non-police functions within the agency. Instead, Governor Rockefeller decided to retain Herman Lindsey as director and reevaluate his position after the legislative session ended in March.[393]

With the agency's top leadership remaining in place, Governor Rockefeller moved to fulfill a key campaign promise, ending wide open gambling in Hot Springs. Rockefeller issued a warning to the Hot Springs gamblers in late February telling them that unless they ceased operations by February 27 he would send in the State Police. The governor also revealed that undercover CID officers were already in the city compiling intelligence on casino operations. These intelligence operations found casinos in Garland and Pulaski County that boasted 118 slot machines, 37 blackjack tables, 12 crap tables, two roulette wheels, and 117 employees serving 1,035 patrons. These findings prompted Rockefeller to warn law enforcement officials in Pulaski and Garland counties that, "it is clear that illegal gambling exists in your county upon such a scale and of such prominence as to be an affront to the laws and the people of the state of Arkansas."[394] When the deadline passed without compliance by the casinos, Rockefeller told Colonel Lindsey to end gambling the best way he saw fit.

A day later, Lindsey designated Majors Struebing and Ken McKee to plan and oversee all gambling raids, with the first occurring on March 1. After obtaining a search warrant from Hot Springs' Municipal Judge Earl Mazander, 25 troopers raided seven Hot Springs clubs, but found only one, a club catering to the black community, with gambling paraphernalia.395 McKee and Struebing were convinced that the delay in obtaining search warrants had allowed time for someone to tip off the casinos to the impending raid. Therefore, the next night the officers chose a different strategy. Undercover officers slipped into three clubs—the Palms, the Frontier, and the Shamrock—where they observed hundreds of people playing slot machines and table games.

The men walked out and called in a flying squad of 12 troopers commanded by Major McKee. The officers raided the clubs, seizing dozens of slots and several table games without relying on a search warrant. The troopers employed the same tactic when they raided the Carousel Club two weeks later and confiscated several more slots.[396]

The search-warrantless raids infuriated Hot Springs Municipal Judge Earl Mazander who ordered the machines to be released to the Hot Springs police department.[397] Major Struebing refused to release them since he knew full well that the local police were fully involved in the gambling racket. Struebing's refusal resulted in contempt of court charges being filed against him by Judge Mazander. Even more damaging to the gambling interests were the reported 26 state troopers currently patrolling within Hot Springs.[398]

Against this backdrop of raids, patrolling troopers, and legal battles between the gambling interests and the State Police, the state Senate began debating the State Police's appropriations bill. The original appropriations bill passed by the Senate in February established a $3.8 million annual budget for the department, but the House had amended the bill in order to increase this appropriation to just over $4.0 million. The increased amendment had to be sent back for approval by the Senate. The return of the appropriations bill provided a golden opportunity for Garland County Senator Q. Bynum Hurst to strike back at the governor's use of the State Police to end wide-open gambling in Hot Springs. To do this, Hurst introduced Senate Bill 491 that called for the elimination of the Criminal Investigation Division within the State Police and a redefinition of the State Police's duties to include just traffic enforcement and a more restricted ability to assist local law enforcement. Hurst promised to kill SB-491 if the department's appropriation bill was amended to include language limiting the State Police's powers to highway patrol and invitation-only criminal investigations. The intent of the bill was obvious to everyone in the state. Seeing the early efforts of Governor Rockefeller and the State Police, Senator Hurst knew this would be his one shot to save gambling in the city. He pulled his sizable faction together and successfully led an effort to block approval of the returned appropriations bill. Unperturbed, the House merely decided to reconsider the Senate's original appropriations bill, which had passed the Senate in February. The House removed their amendment that increased the agency's budget and passed the original, albeit smaller, appropriations bill that did not limit the law enforcement responsibilities of the department.[399] Although it would take almost two years of raids by troopers, this decision to keep the State Police's mission intact sounded the death knell on wide-open casino gambling in Hot Springs.

The 1967 session of the General Assembly produced another important State Police-related piece of legislation, although it proved slightly less controversial. The previous year, the United States Congress passed the Federal Highway Safety Act of 1966, which among other things mandated that the states create a vehicle inspection program or else lose federal highway funding.[400] To satisfy this mandate and guarantee their receipt of $10 million in federal highway money, the legislature tasked the State Police with setting up and operating a Motor Vehicle Inspection Division. Lieutenant W. A. Tudor commanded the 16 troopers and four sergeants who were assigned to the new division where they would oversee vehicle inspection stations around the state.[401] One of the sergeants sent to the MVI section was Dean Friend, who remembered their early efforts at setting up and operating the unit:

> We patterned it after programs in five states … [and] it went into effect on January 1, 1968. We would dummy up cars and go to inspection stations and see what kind of inspections we would get. I was working with a real good friend of mine, Bill Mullenax, south of Hamburg in a town called Portland. We had received some complaints on an inspection station down there. As we pulled in, a car was being pulled out [after an inspection] and it was really ragged. I had them put it up on the rack and the tie-rods were bound with hay wire and it still had a legal inspection sticker on it."[402]

Before the State Police could refocus on stamping out the resilient casinos in the spa city or operating a vehicle inspection program, the probably inevitable change of leadership occurred. On June 1, Herman Lindsey announced his retirement from the department, as did Majors Thompson and Earl Scroggin, who was one of the original 13 members of the Arkansas Rangers in 1935. Highway Patrol Commander Kenneth McKee was an early leader to replace Lindsey following a recommendation for the position from the State Police Commission.[403] Rockefeller directed Major Thompson to poll the leadership within the State Police as to their preference for the new director. Thompson reported back that, "I have not located anyone who does not endorse Major McKee with enthusiasm," which led him to say that he "truly believes his selection to lead this department would be most wise." Even though Thompson recommended McKee as director, he qualified his remarks by stating, "the greatest assets of this department was its troopers and the greatest liabilities was the Supervisors...I believe the greatest needs of this department is young new blood in leadership to direct the many young troopers."[404]

It is conceivable that the director's position would have been offered to Major McKee had it not been for a chance encounter by B. Bryan Larry, a Rockefeller appointee to the state Revenue Commission, and the brother of an old high school and college friend named Lynn Davis. After Commissioner Larey heard that his old friend and debating partner at Henderson State was an agent with the Federal Bureau of Investigation and desperately wanted to move back to Arkansas, he thought of the vacancy at the State Police. Larey approached the governor and set up an interview between him and Lynn Davis in mid June. The two men met for dinner, and as Davis remembered, "We hit it off right away. I flew back to Los Angeles, and the next morning Tom Isley ... called me and said, 'Win wants you to resign as soon as you can. How long can you give them?' I said, 'Well, at least two weeks.' I went down to the special agent in charge and submitted my two-weeks notice."[405]

However, there was a problem with Rockefeller's choice. He had lived out of state for more than six years. In the original legislation creating the State Police, there was a clause mandating that the director be a resident of Arkansas for at least 10 years preceding his or her appointment. Davis clearly failed the residency requirement, but Rockefeller and Davis hoped that the interpretation of "residency" could be defined as something other than maintaining a physical presence inside the state. Davis remembers that they made the counter argument that "residency" should be defined "by the voting method, which meant where the heart was. I knew my heart was always in Arkansas. I loved Arkansas and always intended to come back."[406]

Arkansas Attorney General Joe Purcell did not agree with Davis' interpretation and filed a lawsuit in Pulaski County Circuit Court to overturn his appointment. Still, it would take time for the suit to work its way through the court system, and Colonel Davis had big plans for the State Police until then. He promised to "develop professionalism, make use of new crime and highway safety techniques, and put more emphasis on criminal investigation." When asked about his plans regarding gambling in Hot Springs, he replied, "If the local law enforcement officers failed to handle the case, we would be duty-bound to do so."[407]

A month later, Colonel Davis made good on his promise. Undercover officers entered four Hot Springs casinos—the Citizens, the Bridge Street, the Ohio, and the White Front. After observing the ongoing gambling, the officers left and called Colonel Davis. Davis remembered,

> I got Ken McKee to come down with fifteen marked cars with sirens and red lights on. I had him put someone at parade rest in front of five casinos and at any exit. At any point of egress or ingress I wanted a trooper there. We established a perimeter of defense. I told them to let anybody go. [They could] just walk out, but they couldn't carry any machines or books or anything. Then I called the prosecuting attorney at about 1:30 a.m. He said, "Oh yes, Colonel Davis, how are you doing?" I said, "I need to get a search warrant for these five

clubs." He said, "Okay, no problem I will get you one in the morning. I usually get there about 9:00 a.m." I said, "Well that is fine, whenever you want to come down. We've got troopers in the front and back of all of the clubs." He said, "The hell you say!" I said, "Yes, we have the place surrounded, and it doesn't matter when you get here." He said, "I'll be there in five minutes."[408]

The raid proved to be a huge success. Colonel Davis estimated that they seized almost $70,000 worth of gambling devices at the four clubs.[409] Some of the paraphernalia did not make it out completely intact though. Trooper Mickey Smith and another officer went upstairs at the Bridge Street Club to bring the table games down to the waiting trucks,

> As we started down, the other officer said, "I don't believe I can hold this." I told him to move out of the way and I would show him how to get it down the stairs. I just shoved it, and down the stairs it went. It took off the two front doors on its way. About the time I looked up, Lynn Davis was standing there. I thought, "Uh-oh." He said, "Those things are hard to hold sometimes." I said, "They sure are!"[410]

Close on the heels of these opening shots, Pulaski County Circuit Judge Warren Wood made a surprise ruling that Davis's appointment was legal because he was convinced that the Texarkana native had always considered Arkansas his "home." Due to this, the former FBI-agent-turned-judge argued that the appointment satisfied the legislative intent of the residency requirement.[411] The ruling outraged Attorney General Purcell who filed an appeal with the state Supreme Court, but once again, it would take time for the appeal to be considered by the court. Time used by Colonel Davis and the department to continue its attack on gambling in Hot Springs.

The first week of October witnessed another large raid by troopers in Hot Springs, where they seized more than a hundred slot machines. Probably not surprisingly, 18 of the seized slots bore markings left by troopers on slot machines seized in August. Those machines had been given to the city police department for destruction, but the markings proved that the Hot Springs police department had only made a show of breaking the machines before returning them to their owners.[412]

Any damage that the city officers might have done to the slot machines could be fixed at a large repair shop located in a red barn behind the house of the Southern Club's manager, which was on Second Street. This repair shop was just as critical to the gamblers as any of the casinos. The federal gambling laws passed in the early 1960s had outlawed the interstate transport of gambling paraphernalia, which included new slot machines and even replacement parts, into a state where gambling was illegal. The two federal investigations into gambling at Hot Springs during Faubus's time in office had attempted to determine if just such interstate activity was occurring, so the gamblers were naturally hesitant to risk a third investigation. Therefore, all slot machines had to be maintained and fixed within the state to avoid breaking federal laws.

This critical cog in the gamblers' machine fell on October 8. Trooper Glenn Minton tipped off Colonel Davis to the shop's location. Davis and six other officers headed over to set up surveillance.[413] Early the next morning, the men raided the barn and seized over a hundred slot machines in various states of repair, many of which were being cannibalized for spare parts. This time, the State Police would make sure the machines did not make their way back to the casino floors. They loaded them up in a truck and hauled them to a gravel pit outside of town. They dug a pit with a bulldozer, dumped the slots in and then drove the bulldozer over the top of them. Wanting to make an even bigger statement, Colonel Davis ordered 30 gallons of diesel fuel poured into the pit and then ignited, turning the broken machines into charred clumps of metal.[414]

Since August, the State Police had seized more than 500 slot machines, made numerous arrests, and captured the main slot machine repair shop in the state. These indisputable achievements led Colonel Davis to declare that "This is the end of an era."[415] While this might have been a slight overstatement by the always quotable colonel, no one would argue that wide-open casino gambling in Hot Springs was on its last legs.

It would be a mistake to say the State Police focused solely on illegal gambling in Hot Springs. They also conducted raids in Pulaski County, Washington County, and other areas of the state. In fact, it would be the raids in Pulaski County that led to Colonel Davis's arrest and night in jail. On September 19, State Police officers raided the Westwood Club, a gambling house and bookie joint located in Pulaski County, where they made 12 arrests.

In November, a grand jury began considering charges for the men, all of whom had long records of previous gambling arrests, but each time they had gotten off with a nominal fine. Despite overwhelming evidence that the Westwood was indeed a gambling club, the prosecutor demanded that Colonel Davis reveal the informant used to obtain his search warrants.[416] Davis refused, so the prosecutor asked Judge William Kirby to see if he could use the threat of a contempt-of-court charge to scare the information out him. On December 5, Colonel Davis appeared before Judge Kirby, who said, "The prosecutor tells me that you won't tell him the name of your informant."

Davis replied, "That is right judge. I think he has enough evidence to convict without the name of the informant."

The judge asked Davis one last time if he would tell the prosecutor the name of his informant. Davis again refused, so Judge Kirby ordered the deputies to arrest the director of the Arkansas State Police and remand him to the county jail until he complied with the court's order.[417]

The jailing of the state's top police officer created a nationwide media sensation. As Colonel Davis stared around his jail cell he remembered thinking that,

> "I was finally going to get a good night's sleep because I was in a jail cell and nobody was going to wake me up. I sent the major out to my house to get some sheets to sleep on. My wife ... decided to send ... pink sheets. I am asleep about 1:30 in the morning and I hear [a deputy] whispering my name. I ask what he wanted and he told me

that the *New York Times* was on the phone and wanted to talk to me
… so I went and answered the pay phone and did an interview."[418]

Judge Kirby's decision to have Davis arrested "enraged" Governor
Rockefeller, who called the action a form of "political harassment."[419]
The next day, Governor Rockefeller took the case to the state Supreme
Court for an emergency ruling. After reading a transcript of the court
proceedings, the Supreme Court realized that Judge Kirby had made a
critical mistake during his questioning of Colonel Davis. The judge had
only asked Davis if he would tell the prosecutor the name of his
informant instead of asking him directly the name of his informant.
Based on this technicality, the Supreme Court overruled the contempt
of court charge and ordered Davis freed from jail.[420]

Two weeks later, another state Supreme Court ruling would issue
another important ruling on the State Police and Colonel Davis. After a
delay of several months, the Supreme Court finally reached a verdict on
Attorney General Purcell's appeal of a lower court's decision that Davis met
the 10-year residency rule. The Supreme Court agreed with Purcell and
ruled that Davis did not satisfy the residency requirement, thus making him
ineligible for the position of director. The ruling upset many within the
state, including Lieutenant Governor Maurice Britt, who remarked that
"Lynn Davis exemplifies all that is expected of a law enforcement official …
[h]e has brought professionalism to the State Police. He has carried out his
duties in a bold and forthright manner. He has enforced the laws of
Arkansas in a fair and impartial manner, regardless of race, creed and color
… social status … financial status and regardless of political pressure or
influence."[421] Even the State Police Commission, which had originally
lobbied for the elevation of Major McKee to the top post instead of Davis,
issued a public statement supporting Davis and urging Governor
Rockefeller to seek a change in the department's enabling legislation that
removed the 10-year residency requirement.

At the same time, a number of people were equally happy to see
him go. Garland County Senator Hurst warned against any attempt by

Rockefeller to change the residency requirement.[422] Despite this warning, a bill was passed during the 1968 special session of the General Assembly that lowered the residency requirement to a single year, but by the time it became law, a new director had been appointed.[423]

To temporarily fill the void in the director's office, Governor Rockefeller agreed to elevate Lieutenant Colonel Carl Miller to the department's top spot in January 1968. Colonel Miller had made it known that he would be retiring soon, so the promotion reflected one final reward for the officer's long tenure with the State Police, which began in 1937. When Colonel Miller announced his impending retirement a month later, the State Police Commission once again appointed Major Kenneth McKee as acting director.

During the brief time that Carl Miller and Ken McKee ran the State Police, the department kept up their efforts to stop casino-style gambling in Hot Springs. Led by Major Bill Miller and Lieutenant W. A. Tudor, the State Police had to widen their net after the major casinos temporarily ended wide-open gambling following the Davis raids during the fall of 1967. Now, casino-style gambling had shifted to private homes in Hot Springs. In February, Miller and Tudor took a handful of troopers on a late night raid of a private residence suspected of being a gambling house. When Major Miller knocked on the door and announced his presence he heard what "sounded like a stampede" from the other side. The officers kicked the door open, and Miller remembered finding:

> "A big living room [with] a big crap table sitting in the middle
> …[t]here wasn't a soul in the room. Cigarettes were in ashtrays with
> smoke rising up, money all over the tables, but they were nowhere in
> the room. We had already surrounded the house, so they had to be
> here somewhere. We started looking. There were three bedrooms full
> of people standing with their coats and hats on. One of the sergeants
> looked in there and said, 'Good evening and where are you folks
> going?' [Another] trooper walked down the hall … and opened a
> closet door. He saw all of these clothes suddenly shiver and he pulled
> apart the clothes and [saw] this old boy standing there. The trooper
> says, 'What are you doing in there, feller?' He said, 'Well, everybody

has to be somewhere!' Every time we made one of those arrests, we took them down [to the city jail] and didn't try to keep the press from knowing about it. When you do something like that, the people get leery of going into an illegal gambling place. We did that for about three months, and it was pretty quiet when we got through."[424]

Even though the State Police continued to have success in stopping gambling in Hot Springs, Governor Rockefeller decided to look outside the department for Colonel Carl Miller's permanent replacement. On February 29, Governor Rockefeller selected retired FBI agent Ralph Scott as the new director of the State Police. Scott's selection proved to be a complete surprise since he had no prior relationship with Governor Rockefeller or anyone within the State Police. In fact, Rockefeller's first introduction to Scott was through a letter of application received by the governor on January 31.[425]

Probably not coincidentally, Scott had a similar background as Lynn Davis, but without the residency issues. He was an Arkansas native having grown up in Hempstead County. He had joined the FBI in 1935 serving as a special agent in Detroit, New York, Washington D.C., and Arkansas before retiring in 1963. Following his retirement, Scott spent time as an instructor at Arkansas's law enforcement training academy and as a chemistry teacher at Camden High School.[426]

Colonel Scott had barely moved into his new office when the assassination of civil rights leader Martin Luther King in Memphis plunged that city into virtual anarchy on April 4, 1968. As the ripples of violence spread out from Memphis in early April, police forces around the nation were stretched to the limit trying to bring order amid the chaos. In Memphis, city and county officers were quickly overmatched as an outraged black community took out their anger and frustration over inequality and discrimination on their city and its guardians. On the night of King's murder, the mayor of Memphis placed an urgent request to Governor Rockefeller and Colonel Scott asking for additional men from the Arkansas State Police to cross the Mississippi River and help contain the violence. The Tennessee State Police and the Tennessee National Guard could not promise to arrive in a timely manner due to other instances of unrest in their state. Since Arkansas remained moderately calm, the governor and Colonel Scott agreed to dispatch 30 of the biggest, toughest State Police officers in the department to Memphis. When the men arrived, the Shelby County sheriff deputized them and paired them with at least two other county or city officers to ride in a single patrol car.

What awaited them in the city streets seemed like a war zone. Fires burned, stores were being looted, and all too frequently, gunshots rang out, leading one reporter to described the city as a "jungle."[427] Over the next two days, 229 fires would be set, 30 people would be injured, and 136 people would be arrested.[428]

Uniformed troopers only remained in Memphis for a few days before they were speedily reassigned to Pine Bluff where rioting and unrest had broken out, as well. Incidents of sniping and firebombing pulled in 36 troopers who worked with 50 local officers to seal off four blocks inside the city where most of the unrest was occurring. Once commanders felt that the violence was contained, the officers began to move in. As they approached the Gala Club, shots rang out from the third-story nightclub's windows. Officers returned fire while pressing forward to the bottom floor of the building. A tense search of the building and more than 400 of the club's patrons resulted in the arrest of 38 people for carrying concealed weapons. After the arrests, Pine Bluff's mayor declared a 7:00 p.m. to 7:00 a.m. curfew and stated hopefully, "I think the emotional peak has been reached and passed."[429]

For the next several days, State Police officers were paired with unarmed National Guard soldiers who rode with them while they assisted city and county officers in patrolling the streets of Pine Bluff and enforcing the curfew.

This outburst of violence following the assassination of Martin Luther King convinced Colonel Scott that all of America's police agencies, even the Arkansas State Police, had to repair an image that had been tarnished by past abuses and corruption, even if those transgressions occurred in other departments. Doing so would require the State Police to hire the right people, improve training, and act courteously when dealing with the public, especially in instances of civil disobedience.[430] Scott's comments proved to be prescient, for over the next five years, Arkansas would be beset by racial conflict, unrest, and sporadic violence as the state, like so many other Southern states, struggled through the civil rights era.

Only four months after the rioting in Pine Bluff, Little Rock had a serious burst of racial strife following the death of a black teenager who was serving a sentence at the county's penal farm. To protest the youth's death, members of the black community marched daily for a week. On Friday, August 10, another march was planned by 300 protestors who met at a church on Dunbar Street from which they were to march several miles to the county courthouse on Markham Avenue. Little Rock police officers were assigned to block off traffic along the march route. State Police and National Guard personnel were alerted and placed on stand-by in case the peaceful march turned violent.

The marchers walked to the county courthouse without incident, but during their return, the city police began receiving more and more complaints of vandalism and rock throwing by members of the group. Officers began to move into the crowd to prevent any escalation in the unrest, but this move only served to further anger the marchers. State Police and Guardsmen were called in to help establish a cordon around 80 square blocks of central Little Rock bounded by High, 10th, Wright, and Broadway streets. Also arriving on the scene was former State Police Major Ken McKee who had left the department and was now working for Governor Rockefeller's private security team. McKee met with marchers at a police barricade to help calm its leaders. The marchers dispersed shortly thereafter, but that night the city would see a number of cases of arson, vandalism, and even some sniping as 60 troopers patrolled alongside city officers and National Guardsmen in the cordoned-off section of Little Rock.[431]

The same month that Little Rock smoldered, the State Police was on the cusp of a huge leap forward in technology. In August, the State Police's first computer system, an IBM 2740 Model II, became operational.[432] In a joint effort with the state Revenue Department, the IBM 2740 provided a central database of driver and vehicle records that could be searched almost instantly. Before this, checking a vehicle license was a slow, labor-intensive process, as Major Ken McFerran remembered,

> If I was checking a license in Boone County, I would call a [Boone County] dispatcher and ask them to run me a "28," which was a license check. So the radio operator would copy that down on a piece of yellow pad. He had a printout of all of the Boone County license plates, and he would go through that and find my license plate. He could then tell me who it belong to, where they lived, and what type of car it was registered to. That was relatively fast. But if we got one out of Crittenden County or somewhere, our radio operator would have to call Forrest City and have them contact Crittenden County on the local radio to do the same thing. Then the information would have to pass from Crittenden County to Forrest City to Harrison and then down to me. This could take several minutes and sometimes the next day.[433]

A few months later, an even greater improvement was made to the system when it was connected with the Federal Bureau of Investigation's National Crime Information Center (NCIC) database. This gave officers almost instant access to a suspect's arrest history, wanted status, and other pertinent information. Each State Police District Headquarters was provided with a terminal that could access this information. The first arrest made from a search of the NCIC database occurred when Trooper Bobby Neel stopped a car with a North Carolina license plate on the day after Christmas 1968. The officer ran the man's identification through the system and found out he was wanted in North Carolina.[434]

While Trooper Neel and the rest of the department were reaping the benefits of improved technology, the relationship between Colonel Scott and Governor Rockefeller was falling apart. After being re-elected to a second term in November 1968, Governor Rockefeller began to re-examine Scott's performance. Rumors of the fiery director's demise abounded in the department as the question became not if but when he would be fired. These rumors became fodder for the state's press in March 1969 when Colonel Scott surprised Governor Rockefeller by submitting his resignation. Scott said that the two men had "no cordiality or dialogue" after the director fired one of Rockefeller's closest friends in the department almost a year earlier. As a result of their strained relationship, Scott had become "disillusioned" with some aspects of the job, but he would "hate like hell to leave."[435]

It is very possible that Governor Rockefeller would have accepted his resignation had it not been for events that erupted in Forrest City the day after Scott submitted his resignation. On March 20, nearly 200 students at Forrest City's all-black Lincoln High School walked out of their classrooms and began pulling down lockers, breaking windows, ripping water fountains off the wall, and smashing vending machines, all of which resulted in $17,500 in damage.[436] School officials frantically called for police assistance to stop the students. City and county officers responded, along with 25 state troopers, and after two hours and 12 arrests, an uneasy truce developed that only promised more trouble in the future.[437]

The impetus behind this mini-riot was the firing of the school's popular social science teacher, J. F. Cooley. Tension had been building between blacks and whites in Forrest City ever since school board elections in February saw a pro-segregation faction gain a majority of seats. Thus, when the school board fired Cooley, who represented "for too many of these boys and girls ... the only brother, father, and friend they have ever known," it seemed to confirm their worst fears that integration would be indefinitely delayed.[438]

For the rest of the spring and summer, tensions between the black and white communities continued to increase. In June, a community center catering to the predominately black part of town burned under suspicious circumstances. At the same time, black activists began to arrive in the troubled city to help organize protests. The most vocal of these outsiders was a Memphis man named Lance Watson, although everyone knew him as "Sweet Willie Wine."[439] Sweet Willie was a tall, thin man who sported a goatee and whose left arm was crippled following a childhood fight with polio. This physical handicap did not diminish his ability to motivate and organize the disaffected. His activism took the form of a small group of black militants known as "The Invaders," whose most famous action involved helping organize a strike of sanitation workers in Memphis in 1968.

In Forrest City, Sweet Willie's Invaders worked with a local activist group known as the Committee for Peaceful Coexistence to stage a month-long picketing of Forrest City's downtown merchants. The picketing was a success—if for no other reason—because it kept the issue of civil rights and equality at the forefront of daily conversation in Forrest City and throughout the state. Still, even this level of public attention did not satisfy Sweet Willie, who seized upon the idea of a walk from West Memphis to Little Rock as a way to protest violence against blacks in Arkansas.

The idea for a walk actually originated within the leadership of the Committee for Peaceful Coexistence, who were upset with some of Governor Rockefeller's statements regarding events in Forrest City. After Rockefeller met with black activists and convinced them that he supported their efforts to promote equality, integration, and civil rights, the committee called off the walk.[440] Sweet Willie recognized a good idea when he saw it, so he picked up the abandoned plan, calling it Sweet Willie's "walk against fear."

On August 20, Sweet Willie and his entourage of four Invaders, 12 reporters, and five State Police cars carrying seven officers stepped off from West Memphis on Highway 70. Overseeing the State Police protection detail was the recently promoted Captain W. A. Tudor, who met with Sweet Willie before the walk to discuss security measures, remembering,

> Doug [Harp] and I ... went to West Memphis [to meet with Sweet Willie] ... I told him that we were going to stay with him, and if he listened to what we told him, and we listened to what he told us, we are going to make this trip without a shot fired or a club swung. And there wasn't."[441]

The group planned to walk the 130-mile distance over five days. A difficult feat compounded by the hot Arkansas summer, which saw temperatures in the 90s. Luckily for the State Police officers, the department began buying cars with air conditioning in 1966, so at least they had some respite from the blazing sun. Sweet Willie and his small band of walkers trudged on meeting small groups of supporters who would join them at the outskirts of towns and walk a few miles with them before dropping out and returning to their homes.[442]

After two completely uneventful days, Captain Tudor and Sweet Willie had reason to feel good about the outcome of the march, but the next day would be the first true test of racial attitudes in Arkansas. On this day, the "march against fear" was scheduled to pass through Hazen. Over the previous few weeks, Hazen's mayor had made a number of inflammatory statements warning Sweet Willie to stay out of Hazen. When the march kicked off on August 20, the mayor mobilized dozens of "special policemen" who manned barricades set up along Highway 70 to prevent any of the marchers from leaving the highway. For the first time, the potential for fighting between marchers and onlookers seemed within the realm of possibility. To prevent any embarrassing incidents, 16 troopers and five CID investigators were called in to help escort the marchers through the small town. As the marchers, now bolstered by almost 40 locals, entered the city, they saw the side streets lined with farm implements, wooden saw horse barricades, and combines.[443] Despite this uneasy sight, Captain Tudor remembered, "We walked through Hazen ... and there wasn't a sound made. In fact, Hazen was probably the easiest town we went through."[444]

The next day, Sweet Willie and his fellow marchers arrived in Little Rock where they met with local black activists to attend a rally. The march had been a rousing success for Sweet Willie, who gained a tremendous amount of notoriety due to the front-page coverage provided by the media. The State Police also received a valuable public relations boost when a grateful Sweet Willie told the press that "If police were like them all across the United States, we wouldn't have any police brutality."[445]

Sweet Willie Wine's saga in Arkansas does not end there, though. Just as the march was ending, a group of white citizens in Forrest City formed the Concerned Citizens Committee to protest the presence of "outsiders" in their city and demand a return of "law and order."[446] What they really wanted was for the black activists to leave the city so they could go back to the way things had been before the advent of integration and civil rights. The initial kernels of anger were embedded during the summer-long picketing by black activists of white-owned businesses in downtown Forrest City. These feelings were greatly inflamed by recent allegations that a black man had raped a white woman and that a group of five black men robbed and stabbed a grocery store clerk. Many of the members of the Citizens Committee blamed the local police department for failing to stop the summer-long protests in addition to their inability to find and arrest the perpetrators of these crimes.

The Citizens Committee decided to picket city hall as a way to voice their displeasure with the city administration. Probably of more concern for the local authorities and the black community was the committee's decision to direct its members to conduct an armed motor-patrol on the city streets where they would communicate with other citizen patrols via two-way radios installed in their cars.[447] The stated goal of this patrol was to assist city police officers in enforcing the law.

On the morning of August 26, a planned Citizens Committee march drew a crowd of almost a thousand whites who congregated at city hall carrying signs that read, "We Demand the Return to Law and Order" and "Remove the Scum and Animals from Our Town."[448] After a long day of protesting, the crowd had turned even more surly and ready for a fight. It was at this time that Sweet Willie Wine and a handful of his fellow Invaders chose to come to city hall to check on one of their brethren who was confined in the city jail. Sweet Willie represented the epitome of the "outsiders" that the Citizens Committee despised, especially after his recent "march against fear." So when he appeared in their midst, it was not a matter of if he would be attacked, but who would strike the first blow.

Members of the crowd grabbed Sweet Willie and threw him up against a parking meter, raining blows against the man. The crowd attacked four other people, as well, including the publisher of a local newspaper who remarked later, "I know what fear is now."[449] With great effort, Sweet Willie and the other targets of the crowd were able to scramble free with some help from local police. During the fighting, Sweet Willie suffered a fractured elbow, but luckily, most of the injuries were confined to bumps and bruises. Even after this confrontation had ended, the jumpy crowd continued to mill about, only dispersing after more than 50 State Police officers arrived at 10:00 p.m. to reinforce local officers. One Forrest City businessman summed up the situation quite accurately, telling the press that, "This town has gone mad."

Governor Rockefeller agreed with this sentiment and called out 160 members of the National Guard to reinforce the more than 80 state and local officers operating in Forrest City. The Troop Commander of the Forrest City District, Dwight Galloway, commanded the State Police contingent and assigned the troopers to man roadblocks and conduct roving patrols the night of the 26th in an effort to enforce the nighttime curfew.

The next afternoon, crowds of white and black residents began to gather on opposite street corners around city hall. Both groups hurled insults and taunted the other side, while standing in the middle absorbing it from both sides were State Police, local officers, and National Guardsmen. When the tornado siren sounded at 7:00 p.m. to signal the start of curfew, officers began dispersing the crowd and eventually arrested five white demonstrators for carrying concealed weapons. For the next week, troopers remained in Forrest City and patrolled the streets dispersing crowds and helping to prevent further violence.

Through September, tensions remained high in Forrest City, especially toward outsiders and the news media. Two reporters from the *Arkansas Gazette* were actually struck by members of the Concerned Citizens Committee.[450] This action seemed to represent a turning point in the city since it forced the moderates in both the black and white communities to open a dialogue and organize a large, bi-racial rally to end the violence.[451] Following the rally, the widespread unrest came to an end.

Exactly 12 months later, another east Arkansas community would undergo the same sort of racially motivated unrest that required the intervention of State Police officers to prevent an escalation. On September 8, 1970, students at Earle's all-black Dunbar School walked out of class and began marching toward Earle's white high school. The small school system was in the first year of its long-term integration plan, and black students were dissatisfied with the sub par conditions of their school and the seemingly prejudicial attitudes of several of their white teachers.[452] As the teenagers made their way across town, a small group of state troopers stood in their path. One of the officers, Mel Hensley, remembered:

> The first day we went to Earle, there were at least 200 [demonstrators] and just three of us. There was myself, Glen Bailey ... [and] Sergeant Cooper. We were standing on the sidewalk, and I said, "Sarge, what are we going to do when they get up here?" He said, "I don't know. We just hope they stop." We were outnumbered by a long ways, and we just can't start shooting high school kids. We were lucky. When they got across the street, they just stopped. They sang their songs and carried on for a bit and then went on back up the street.[453]

Several hours later, a number of the students were arrested for marching without a permit. The arrests upset members of the black community, who organized a nighttime march several days later to protest the officers' actions. Twelve State Police officers were called in under the command of Captain Galloway where they joined forces with city and county officers in an effort to contain the almost 200 protesters. Before the officers could move to intersect the marchers, 30 white men armed with shotguns appeared in their path. The marchers hesitated, unsure what to make of this unexpected threat. Then the white men began firing their weapons into the air and moving toward the marchers who turned and fled in disorder. A few did not escape quickly enough, including the leader of the march, Reverend Ezra

Greer and his wife, who were struck several times by fists and feet.[454] Officers moved in to separate the two groups. For the next few weeks, additional State Police troopers were assigned to patrol within Earle where the lack of motels forced them to sleep on cots set up at the local John Deere dealer.[455]

Before the troopers had time to settle back into their regular patrols, inmates at Cummins Penitentiary began to riot. Throughout 1970, inmates at both Tucker and Cummins had been giving their wardens fits. In May, prison guards at Tucker had to use tear gas to remove striking prisoners from their barracks. But the most serious incidents occurred at Cummins. On November 2, 18 prisoners seized four hostages—two free-world guards and two trusties. The prisoners threatened to kill the four unless the prisoners were released from prison. After 13 hours of negotiation, the prisoners released their hostages unharmed. A few weeks later, the prisoners turned on each other. Just a few days before Thanksgiving, 500 of Cummins' 1,160 prisoners began fighting. The fight erupted between black and white prisoners who were angry over the forced integration of the prison, which had started earlier that year. The situation was made even more complicated since Cummins was in the middle of its transition from the trusty guard system to a completely free-world system. Therefore, the new free-world guards were only half-trained and had little to no experience in dealing with such critical situations.

The warden and Governor Rockefeller urgently requested as many troopers as possible be sent to Cummins to stop the riot. By 9:20 p.m., 75 troopers had arrived and forceably separated the two groups of prisoners, sending the whites to the gym and the blacks to the barracks. Twenty-five troopers took over responsibility for guarding the prisoners that night, even going so far as to assume control over the towers and the front gate. The remaining 50 men were ordered to report back to the prison at 6:00 a.m.

The next morning, the inmates filed into the cafeteria for breakfast. A fight broke out between two rivals, but this time troopers armed with shotguns were ready. The troopers lined up facing the prisoners, jacked a round into their shotguns, and leveled them at the suddenly quiet crowd. The willingness to use force convinced the convicts that it would be in their best interest to follow instructions, so they returned to their barracks without incident. The State Police spent the next two days searching the prison, where they uncovered almost 500 homemade weapons. By November 25, most of the troopers had returned to their regular posts, although several did make a surprise return on December 1 to re-inspect the prison. This time, they brought metal detectors, which helped them locate another large quantity of homemade weapons.

After all of the special assignments and civil unrest the department responded to between 1967 and 1970, it seemed easy to forget that their main responsibilities remained highway patrol and criminal investigation. Yet the Rockefeller era would present more than its fair share of significant highway patrol and investigation related events.

The most groundbreaking of these occurred in 1967 with the hiring of the State Police's first black trooper, Marion Taylor. Then-Major Bill Miller, who ran the department's Motor Vehicle Inspection Division (which included safety and driver's license responsibilities as well), remembered, "I think they were a little leery of putting him on the road by himself. So Herman [Lindsey] asked me if I would take him and ... I said I would be glad to have him. I put him to work and he did a fine job for me."[456] Trooper Taylor worked primarily as a safety education officer where he traveled around the state and gave presentations, lectures, and demonstrations on safe driving.

Assigning troopers to focus primarily on safety education did not hold much favor with Colonel Scott. Especially after he pushed through a change in policy that reduced shifts from the decades-old practice of six-10s—six 10-hour days—to five 10-hour days a week in 1969. The reduction in regular hours did not necessarily mean that officers worked significantly fewer hours since they remained on call 24 hours a day. This often meant their shift would extend far beyond the 10 hours the policy required. But by reducing the number of hours troopers are on patrol, he had to find a way to increase the number of total shifts to maintain the same levels of coverage. One way would be to eliminate the Safety Section and transfer its officers to Highway Patrol. Colonel Scott also began a push to remove driver's testing from the State Police's purview, as well. He argued that transferring this responsibility to the Revenue Department would free up almost 40 troopers for highway patrol. The key impetus behind the reassignment of safety officers and the push to remove driver's testing from the State Police was the seemingly unstoppable rise in traffic-related fatalities. After a large decline in deaths in 1967, 1968 saw fatalities rise over 700 for the first time in history.

Hand in hand with assigning more officers to highway patrol, Colonel Scott attempted to institute new patrol techniques. Lacking a background in highway patrol, Scott turned to numerous books and manuals that described the latest experiments at traffic enforcement, some of which caused more than a little head shaking among the department's long-time officers.[457] Others found some support among the veteran officers, one of which was known as Operation Pacesetter. In the Pacesetter operation, every State Police officer would be assigned to highway patrol where they would drive the state's highways not to stop people, but to let traffic back up behind them while they drove the speed limit. Another was known as a round robin operation, which remained a fairly regular tactic for years afterward. The round robin, as described by Captain G. B. Harp, required

> Everybody [to be] assigned a particular area during a holiday. Nobody took a holiday off. Everybody went into uniform and worked, even the Criminal Investigation Division. Everybody had a 20- or 30-mile stretch of road [to patrol]. The reason it was called a round robin was you would drive from point A to point B and back and forth all day. That really increased visibility."[458]

One change implemented during the Rockefeller/Scott period that won the praise of no one was the Highway Patrol's brief experiment in

1969 with wearing a western style hat similar to the one favored by Governor Rockefeller. The vast majority of officers preferred the traditional campaign hats, so the hats did not last long.

The latter half of the 1960s would prove to be a busy one for the Criminal Investigation Division, as well. Their first high-profile investigation exploded into a national news story and later a major motion picture. In January 1968, three skeletons were dug up just outside the fence at Cummins penitentiary.[459] The head of the state's penitentiary system at the time was Thomas Murton, a Rockefeller appointee who had been recruited from Southern Illinois University where he was a criminology professor. The discovery of the skeletons prompted Murton to tell the press, both state and national, that the skeletons must have been the bodies of inmates murdered at the prison. The reputation of Arkansas' prisons was already poor, but Murton's accusations reduced them to a new low and greatly embarrassed Governor Rockefeller. CID officers were called in to investigate, and the skeletons were sent to the state medical examiner for inspection. The identity of the skeletons was never determined, but an examination of the bones found that none of the three died a violent death. Investigators theorized that the three were prisoners who died of natural causes and were buried outside the penitentiary in an old prison graveyard. Further testing performed on the bones determined that the three people had died in the late 1800s.[460]

The hiring of Colonel Scott also led to a number of procedural changes within the CID, the most important of which was the implementation of a standard reporting system. Before this, investigators kept their own case notes and files and would submit reports that followed no established format. Colonel Scott's background in the FBI convinced him that a more organized, formal reporting system needed to be established. Scott assigned his administrative assistant, W. A. Tudor, to prepare standard reporting forms based on the FBI's system. The change did not sit too well with some of the more senior investigators who preferred to work cases the way they had

always done it—often equated to minimal paperwork and storing most
of their case notes in their shirt pocket. In addition to preparing
standard forms for all aspects of an investigation, the CID also
implemented a central transcription and typing center that officers
were required to use. Ken McFerran, who had just transferred into CID
when these changes were implemented, remembered that "when I went
in they gave me a recorder. You take your notes on [a] yellow pad and
that night dictate everything and mail the tape to Little Rock [where]
they type it up. That may have been the biggest change that the
Criminal Division ever had."[461]

Another major change also proved controversial within the CID. In
1969, Colonel Scott began implementing a reorganization of the State
Police that would place more responsibility and authority at the district
level instead of in Little Rock. Chief among the changes was placing
CID investigators under the direct oversight of a district Highway
Patrol commander. Scott argued that such a move would allow for a
more efficient use of personnel and result in better oversight. On the
outside, such an explanation seems logical enough, yet anyone with an
understanding of the tremendous degree of independence and
authority that already rested with a Highway Patrol district commander
would certainly be puzzled by this "official" reorganization. District
commanders of this era were "God," as one trooper so succinctly
described them, and often the decisions and policies developed in
Little Rock would only be implemented if the local commanders
completely agreed with them.[462]

Therefore, it seems that Colonel Scott's real intent was to reduce
the authority of the Criminal Investigation Division by subordinating
their investigators to Highway Patrol commanders. This seems to be
confirmed by Scott after he left the department and made it clear that
he felt the State Police should commit their scarce resources on
highway patrol and not investigation.[463] While this debate had been
around for decades prior to Scott's tenure, it did not take into account
just how far apart the two major divisions of the State Police had

become. The investigators did not wear a uniform and were rarely seen by the highway patrol troopers. This created a detachment between the two groups of officers and even some animosity at times. When Scott decided to subordinate the investigators to the Highway Patrol, it appeared to question the investigators' ability and work ethic.

The death of an officer always proved that despite some superficial differences between the two major divisions, they still remained members of the same close-knit family. A tragic example of this occurred for the fourth time in the department's history in July 1969. Just after midnight, Trooper Allen Bufford pulled over a car for speeding a few miles outside Batesville. Everything seemed routine as the officer stood beside the driver's door writing the woman a ticket. The passenger, a parolee from Cummins Prison named Jesse Ring, asked Trooper Bufford if he could get out of the car to use the bathroom. The officer told him to go ahead and continued writing the ticket. Then, inexplicably, Ring circled around behind the officer, placed a .22 caliber derringer to the back of Trooper Bufford's head, and pulled the trigger. The officer slumped to the ground, and Ring pulled the trigger a second time, sending another round into the officer's body. That night, Trooper Bufford had a friend riding with him, and when the friend saw Ring shoot the officer, he got on the radio and called for help. When officers arrived, Ring was placidly waiting for them and was arrested without incident. Ring was convicted and sentenced to life in the penitentiary for the murder of Trooper Bufford, who at the time of his death left behind a pregnant wife and young daughter.[464]

By the time Scott's reorganization was completed in 1970, Governor Rockefeller's time in office was growing short. A surprisingly strong candidate for governor named Dale Bumpers had emerged from a crowded field of Democrats that included Orval Faubus who was seeking a return to politics after a four-year hiatus. When Bumpers and Rockefeller squared off in the general election in November, the lawyer from Charleston handily defeated the millionaire governor, and once again the director's watch was on.

Initially, Governor Bumpers seemed reluctant to make any changes in the director's position. He was more focused on a state government-wide reorganization. During its 1971 session, the state legislature conceded to Bumpers' desire to reduce the number of state agencies from an unwieldy 67 to a more manageable 13.[465] One of the 13 new state agencies was the Department of Public Safety (DPS), which would include under its umbrella of responsibility the Alcohol Beverage Control Commission, the Arkansas Law Enforcement Training Academy, the Arkansas National Guard, and the Arkansas State Police, otherwise known as the Police Services Division.[466] On paper, the State Police director reported to the DPS director, but the DPS did not have the power to discipline or fire the director, so in practice the DPS director's authority over the State Police was minimal.

Governor Bumpers may have wanted to wait until closer to July when the DPS officially came into existence before he either reappointed Ralph Scott or named a new director. However in February, the decision was essentially made for him after Colonel Scott made a serious error in judgment by firing Major Melvin Delong in the middle of a legislative session for allegedly undermining his authority.[467] After more than 20 years with the department, Delong had established close ties with a number of very powerful politicians in the state legislature who spoke up in his defense. It stretches reason to believe that it was mere coincidence that Colonel Scott submitted his resignation the day after he fired Delong.[468] Governor Bumpers "reluctantly" accepted Scott's resignation, which was a decision strongly criticized by the state's press. The editors of the Gazette warned, "What Bumpers may not understand is that a good State Police director is hard to find."[469] Scott did not leave without issuing a few final observations. "This is a political job," he said. "I knew that when I took it [and] I never expected it to last quite as long as it did."[470]

In late April, Harold Brueggeman, a retired FBI agent living in Hot Springs, was named DPS director. This appointment allowed Bumpers to move forward and name a permanent replacement for Scott. One of the early applicants for the position was Scott's assistant commander and current acting director, Bill Miller. As Miller recalled, "I liked four years of having enough to retire. Usually Governors get four years [in office] and he seemed like he was a pretty sharp young man and I thought Dale would make the four years. I was going to take a chance and apply and then that would give me a chance to retire [as director]."[471] Governor Bumpers was duly impressed with Miller's application, and on the day he appointed Breuggeman to DPS director, he informed Miller that he would be appointed State Police director in a few weeks. The decision pleased Miller, but he still had a few reservations that needed to be worked out:

> We talked one day before I was appointed and I said I wanted it [director's job] on the condition that I report directly to him and not his subordinates. That was one of the problems with the Faubus administration. There were people in his administration that would call us and tell us to do things. Because they were in the Governor's office we felt like we had to do them.[472]

Bumpers agreed to the stipulation, and on June 16, 1971, Bill Miller became the State Police director.[473] One of Colonel Miller's first actions as director was to return CID to a separate command structure that operated out of Little Rock instead of subordinating them to their respective Highway Patrol district commanders.[474]

Miller's tenure as director got off to a volatile start shortly after Governor Bumpers removed the "acting" portion of his title in June. On June 10, black activists began to coordinate a boycott of downtown merchants in the town of Marianna. The black community was upset over the lack of minorities in government and business positions in Lee County since they made up an overwhelming majority of the population. Also, the school board's decision to make the former principal of Marianna's all-black school a vice principal at the new integrated school angered many within the community. By early

August, downtown merchants were feeling the effects of the boycott as sales were off by double-digit percentages and even led to the closure of three businesses.

White citizens in the county decided to strike back at the protesters by forming a "Good White Citizens Council of Lee County" that would patrol the downtown streets to ensure citizens "will be protected and treated with proper respect and courtesy."[475] The creation of a Citizens' Council combined with three cases of suspected arson in the previous few weeks convinced Marianna's mayor there was an increased probability of violence within the city. Thus, the mayor declared an 8:30 p.m. to 5:00 a.m. curfew in the city, and Lee County Sheriff Langston asked for additional State Police officers to be assigned to the county to help enforce the curfew. The sheriff surmised that "when you have a three-man sheriff's office and a five-man police office, you can hardly watch every store in the county."[476]

Even with this increased police presence, racial violence broke out on August 5 when small groups of white men punched and kicked an *Arkansas Democrat* reporter, a lawyer for the boycotters, and a boycotter. The next day, white residents angered over the *Democrat's* coverage of recent events chased two more of their reporters out of town. The editors of the *Democrat's* main competitor, the *Gazette*, sympathized with their media brethren arguing that the "Physical abuse against at least five men…by crowds of whites in the Courthouse square demonstrates the breakdown of law and order at the local level."[477]

The ninth of August saw a crowd of whites gather in the courthouse square where they surrounded a car containing a reporter and cameraman from Little Rock's ABC affiliate, Channel 7. Members of the crowd opened the car's door and grabbed the man's camera. Escorting the two reporters were three State Police officers in a marked police car.[478] One of those troopers was Dale Miller who remembered,

> Captain [Dwight] Galloway was the commander down there and he told me to take two other troopers and follow this camera crew around to make sure they got their pictures. They [white crowd] saw

them and even with three troopers in a marked car behind them, they blocked the road in front of the courthouse and drug the photographer out and tried to get his film and camera. We got there and I arrested one old boy and threw him in the back of the car...[and] escorted them out of the city limits and these whites went out there and blocked Highway One. These whites had pickup trucks blocking the road. We called Captain Galloway and he said that he didn't want any more trouble. I asked the people if we gave them the film would they let us pass and they said they would. Those dummies. The camera guy gave them some blank film and that night on the news, I think Channel 7, showed them (camera crew) driving through there and then being pulled out of the truck. I had to let the boy I arrested go...[t]hat was a low day."[479]

The willingness of the crowd to openly challenge the troopers' authority angered Captain Galloway who told the press, "We don't intend to condone such actions by any group." That evening Colonel Miller dispatched almost 30 additional troopers and two CID investigators to Marianna to provide what Captain Galloway called a "show of force." When another television news crew requested a State Police escort, Galloway took no chances and sent 12 officers along.[480]

Over the next few weeks, both whites and blacks within Lee County met to try and resolve their differences and put an end to the violence. Their efforts were at least superficially successful since the threat of unrest and mob violence became less and less prominent. On August 15, 10 troopers were released from this special assignment and the next day the mayor lifted the curfew.

The state was not through with racial unrest after the situation at Marianna settled down. In March 1972, fighting erupted between black and white students at Arkadelphia High School during which 12 students were injured and much of the school's property was in "shambles."[481] City police arrested three black students who were charged with inciting a riot and then placed in the Clark County jail. As word of the arrests spread through the black community, an estimated 250 protesters went to the jail. State Police hurriedly dispatched officers stationed in southwest Arkansas to beef up security at the jail while a larger contingent was pulled into Little Rock before being hurried south, but it would take time before they would be able to reach Arkadelphia.

Until they arrived, only a dozen or so troopers faced an increasingly restless and physical crowd who appeared determined to free the three young men. Rocks and bottles began to fly, striking near the officers, hitting their patrol cars, and breaking windows in nearby buildings. This escalation convinced the officers that they had to be more aggressive since they were so outnumbered and were unsure how long it would take for reinforcements to arrive. So, the troopers formed a wedge and advanced into the crowd, which allowed them to physically disburse the protesters and prevent any attempts to free the prisoners.[482]

A very similar situation developed in Eudora in 1976. More than a hundred black and white high school students began fighting during their lunch hour. Since such a small town had few city police officers, 12 state troopers were rushed in to restore order between the bottle and rock-throwing students. For more than a week, the school remained closed and the town under a curfew as troopers patrolled within the city to head off a repeat of past racial disturbances.[483]

Narcotics investigations were becoming another focal point for CID officers in the early 1970s. The State Police's first efforts at combating illegal drug use began in 1968 when Governor Rockefeller tapped CID Lieutenant Howard "Bear" Chandler to use his squad of special investigators to begin undercover narcotics investigations. While all officers began to note an increase in drug usage during the late 1960s, widespread and heavy abuses appeared to be rare in Arkansas. As Lieutenant Chandler recalled being asked during a training session with the Federal Bureau of Narcotics and Dangerous Drugs what kind of drug problem Arkansas had, he responded "we didn't have one, but the agent said, 'You just think you don't have one. You will find out you do have one.' All we were getting before that was a pill or two off a truck driver."[484] One of the first men hired by Lieutenant Chandler was Conrad Pattillo, who was sent in 1969 to work undercover narcotic investigations. Pattillo remembered that as a college student,

> I saw on the career placement bulletin board at Philander Smith [College] a notice that the State Police were looking for individuals to come to work in the Investigations Division. Little did I know that they meant working undercover in narcotics ... They were looking for an individual of color to get out and infiltrate into the drug culture.... When I came on board I was assigned to Sergeant [H. H. "Duke" Atkinson] who had been working narcotics for awhile. I did not have any previous training for that job assignment. I stayed there about three or four months, and then I went to troop school for my formal training.... We were concerned about the drug traffic in the truck stops because truck drivers were using amphetamines to stay awake. Then we would get information about situations in areas outside of Pulaski County. You see, I was known in Pulaski County. I had grown up here and [gone] through the school system, so the black community knew me and knew I was getting into law enforcement. I went to the outlying areas like Texarkana, Fort Smith, Jonesboro, and Camden to work undercover.[485]

By 1973, the realization that the state did indeed have a rising tide of drug cases dawned on the State Police and the legislature. That year the legislature provided the department with specific funding to hire five undercover narcotics officers.[486] In July 1973, the State Police activated their first unit dedicated solely to narcotics investigation. As the unit's first commander, Ken McFerran, wryly noted, "With these five, we were supposed to solve the drug problem in the state of Arkansas."[487] The five new officers were trained by State Police and federal drug enforcement agents following which, McFerran remembered, "We outfitted them in these old junk cars and took their identity away from them and gave them new driver's licenses and all that. If somebody had shaken them down, they could prove they were somebody else."[488] These five officers were dispatched around the state where they setup residence and attempted to insert themselves into the local drug scene. As one officer remembered, it did not take long before "we were buying dope by the pound."[489]

Unfortunately, for the investigators to actually buy pounds of drugs, they had to secure the financial assistance of federal, city, or county agencies since the legislature set aside just $10,000 in buy money for 1973-1974.[490] Jerry Reinold worked undercover for the State Police in the mid 1970s and remembered that

> Back then, a pound of marijuana cost $125 or so. The buy money from the State Police normally wouldn't exceed $25. We relied heavily on the D.E.A. We made a lot of dope deals for $10 or $15. It wasn't just for marijuana. LSD, or what we called "window pane acid," was a big deal back then. You would pay a dollar a hit. Still it was hard to convince someone you were a high roller when you could only buy $25 of dope. We ran into big problems because of that. What we began to do was a buy-bust operation. You would go buy an ounce that cost $10 or $15 dollars. Then you would go back and order up two or three pounds. We didn't have the money to pay for that much so we would do "flash rolls." This was a wad of money where 99 percent were one dollar bills, but on the outside was a larger bill. This money was never actually spent. It was just to show the dealer, and when the dealer produced the drugs, we would bust them."[491]

Two years after the creation of the Drug Abuse Enforcement Section, its officers would play a key role in the biggest drug bust in Arkansas history to that time. In 1975, D.E.A. agents learned that a group of erstwhile drug runners from Arkansas and Oklahoma were attempting to lease a DC-6 aircraft so they could fly a large shipment of marijuana from Columbia to a small airport in Oklahoma where it would then be driven to Arkansas and parceled out to dealers around the country. The D.E.A. had several well-placed informants within this group and were even able to have one of their undercover agents fly the DC-6 from Columbia to the United States.

Once the marijuana arrived in Oklahoma, the D.E.A. coordinated their efforts with State Police officers in Oklahoma and Arkansas who helped them tail the marijuana using six cars and four airplanes. One of the officers riding in the airplanes was State Police Narcotics Officer Ken McKee, who played a major role in the planning and execution of the operation. The officers allowed the marijuana to reach its intended destination, a farm in Goshen where it was stored in a barn until deals could be finalized with buyers from around the country. Once several buyers had arrived to pick up their share of the drugs and had departed with D.E.A. agents following them, the order was given to raid the farm. At 12:30 a.m., State and federal officers stormed the farm where they seized 8,584 pounds of marijuana and $75,000 in cash while making nine arrests, including the ringleaders of the plot, Larry and Barbara French and Guy Payne. For the rest of the night, State Police and federal officers loaded the hundreds of bales of marijuana into rented vans to be transported to an incinerator in Siloam Springs. Then-Trooper Keith Ferguson was one of those tasked with moving the marijuana and remembered "loading 50-pound bales of marijuana into vans until I was drenched in sweat."[492] Later that day, officers in Maryland, Connecticut, and Colorado arrested couriers transporting the remaining portion of the shipment, which brought the total amount of marijuana flown into the country at almost 10,000 pounds.[493]

While the CID continued to have success even with limitations on buy money, the Highway Patrol faced the daily reminder of the seemingly unstoppable rise in traffic-related fatalities. After a large decline in 1969 to 602 fatalities, the number of people killed in traffic-related accidents continued to rise through 1972 when a record 760 people died. Stunned by the carnage, Governor Bumpers tagged the year as the "slaughter of 1972" and the State Police began to try new tactics to lower the death toll. For many people within state and federal government, the best way to lower traffic fatalities was by targeting drunk drivers. As a result, the federal government awarded grants to help police departments catch drunk drivers. This program funded a special squad of six State Police officers who were assigned to the Alcohol Safety Awareness Program, or ASAP. These officers would provide intensive patrol in high-fatality areas for as long as a week, where they would set up roadblocks and concentrate solely on making DWI arrests.[494]

In October 1972, Colonel Miller asked troopers to volunteer to work a sixth day each week during the month. Since the officers were on salary and this was before compensatory time policies had been implemented, they would receive nothing for working the extra day. Also, the troopers were instructed to not issue any warnings during October as a further reminder of the seriousness of the situation. While the request to work the extra day reportedly upset a few officers, more than 90 percent agreed to work the extra day.[495]

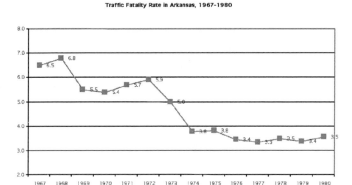

Traffic Fatality Rate in Arkansas, 1967-1980

Governor Bumpers hoped that his funding request to the legislature in early 1973 for 60 additional troopers would be approved so the department would not have to request its troopers work special traffic-enforcement operations. The initial State Police budget ran into trouble after Senator Max Howell amended it to include a restriction on the number of CID officers that the State Police could employ. After the senator agreed to remove the amendment, the legislature approved the 60 new positions, but only provided funding for 30.[496] This meant the department would employ 572 people of which 340 were troopers.

Even with the additional funding, the department struggled to recruit qualified personnel in the early and mid 1970s. The primary complaint voiced by applicants and troopers alike was the low pay. In 1973, troopers earned $7,020 in salary and received an annual clothing allowance of $680 and a meal allocation of $840.[497] These levels mired the officers near the bottom of national State Police pay rankings. The situation got even worse in 1974 when the Internal Revenue Service ruled that the meal allocation payments must be counted as pay, instead of a job-related expense, and thus taxed. The low pay and change in accounting for meal allowances convinced a number of veteran officers to resign in 1974.[498]

The low pay also severely handicapped the department's ability to recruit black troopers. Five years after Marion Taylor became the first black trooper in 1967, the State Police boasted only four black officers. Colonel Miller and the head of the department's Personnel Section, Major L. E. Gwyn, pushed for more black troopers, but they found it tough to compete with the private sector when it came to pay and benefits. The issue of minority recruitment would continue to plague the State Police, but it would not become a legal requirement to do so until after Colonel Miller retired, which was not far off.

In 1974, Colonel Miller's time as director was running short. Governor Bumpers had chosen to forego an attempt at a third term as governor and instead picked an even more daunting political challenge, to run for the United States Senate against a legend in Arkansas politics, J. William Fulbright. This decision opened the door for a United States Congressman named David Pryor to make a run for the governor's office. Both Bumpers and Pryor won their respective elections in November 1974.

Colonel Miller enjoyed a good reputation as State Police director and there seemed to be no pressure to replace him even though a new governor would be moving into the mansion in January. Still, he remained committed to his original plan to retire after he became eligible for his pension in early 1975. Before he could retire, he had to face what would undoubtedly be his worst day as director, the death of one of his officers.

On a cold, blustery day in late February, Larry Hutcherson and three other prisoners at the Monroe County jail in Clarendon escaped. At the time of the escape, the only guards at the jail were a handful of trustees, which presented an easy target for the four prisoners who had armed themselves with sharpened spoons. The prisoners forced the trustees into a jail cell and grabbed two rifles and a .357 magnum pistol on their way out. As fate would have it, Trooper Ron Brooks, a member of the department's Motor Vehicle Inspection Division, was leaving the Monroe County Courthouse at the same time the escapees were running out of the jail. Trooper Brooks' chased three of the escapees into an alley six blocks away where he fired a warning shot into the air and ordered the fugitives to lie on the ground. Two of the fugitives—Hutcherson and Butler—complied, while the third continued to run down the alley. Brooks handcuffed the two men together and ordered them to stand up. As the two men stood, Hutcherson grabbed the .357 magnum pistol he was lying on and shot Trooper Brooks in the head.[499] Officers responding to the jailbreak discovered Trooper Brooks's body fairly quickly and caught Hutcherson and Butler as they attempted to steal a nearby vehicle. The news of the trooper's death brought out every available officer, on- or off-duty, to work roadblocks and patrol Clarendon's streets in search of the two remaining fugitives. By the next day, all four would be in police custody. For the murder of Trooper Brooks, Hutcherson received a life sentence in the state penitentiary. The department mourned the loss of such a tremendous man whose fellow officers particularly remembered Brooks's skill as a singer, songwriter, and musician. His song "A Little Boy's Christmas Prayer" had been a local favorite for a number of years.

The State Police would be jolted out of its mourning in May when Governor Pryor made a surprise choice for the department's next director. Early leaders for the position appeared to be Major Tommy Goodwin, the Highway Patrol commander, and Lieutenant Colonel Melvin Delong, the politically well-connected assistant director. On May 6, the day Governor Pryor had scheduled to announce his selection, all outward signs hinted that Colonel Delong would be promoted to director. It appeared so certain that the *Arkansas Gazette* ran a front-page story announcing the promotion before they even heard the official announcement. In fact, the decision had been made almost a week earlier, and Pryor's choice was not Melvin Delong.

Governor Pryor's choice as director was Doug Harp. Harp had joined the State Police in 1965 after which he worked in Highway Patrol, Motor Vehicle Inspection, and CID before moving into Governor's Security when Governor Bumpers entered office in 1971. Shortly thereafter, Harp took over command of the security detail and was promoted to lieutenant in 1973. During Governor Bumper's Senate campaign, Harp had several occasions to meet candidate Pryor, so when the new governor took office in January, Lieutenant Harp stayed on as commander of his protection detail. Over the next four months, the two men developed such a close relationship that Pryor decided to promote this 34-year-old lieutenant ahead of four majors, 15 captains, and 11 lieutenants. Harp remembered how he learned about Pryor's decision:

> [Governor Pryor] told me, "On Thursday, I am going to hold a press conference and name you director of the State Police." I got up out of my chair, and I said, "You aren't appointing me to anything." He said, "I know what you are thinking—that in two or four years you will be out of a job." I told him that was exactly right. He told me to take the rest of the day off and go and talk to my parents and my wife or whomever as long as they weren't in the State Police. I went to the mansion, and the first person I told that I knew I could trust was a trooper at the mansion. Then I went and called my wife. At that time, the State Police had a house at the headquarters that the director could have, and sometimes I would have my wife with me when I went to headquarters to gas up. I called her and said, "You know that house that I told you we were going to move into one day?" She said, "What house?" I said, "The house up by the State Police headquarters? We are going to be moving in there because David Pryor is going to appoint me as director of the State Police." It took awhile to convince her I wasn't joking because it was so out of the blue.[500]

For Pryor, appointing Harp represented "fresh leadership" and a "new approach" for the State Police.[501] Many outside observers applauded the decision. The editors of the *Benton Courier* called Harp a good choice since so many of the department's top officers are "holdovers from the Faubus days."[502] Within the department, the decision "rocked" and "startled" the State Police, where most had assumed Melvin Delong would simply be elevated. Even Harp conceded that his appointment was "something nobody expected."[503]

Once Colonel Harp had settled in, he began to implement a number of changes in the State Police's organization. First, he ordered that an internal affairs section be created to conduct background investigations on applicants and to investigate complaints against officers. The next major change involved the CID. Until this time, all investigations were supervised from commanders assigned to Little Rock. As long as the number of investigators remained small, such an arrangement posed few real problems, but by the middle of the decade, the Criminal Investigation Division had grown too large for such an arrangement. Therefore, under the guidance of Colonel Harp and CID Commander Major Tudor a plan was devised that divided the state into five CID companies, each identified by a letter (A, B, C, D, and E). Each CID company had its own commander, a lieutenant who then reported to a major in Little Rock.[504] While this arrangement helped streamline the flow of information and improved oversight, it did little to ease the burgeoning workloads of the investigators. David Rosegrant was a CID officer assigned to eastern Arkansas and remembered that his work week ...

> could run 60 hours or more.... Each [CID Company] was responsible for a geographic area. The Dumas Company was responsible for Arkansas, Lincoln, Desha, Ashley, and Chicot counties, but we had only three or four investigators to cover the entire area. You were expected to answer calls in your area on the weekend. Later, we changed that policy, but in the beginning you answered the calls in your county. Many times, I worked seven days a week, and you could get called out on an afternoon and not get back till the next day....

You were constantly being called out. You had about 12 different agencies calling on you, and something was bound to happen.[505]

Along with an expanded and reorganized CID, additional officers were added to the narcotics and fire marshal sections.[506]

As important as these changes were, the most critical to the future of the department occurred in November 1975 when the State Police hired their first female recruit, Barbara Cart. Cart had recently graduated from the University of Arkansas at Little Rock with a degree in political science and planned to attend law school before she submitted her application to be a State Police officer. In retrospect, it seems that Cart's desire was to be more of a trailblazer than a trooper, since her time with the State Police proved brief. Still, her hiring represented a major change in policy that had to overcome a tremendous amount of opposition at every level within the department. The most visible officers to express some public concern about women working highway patrol were Colonel Harp and Major Goodwin, both of whom worried about the ability of a female trooper to defend herself during physical confrontations on the highway.

The State Police expected to overcome these fears gradually by slowly hiring more women for both investigation and patrol duties, but in 1977 these plans were interrupted by the United States Justice Department. In September, the Justice Department filed a federal lawsuit against the State Police charging the department with discriminatory hiring practices. According to the initial suit, the demographics of the State Police needed to match the demographics of the state of Arkansas. Meaning, 18 percent of the State Police's personnel should be black and 50 percent should be female since those were their respective shares of the state's population. Since the actual percentages working in the State Police came nowhere close to this, the suit alleged that the department's hiring process unfairly eliminated females and blacks from eligibility.[507]

A surprised Colonel Harp defended the hiring process by saying 54 percent of all new hires had been black or female since he had become director. While this was true, the department still had just eight black troopers and even fewer female officers. The day after the Justice Department filed the lawsuit, Colonel Harp suspended the hiring process to evaluate and plan a strategy that addressed the suit's primary requests, which were to set hiring goals for blacks and females, to create a marketing program that attracted qualified black and female applicants, to prepare a new written test, and to hire and compensate past victims of discrimination.[508] If the State Police did not comply with the Justice Department's request, they would lose thousands of dollars in federal grants. Even worse, if the courts ruled against them, the very real possibility existed that the federal government would assume the duties of hiring and firing officers while assessing huge back-pay settlements to minority applicants who failed the written examination.[509]

For the next three months, the department negotiated with the Justice Department over a hiring plan that fully complied with federal guidelines. By January, the two sides had reached an agreement on a Consent Decree that said the State Police would establish a goal of hiring blacks and females in the same percentage as blacks and females between the ages of 20 and 34 in Arkansas' workforce. Also, the agreement required the department to reformat their written test, remove height and weight restrictions on new recruits, and pay up to $50,000 in back pay to new hires who were deemed to have been discriminated against in the past.

Another important component to the settlement was an agreement that the State Police would conduct a massive minority and female recruiting campaign. Long-time State Police Commissioner and then-Chairman J. E. Dunlap noted that they were "embarking on one of the most ambitious recruiting programs" in department history.[510] Still, the State Police would find it very difficult to fulfill their goals. Ken McFerran, who oversaw the Personnel Section for 12 months during a period spanning 1979 and 1980, recalled,

All through the history of the State Police we had white kids lining up to be a trooper. All you had to do was take names and cull through. When it opened up to minorities and women it was a new world. I am not sure that I ever talked to a black officer or recruit that had wanted to be a police officer [from a young age]. It was often from the other side of the fence. It was the attitude where they lived that if someone voiced an opinion that they wanted to be a police officer he was ostracized. At least that was what they would tell me. Of course women were out of the loop entirely. Very few women even thought about being a police officer and a state trooper in particular.[511]

For the rest of the 20th century, the State Police struggled to reach the goals established by the consent decree. But since the decree set "goals" instead of a quota, the State Police were never penalized by the Justice Department for their failure to hire and retain more minorities and females. What the decree did mandate was that the State Police put forth a good faith effort to meet those goals. In 1980, Katherine Ransel, a lawyer with the Justice Department, reviewed the State Police's new hiring practices and told Colonel Harp that she was "pleased with what was being done."[512] For the next 20 years, the honest efforts expended by officers in the Personnel Section convinced the Justice Department that the State Police continued to respect and comply with the intent of the decree, so additional lawsuits were never filed.

While 1977 will be remembered for the Justice Department's lawsuit, it was also the year that the state legislature approved a $4 million bond issue guaranteed by an increase in the vehicle inspection fee to pay for construction of a new State Police Headquarters.[513] For the previous 40 years, the State Police's main headquarters had been housed in the old penitentiary buildings located on Roosevelt Road. By the late 1970s, this facility had seriously deteriorated with its out-dated and overloaded electrical system posing a particularly dangerous threat. Eighteen months after the bonds were approved, construction started on the new headquarters located in west Little Rock on Natural Resources Drive. When it was complete in 1981, it provided a huge upgrade in space for the State Police and the other state agencies that shared the building—including, most infamously, the State Crime Lab and its morgue.[514]

The year 1977 would end on a sad note when Sergeant Kelly Pique was killed in a traffic accident on Highway 64 in Cross County. On December 8, a semi truck and trailer lost control on the rain-slicked highway and crossed into oncoming traffic where it struck Sergeant Pique's patrol car head-on.[515] His fellow officers remembered Pique's friendly manner, as John Purcell recounted, "I couldn't drive through Forrest City and not expect to hear Kelly say [over the radio], 'Hey Ace, where are you going? Pull over there a minute.' He might just have a joke or something funny to tell you."[516]

The following year promised to be one of change for the State Police since Governor Pryor had decided to run for United States Senate instead of seeking a third term. For his replacement, the voters chose Bill Clinton, a rising star in Arkansas' Democratic Party who was at the time the state's Attorney General. Governor Clinton, who had worked closely with Colonel Harp and the State Police during negotiations over the Consent Decree, broke tradition and decided to retain Harp as director instead of replacing him with his own appointee. The decision to keep Harp upset a number of legislators who were still angry that Melvin Delong had not been elevated to the director's position in 1975. In an effort to appease this powerful group of legislators, Clinton agreed to appoint their choice to head the DPS, to which the State Police was technically subordinated. That choice would lead to a year of controversy and conflict that only helped to put the final nail in the coffin of the DPS.

Clinton's choice as DPS director was the Chief of Police at Jacksonville, Tommy Robinson. Robinson had been a trooper for several years in the 1960s before going on to work for the United States Marshal Service and the University of Arkansas police department. He was hired as the Chief at Jacksonville in 1975. Knowing full well that he had substantial political support behind him, Robinson set out to accomplish two closely related tasks: one, to take control of the State

Police, and two, to get Doug Harp fired. One of Colonel Harp's most vocal critics at this time was the acerbic editor and columnist at the *Arkansas Democrat*, John Robert Starr. In his memoirs, Starr remembered that Robinson "made ousting Harp a top priority in his department" and that he fed the news media information that later turned out to be entirely false. One of Robinson's charges was issued shortly after being appointed in 1979 and claimed that officers working in Troop A were experiencing severe morale problems.[517] Starr called the story "about as one-sided as a story could get." Another involved charges of a physical confrontation between a State Police lieutenant and a citizen, about which Starr said, "Robinson dogged [the investigating reporter], urging him to stay after the story" even though it had little merit.[518] As Colonel Harp remembered, "We really got off on the wrong foot ... because he told me I was being insubordinate. I told him that I was but that he couldn't fire me and that he shouldn't ever forget that. The war was on then. About every two weeks, Clinton would call us over. I let him know that I only cared about taking care of the people in the State Police."[519] The public mediation sessions with Governor Clinton accomplished little real change since, as John Robert Starr wrote, it was "foolish ... to believe that one could order a cobra and a mongoose to love one another."[520]

By summer it was clear that Robinson would not be able to get Harp fired, but he continued his efforts to exert control over the State Police. In August, he created a Special Investigation Unit under his direct command and staffed it with three State Police officers. Robinson stated that the intent of this special unit was to investigate white-collar crime.[521] Also, Robinson had begun meeting independently with troop commanders, an action few appreciated. The Highway Patrol commander at that time, Major Buren Jackson, remembered telling Robinson exactly what the troop commanders thought of his efforts to run the State Police: "You know how those commanders look at you? They have been here for 30 years and they have seen people like you come and go. You are here today, you may be here a year or even two years, but you will be gone eventually. You are just another experience in their life."[522] Another critic was the State Police Commission, which publicly questioned Robinson's efforts in their September meeting.[523]

Tommy Robinson's reign as director of the DPS came to an end in the spring of 1980 when he resigned to run for Pulaski County sheriff. He would win the election and as a sheriff would have additional confrontations with the State Police.

Even though Colonel Harp's fight with Tommy Robinson provided most of the State Police-related headlines in the final years of the 1970s, there were actually a number of major changes occurring beneath the surface. The most visible change happened in 1978 when the State Police radically changed the look of their patrol cars. Instead of the traditional blue body and white top, highway patrol cars became solid white with blue markings. There were a couple of impetuses behind the change. In the 1970s, three car companies made police cruisers, and the State Police's fleet contained some of all three makes. Unfortunately, each company used a slightly different shade of blue, which resulted in an uneven appearance among the fleet.[524] Also, Colonel Harp recalled,

> At times we would get complaints about our troopers, but when we investigated them, we found out that it was a city marshal or someone who had bought one of these used white over blue cars. I felt like we really needed to identify our cars from everyone else so I changed to an all white car with blue striping with our emblem on the doors.... We chose white because it is easy to keep clean and would make the blue striping stand out. Plus, when you take the stripes off it became just a white car. I think it looked better."[525]

Internally, officers assigned to administration were working on two key documents in the mid and late 1970s, a new policy manual and a complete reorganization of the State Police. The first attempt at a policy manual began during Colonel Scott's tenure, but the resulting document remained more of a hodgepodge of general rules and guidelines than a comprehensive, detailed discussion of the department's policies. One of the policy manual's primary goals was to standardize the operation of all 12 Highway Patrol Troops and five CID Companies. One of the officers assigned to prepare the policy manual, Bill Young, remembered that, "We had 12 separate fiefdoms out there, and every troop commander felt like he should run his troop the way he wanted. Discipline wasn't the same, operational procedures weren't the same, and little things like what was reported wasn't the same from troop to troop."[526] In an effort to win over the historically independent troop commanders, Colonel Harp met every few months with them to discuss the latest draft of the manual and work out changes. Although, the final version still met with some opposition, its completion marked another important step toward a more professional police agency.

A major restructuring of the State Police's organization in 1980 followed the completion of the policy manual. The plan divided the department's enforcement operations into three geographic regions: northwest, east, and south. Each region had a single commander holding the rank of major who was tasked with overseeing every aspect of the State Police within his or her region, which included four Highway Patrol Troops (after 1976 they were known as "Troops" instead of "Districts") and one CID Company.[527] In his annual report, Colonel Harp argued that the "new regional concept helps assure uniform enforcement efforts throughout the state of Arkansas, balances the responsibility of the administrators of the State Police, and improves the ability of the department to offer services to the citizens of the State."[528] Another reason also existed, as Harp remembered later:

> I felt that if the State Police was to continue to grow, it had to give people opportunities. I had a feeling that if you were a trooper with a lot of ambition, but you could only see down the highway, then it wouldn't be very appealing. Also, the Highway Patrol commander can't take care of 75 counties and 12 troops. So we started looking at dividing the state geographically. We needed some control on a regional level.... The structure before was too broad. You might have a guy running something who would only go and see you if there was an emergency. At that time, I had the money and the

rank allotted, and if we opened it up we would give these troopers an avenue to move up."[529]

By the end of the 1970s, Colonel Harp had more officers and civilian personnel to think about than at any other time in the department's history with almost 600 authorized positions. Plus, these officers had more work than ever before. In mid 1970s the country suffered through a severe energy crisis following a Middle East oil embargo. This crisis led the federal government to lower the national speed limit to 55 miles per hour. In an effort to better enforce this new limit and thus conserve energy, the Department of Transportation and other federal agencies made grants available to states to conduct rigid traffic enforcement programs. The State Police took full advantage of these new funds to pay for more troopers and for new traffic enforcement equipment like moving radars. Prior to this the State Police owned a few radars, but most of the time, if troopers wanted to use radar, they would have to borrow it from the local sheriff or police department. This practice led to some problems in court since the troopers were not necessarily certified in the operations of these various models of radar nor were they responsible for their maintenance or calibration. Therefore, in 1979 the department began purchasing new radar units and started an intensive certification and training program.[530] Also, federal funds were used to purchase new unmarked, "sporty" police cars and airplanes to be used for a more stealthy method of traffic enforcement.[531]

While all of these new tactics began to have an impact, none of them would have prevented the deadliest traffic accident in Arkansas history from occurring on June 5, 1980. A Central Texas Bus Lines bus holding 33 people was northbound on Highway 7 on its way to Branson. The bus never should have been on the twisting curves and steep hills that made Highway 7 so dangerous, but a driver unfamiliar with the area had chosen the wrong route. This bad decision became deadly when a critical part of the bus' braking system failed as the bus began its descent into the small town of Jasper. With no brakes, the bus quickly accelerated. The driver swerved into the shallow ditch against the mountain on the right side of the road, but the impact threw several passengers and the driver out of the open bus windows. Now driverless, the bus crossed the highway and plunged over a steep embankment. Twenty of the 33 occupants died in the accident.

The State Police's 1980 reorganization plan also placed two key groups outside of the regional commanders' purview, officers assigned to Organized Crime and Intelligence (OCI) and Rape Investigations. The OCI office used undercover officers to investigate "cases involving extensive and long-term intelligence gathering activities."[532] The group took over the undercover narcotics operations from the Drug Abuse Enforcement Section of the CID, although narcotics investigations were not the only cases they worked. One of their former investigators, John Chappelle, remembered his time with OCI:

> The first thing they told me in Organized Crime was to quit shaving. The next thing you know, I had a full beard and a full head of hair. I didn't know the first thing about buying dope. I had handled dope seizures on the highway, but nothing else. I taught myself the techniques and made it work for me. We had a warehouse over on Bethany Road, something like 130,000 square feet, and we ran the first sting operation in Arkansas. During that sting operation we ran the first reverse. This meant that I sold dope to the bad guys instead of buying dope from the bad guys.... That was quite a deal. No one else knew what we were doing. When the sting rolled out, we arrested 365 people. We filled that warehouse up with stolen merchandise. After we made these arrests, we took all of this stuff over to the Hall of Industry at the Arkansas Stock Show grounds. We had troopers all around it, and the way you got in to see if it had your stuff was a police report showing [you] had been burglarized. You would hear people yell out when they found their property. It was so gratifying to us.

The Rape Investigation office actually consisted of just one State Police officer, Mary Margaret Kesterson, who assisted local officers in all 75 counties investigate cases of rape, sex crimes, and child abuse. The demand for an investigator of Kesterson's skill and ability grew exponentially throughout the next decade, leading to additional officers being assigned to her group. In the mid 1990s, the group's success encouraged the legislature to move civilian social workers into the State Police to bolster their efforts.

As the State Police finalized their reorganization plan, events were set in motion 2,000 miles away that would test the department and its troopers like no other event in its history. In late 1979 and early 1980, Cubans unhappy with life under Fidel Castro's Communist government began seizing every opportunity to flee the country. Large groups of Cubans overran the gates of several Caribbean and South American countries' embassies in Havana seeking asylum and a chance to emigrate. Castro's police forces proved woefully insufficient to stop these repeated and embarrassing attempts, so on April 20, 1980, Castro announced that anyone wanting to leave Cuba and resettle in the United States could do so by boat through the port of Mariel.

The next day, the first voyage of a so-called "freedom flotilla" departed Mariel for the shores of the United States. Initially, President Jimmy Carter encouraged the immigrants, saying, "We will continue to provide an open heart and open arms to refugees seeking freedom from Communist domination." But as more and more Cubans began to arrive in the United States, most without any familial ties at all, he began to temper his enthusiasm. The flood of refugees, 94,181 in May alone, quickly overwhelmed local resources, so the federal government began to look around the country for additional refugee camps and processing centers. On May 7, they selected four refugee camps, one of which was Fort Chaffee in Fort Smith.

Fort Chaffee represented a logical choice since five years earlier this large World War II era facility had successfully processed thousands of Vietnamese refugees who fled to America after the end of the Vietnam War. This time would prove to be a very different experience. Mixed in among the Cuban refugees, most of whom were good, honest people simply seeking a new life in America, were a number of less desirable refugees, all of whom had been inserted into the flotilla by Castro. One of the Cuban refugees remembered that "Before boarding the boats, we were sorted into categories and sent to empty warehouses: one for the insane, one for the murderers and hardcore criminals, another for prostitutes and homosexuals, and one for young men who were undercover agents of State Security.... The boats were filled with people taken from each of these different groups."[533] To prevent United States Immigration officers from detecting the criminal backgrounds of these undesirable refugees, the State Security Service altered their passports to remove any trace of criminal convictions. The number of convicted felons who were sent to Fort Chaffee remains unknown, but before the final Cubans were processed 18 months later, two murders and more than 450 assaults had occurred within the refugee community.[534]

On May 9, the first planeload of 128 Cubans landed at Fort Smith Regional Airport. State Police officers escorted the buses carrying the Cubans to Fort Chaffee past Ku Klux Klan members who lined the highway near the entrance protesting their arrival. This was a picture the State Police had become all too familiar with following a fairly large revival in the popularity of the Klan in the late 1970s. This revival seemed to culminate in 1979-80 with a series of large public rallies, including one at the University of Arkansas at Little Rock that required a large contingent of State Police to separate the Klan from its equally vocal and angry opposition.

Over the next two weeks, the number of Cubans inside Fort Chaffee continued to grow, reaching just over 19,000 by the end of the month. Within the Fort, little had been done to prepare for such a huge population, which had grown to the ninth largest population in the state.[535] Soldiers from newly arrived engineering units worked feverishly to upgrade and repair almost 200 40-year-old barracks, but the most they could really do in such a short amount of time was provide the basic necessities. Additional military police were also transferred into the Fort, including Spanish-speaking National Guardsmen from Puerto Rico. Still, soldiers fluent in Spanish proved too few, which merely increased the difficulty of an almost impossible situation. As one MP noted, "It gets frustrating when I can't understand what the refugees are trying to tell me. I can't help them."[536] Military Psy-ops personnel also attempted to create a sense of community among the refugees by establishing a Spanish-language newspaper and scheduling entertainment and educational opportunities.[537]

These efforts failed to bring much satisfaction to the refugees who quickly tired of being confined to the base and were frustrated over long delays in their processing. Over the next few weeks, Cubans would slip past the MPs and would meet friends and relatives who had driven from Florida to pick them up. Gene Irby, a sergeant at the time, remembered being assigned to patrol the perimeter of the Fort where "you would see cars parked on the surrounding roads at night with Florida license plates."[538]

Tensions continued to rise inside the Fort, so much so that its commander began to restrict the movement of his soldiers on the base on May 20. Less than a week later and half a country away, Cuban refugees in Florida's Eglin Air Force Base attempted to break out of the front gate of their compound. The attempted exodus was stopped after Air Force police officers, Marines, and Florida Highway Patrol officers pushed the refugees back. This incident seemed to embolden the refugees at Chaffee since the next night they staged their first mass breakout. That night 350 refugees walked out an open back gate into the Jenny Lind community. The commander of the Fort Smith Troop (Troop H), Captain Deloin Causey, called in every available trooper to help round up the escapees, and after almost eight hours the troopers, deputies, city police, and federal officers who rushed to the scene had found and returned most of the Cubans.[539]

The breakout of the refugees increased the fear and resentment of residents living near the Fort in communities like Jenny Lind and Barling. "People around Fort Smith are exhausted, irate, and afraid," according to Governor Clinton, which was easily confirmed since gun stores in the area were experiencing a huge boom in business.[540] One gun dealer reported selling almost 50 handguns in the week after the Cubans first left the base on May 26.[541]

Inside the Fort, the Cubans remained angry, and over the next few days they continued to protest. A thousand refugees gathered at the front gate on May 29 to protest, while just outside the gate, small groups of Klansmen, Cuban-Americans, and local residents picketed and shouted slogans.[542]

With such unrest going on inside and outside the Fort, Captain Causey began to take measures to ensure that another mass breakout did not occur, since area residents had been arming themselves and vowing to protect their homes from any further excursions. Fifteen additional troopers were called in to supplement the existing contingent of 20 officers patrolling the perimeter of the Fort. Also, officers were expected to be ready for immediate deployment even if they were off duty, as Trooper Buddy Acoach, a member of Troop H's sniper team, remembered:

> We had a Troop meeting, and Causey told us that he didn't want anyone going anywhere and to keep our stuff in the car. We were to let headquarters know how to get a hold of us if they needed to. He looked at me and the other sniper, who were the only two with walkie-talkie radios, and told me that wherever I went I was to have the radio on and listening. He told me that if anything significant happens at all that I am supposed to get in my car and come here [to Fort Chaffee]. He said, "I don't want to have to call you. I better look up and see you there." June 1 was a Sunday because my wife and I talked about me going to church that morning, but I thought that I had better stay with the radio because there had been too much going on. We were sitting outside drinking a cup of coffee and the radio traffic started getting a little more of this and a little more of that. Captain Causey was already out. I told my wife, "Well, I am going to go ahead and get in my jumpsuit and head on over." We were wearing one-piece jump suites. I hadn't more than gotten in my car and it started."[543]

The morning of June 1, 300 Cuban refugees once again began demonstrating near the Fort's front gate. One of the refugees' leaders shouted, "Carter is bad, the police are bad, and we should set fire to the barracks!" As the demonstration got larger and more vocal, Captain Causey called in additional officers, but before it could get out of hand, another Cuban persuasively argued that they should remain patient and use restraint. By 12:00 noon the situation seemed to return to normal when the Cuban protestors left to attend lunch, which allowed Captain Causey to let his troopers stand down and get a bite to eat at a nearby restaurant.

The calm would be shattered shortly after 1:00 p.m. when a crowd of 300 refugees began marching on the front gate and brushed past the handful of military police manning the gate. Captain Causey recalled his troopers and issued an urgent request to Little Rock that additional help to be sent to Fort Chaffee as soon as possible. By this time the recalled troopers began to arrive, their cars screeching to a halt on Highway 22 where they jumped out with their nightsticks at the ready.

Once outside the gate, the Cubans fanned out along a railroad track that ran between the Fort and Highway 22, and they grabbed additional rocks and debris and began throwing them toward the waiting line of officers. Rocks pelted off the patrol cars, breaking windows and denting metal. The barrage also slammed into the officers who had precious little protective equipment to deal with such an onslaught. Their only recourse was to grip their batons and duck their heads in an attempt to avoid the barrage while warily watching the shouting mob advance ever closer to their position. When the two met, the battle became personal and violent. The wave of Cubans washed over the thinly spread troopers as they swung at the officers with sticks, threw rocks and, most frighteningly, grabbed at holstered service revolvers. Troopers swung their batons and pushed at the Cubans, trying to protect themselves and stop the mob from reaching Barling. But there were 20 Cubans for every trooper, and the situation quickly spiraled out of control. As this teeming, yelling, brawling mass reached a crescendo, a loud blast cut through the chaos. A trooper had grabbed his shotgun out of his patrol car and fired when several Cubans attempted to wrest his service revolver from his holster. The shot changed the nature of the fight and swung the tide back to the State Police. As other officers also fired shots from their weapons the Cubans quickly retreated back into the Fort pausing only to throw rocks and other projectiles at the officers. In the fighting, three Cubans were injured by gunfire and 15 State Police officers were hurt, three of which were serious enough to require a trip to the hospital.[544]

Luckily, as the fighting was dying down and the troopers were being taken to the hospital, a second wave of officers from Springdale's Troop L began to arrive. One of those was Les Braunns, who was at that time a trooper assigned to Madison County and who remembered,

> I was on Highway 23 south of Huntsville on a Sunday afternoon, and Joe Simms was the radio operator. He called all units in Troop L to "10-19" to Fort Smith, and I remember him saying, "and don't spare the horses." We got down there after the initial surge on the fence. I remember pulling up and looking at the guys, Phil Straub, Bob Gibson—I think Rocky Baker came down there on Highway 71—and you could hear those old cars' motors popping and pinging because we had been running so fast. I was running about a 120 [miles per hour] when I left out of Ozark.[545]

Inside the Fort, the Cubans began destroying buildings and setting barracks on fire as the military completely lost control. Cuban families fled to the wooded portion of the Fort in order to escape the violence and fires, while helicopters circled overhead blaring demands to the Cubans to end the unrest.

At 8:00 p.m., the Cubans tried once again to leave the Fort by the main gate, but this time the State Police were re-enforced by troopers from all over the state, along with National Guardsmen and city police, who used nightsticks and gunfire to easily rebuff the refugees' attempt to push past. That night federal agents and regular soldiers from Fort Sill entered the Fort and wrested control from the rioting Cubans, a move that effectively ended the Cuban Refugee Crisis.

These afternoon riots and escapes by the Cubans heightened the fears of Barling residents who lived a short distance from Fort Chaffee's main gate. A crowd numbering almost 500 began to gather on Highway 22 near the edge of town, many of whom were armed and all of whom were frightened and angry over the possibility of Cuban refugees streaming into their town and threatening their homes. The last thing Captain Causey needed was an angry mob of armed citizens at his back and an angry mob of Cuban refugees at his front, so he addressed the crowd telling them, "Give us a chance to control it. If we can't, I will welcome your help. I can't guarantee you that we can keep 20,000 of them under control, but we're damn sure going to try."[546] Captain Causey succeeded in dispersing most of the crowd by 10:30 p.m., but six of the more recalcitrant had to be forcibly removed by officers. Despite Captain Causey's reassuring words, Barling residents remained armed and alert as they sat on their porches and even rooftops ready to defend their homes.

In the immediate aftermath of the riot, the Fort's commander, General James Drummond, criticized the State Police for their strong reaction to the June 1 breakout. Such charges angered Colonel Harp who told him, "That white line on the highway is a dividing line. On that side of it is your responsibility and on this side of it is my responsibility. You need to control these people or when they cross that white line we are going to control them. We aren't going to overdo it, but we are going to protect ourselves and the citizens of this community."[547] These sentiments were echoed by one of the troopers there on June 1, Tom Morrow, who remembered that, "What happened in [Fort Chaffee] was the Army's business. What happened beyond the gates was our business. We took care of our business."[548] Governor Clinton agreed, telling the press that "had it not been for the State Police, local law enforcement officials and the National Guard, I am convinced that tragic violence would have engulfed the area." Any criticism of the State Police was put to rest in October 1980 when the Department of Justice released their investigation into the riot, which praised the State Police and found "no evidence of excessive force."[549]

Undoubtedly, the people most appreciative of the State Police's efforts on June 1 were the residents who lived around Fort Chaffee. Trooper Lyle Smith recalled that "I ate better than I ever have in my whole life. The people of Barling fed us very well.... [They] would set up picnic tables and bring us everything in the world to eat and drink."[550] Trooper Braunns remembered, "You would go into a coffee shop, and someone would pay your way out before you even got up to the counter. It was their way of saying thank you."[551]

Within the department, troopers pointed to the cool head and steady leadership of Troop H's Captain Causey as the real reason for the State Police's success in stopping the Cubans from reaching Barling and thereby preventing an untold level of violence. One trooper who would later become a troop commander himself said, "I can only hope I would have the forethought, the patience, and the overview that he had to handle something of that magnitude. The guys loved him, and he was a great leader." Another trooper paid Causey one of the ultimate compliments that a commander can receive when he said, "I would go with that guy anywhere."

While the State Police basked in the public's appreciation, Governor Clinton received the brunt of their anger. It was his misfortune that 1980 was an election year, so the images of rioting Cubans and burning buildings had no opportunity to fade. This public relations nightmare and Clinton's support of a large increase in the car license fees combined to hand his Republican opponent, Frank White, an easy issue to use against him. The refrain "Cubans and Car Tags" played endlessly to receptive audiences around the state and helped turned the young governor out after a first term.

The State Police would not be able to bask long in the positive publicity from the Cuban Crisis, since just three months later the department suffered through the death of another officer in the line of duty. On September 19, Sergeant Glen Bailey headed out for a routine patrol along Interstate 55 in his unmarked patrol car. Inside his unit, Bailey had one of the new moving radars that the department had made such an effort to obtain over the previous few years. At the same time, an escaped prisoner from Tennessee named Clay Ford was driving south on Interstate 55 at speeds regularly topping 100 miles per hour. The two met just north of West Memphis where Bailey's radar clocked Ford's car at 106 miles per hour. The officer quickly crossed the median and initiated a pursuit while calling for officers to set up a roadblock on the U.S. Highway 64 off ramp.

When Ford reached the off ramp, Trooper Larry Jackson was waiting. Ford quickly brought his car to a stop and slammed it in reverse, seeking a way out, but Sergeant Bailey's patrol car blocked him in. Bailey and Ford jumped out of their cars, and as they neared one another, Ford pulled out a small caliber pistol and fired a single shot, striking the officer near the heart. As Sergeant Bailey staggered back, Ford sprinted away from the scene into a nearby neighborhood. Trooper Jackson rushed after the man where the two exchanged shots, one of which struck Ford in the lower back. Ford's flight would not last long when Marion's chief of police caught him hiding in a backyard a short time later. Meanwhile, a deputy sheriff had arrived at the scene of the shooting where he put Sergeant Bailey in his car and rushed him to the hospital. Even though the bullet was fired from a small caliber pistol, the placement of the wound near the officer's heart proved fatal.[552]

Fellow officers remembered that "There wasn't a finer man than Glen Bailey. He was always laughing and had a funny story to tell. People just liked to be around him." Trooper John Purcell remembered seeing Bailey at the shooting range where he "would show up, and he probably hadn't seen you in two or three months, and he would ask about your family. He wasn't making conversation. He gave a damn. If you were having problems, he wanted to know about it, and if he could help you, he would."[553]

The defeat of Bill Clinton in 1980 represented a transition for the State Police, not so much due to a clear break in attitude or operations, but because of the man who would become director a few months later. Tommy Goodwin would return to the State Police four years after retiring as Highway Patrol commander where he would hold the department's top spot for the next 13 years. The agency that Goodwin took over in 1981 had more officers than at any time in the State Police's history—officers who had passed through a veritable trial by fire since 1967 when Winthrop Rockefeller became governor. In the intervening 13 years, the State Police responded to a seemingly continuous succession of events that tested their officers' resolve while placing them in a position where failure would threaten the reputation of the state and department, and more importantly could risk the lives of the officers and the citizens they were charged with protecting. Most distressingly, the period saw the death of four officers, three by gunfire, which was more than the number of officers killed in the 31 years between the State Police's creation in 1935 and the defeat of Governor Faubus in 1966. Yet, the final product was a well-trained, veteran department whose shared set of experiences melded them into a cohesive and confident family of men and women ready to respond wherever the next challenge might arise.

Chapter Six

The Goodwin Era, 1981-1993

The people of Arkansas really got some bang for their buck with that one.
> —State Police Major John Chappelle
> regarding Colonel Tommy Goodwin

"If 400 cops come in shooting, we would kill a lot of cops."
> —Jim Elllison, the leader of the Covenant, the Sword
> and the Arm of the Lord, regarding any attempt
> by officers to raid the CSA compound in Marion County.

When James and Sandra Warren heard Frankie Parker yelling outside the front door of their Rogers, Arkansas, home for their daughter Cindy, they knew better than to open the door. The relationship between their daughter and ex-son-in-law had been volatile, even violent, and by the sound of Frankie's yelling things were not any better this November evening. Unfortunately, Frankie Parker refused to be denied. He kicked the front door open and ran into the house, only to find that Cindy was not there. In a rage at not finding the object of his anger, he murdered the only people he saw, James and Sandra. As it would turn out, Frankie was just getting started.

Frankie drove across town to his ex-wife's house, and this time he found her. He shoved her into his car and headed back toward the center of town. Frankie was not only angry with his ex-wife, he was also upset with the Rogers police department. In October, Frankie claimed that his ex-wife had shot him in the lower back, and he became upset after the police department did not arrest Cindy for the shooting. So when he pulled up to the Rogers police department and jerked Cindy out of the car, he had two impulses: to bring in the woman who had shot him and to exact some revenge on the police.

Working the front desk on November 5, 1984, was Officer Ray Feyen. He saw the pair walk in and asked, "Can I help you?" Parker responded by firing three rounds from a nine-millimeter pistol at the officer—one striking him in the leg, one in the lower abdomen, and the third stopped by his bulletproof vest. Parker pulled his wife behind him and walked toward the jail leaving Officer Feyen writhing on the floor. The only other police department employee in the building that night was dispatcher Monty Baulk. When Baulk heard the gunshots, he ran to the front desk and dragged Feyen to a safer position in a microfilm room before running out the backdoor to a nearby fire station for help. Also inside the building were two janitors and the mayor's secretary, who heard the gunfire and locked themselves in an upstairs office.

State Police Sergeant Keith Ferguson was just ending his shift and pulling into his driveway when Baulk's warning was sent out over the radio. Sergeant Ferguson backed out and sped over to the police department. He pulled up next to the only other officer at the scene, a Rogers policeman, and asked for a status report. The officer said the shooter was somewhere inside the building and that the wounded officer was in a room on the ground floor. The officer told Ferguson he was waiting for the Rogers S.W.A.T. team to arrive before he entered the building. Ferguson remembered,

> Once I found out, I acted out of impulse and ran up to the window of the room where the officer was. I broke out the window and tried to pull Ray out, but I wasn't man enough to do it by myself. Then a Rogers officer ... named Terry Woodside came up alongside the building. I told him I needed his help getting Ray out, so we flipped a nickel and he lost. He crawled in the window and pushed Ray while I pulled and we were able to get him out of the window and to the EMTs. Then I helped Terry out of the window. Then the Rogers' Chief of Police arrived, and he told me to go to the back of the building to a small concrete building that was an evidence collection facility for the police department. The position allowed a clear view

of the back door. Charlie Brooks, who was the sniper for the State Police SRT team, was also sent back there, and we were standing by this building, which was about 20 yards away from the back door.[554]

For the next hour, additional officers arrived and attempted to open negotiations with Parker while the S.W.A.T. team worked to get the three civilians out from the second floor offices. Parker not only talked to police officers, but he also talked to several reporters who called the police station, telling the local Associated Press reporter that "I am the one that's doing all the shooting." Parker also warned the police that he was not going to come out alive. Officers were aware of Parker's murderous evening and took him at his word. After almost an hour, the civilians were removed from the building, and Ferguson remembered,

> While we were waiting, we would see Frankie every once in a while peeking around the corner of the door at us. Then Les Braunns got there with us and he took a position on my left. When the secretaries were out, the captain came up behind us and gave us the order to eliminate Frankie if we saw him. They had been trying to negotiate with him and nothing worked. He was in there calling everybody under the sun on the police department's communication net. We finally saw him again and I shot high and Charlie shot low. I hit him in the neck, which caused a flesh wound, and Charlie hit him in the butt, which also caused a flesh wound.

Parker continued to hold out for almost another hour before surrendering to police, who found his ex-wife, Cindy, shot, but thankfully alive inside the station. A jury found Parker guilty of the first-degree murder of James and Sandra Warren and sentenced him to death.[555] For his actions that day, Sergeant Keith Ferguson would be named Trooper of the Year.

* * *

Frank White's election in 1980 signaled another change in the State Police. Shortly after the conclusion of the 1981 session of the General Assembly, White began searching for a replacement for Colonel Harp. By May, he narrowed down his choices to the current State Police Major

Richard Rail and retired Highway Patrol Commander and the current Chief of Police at Springdale, Tommy Goodwin. On May 28, White made his decision known when he publicly appointed Tommy Goodwin to succeed Doug Harp as director.[556]

The challenges facing the State Police's new colonel began even before he could get settled into his office. The legislature, with Governor White's backing, ended the decade-long attempt to wedge the State Police under a Department of Public Safety by voting to eliminate the DPS by July 1, 1981. The demise of the DPS was a welcome change for the department, but more pressing concerns prevented them from enjoying it. In what would become the toughest financial test since 1963, Governor White and the legislature slashed the State Police budget after falling tax revenue proved insufficient to cover the department's operating expenses. This was especially true for the cost of gasoline, which had risen precipitously in price. The State Police responded by curtailing officers' mileage to just 80 miles per day, which essentially ended moving radar patrols as a method of speed enforcement. Also, Colonel Goodwin instituted a hiring freeze and delayed the purchase of any new automobiles until revenues increased. Even with these cuts, the State Police faced a nearly $800,000 dollar deficit by June 1982. The dire situation required additional cuts in expenses, a reduction in the number of authorized positions, and a cash infusion from the governor's emergency fund to maintain operations.[557] Throughout Frank White's two-year period as governor, the State Police struggled financially. The effects were so severe that by July 1982 there were 70 vacant positions within the department, and mileage restrictions would not be lifted until the summer of 1983 when new appropriations from the legislature went into effect.[558]

By this time, Governor White had been defeated in his bid for re-election by a humbled and politically wiser Bill Clinton. As in his first term as governor in 1979-1980, Governor Clinton chose to retain the current director of the State Police, a position that Tommy Goodwin would hold through the rest of Clinton's time in Arkansas.

Despite the financial handicaps that limited the operation of the Highway Patrol in the early 1980s, the State Police instituted a number of new programs during this period that would provide immediate and long-term results. The impetus for these new programs was the increase in drug use in Arkansas and the United States, which Colonel Goodwin argued had "dramatically" changed the State Police's mission over the previous decade.[559] The department's marijuana eradication program garnered the most headlines of any State Police activity during the 1980s. Concerted efforts by state and local officers to locate and destroy marijuana-growing operations actually began in the late 1970s where the commander of the narcotics section, Lieutenant James Beach, said he and his officers "spent half our time in marijuana fields." Large-scale growing operations began to pop up in the state during this period because of the increased difficulty of transporting drugs across the United States-Mexico border and through Texas after that state's Department of Public Safety created a drug task force that had tremendous success at catching drug runners.[560]

The State Police's efforts to eradicate marijuana-growing operations became public knowledge in 1977 after two hunters stumbled onto a huge plot of marijuana planted near the Newton County line in the Ozark National Forest. The hunters tipped off police, and the State Police's narcotics section conducted aerial and ground surveillance missions of the 15 separate plots encompassing almost six acres of cultivated marijuana. Just as the drug reached full bloom, narcotics officers and forest service employees moved in to destroy the plots, which yielded 113,000 plants valued at $10 million.[561]

The marijuana eradication program officially started in 1981, but in 1983 the federal government expanded their support of these types of programs by providing grants, training, and additional equipment to agencies like the State Police. This support led to an even higher level of participation and increasing numbers of marijuana plots destroyed. Despite these increased efforts, the head of the eradication program in the State Police, Captain Casey Jones, guessed that they were still only able to "get somewhere between nine and 10 percent of the marijuana grown in the state."[562] The Forest Service agreed with Captain Jones and estimated that $200 million worth of marijuana were grown each year in Arkansas, which ranked it second only to California in the amount of marijuana produced. Contrary to popular belief, marijuana was grown throughout the state and not just in the rugged northwest corner. As shown by statistics from 1983, the State Police seized plants in all but three of Arkansas's 75 counties.

One of the main avenues of assistance offered by the federal government was D.E.A. training on how to spot marijuana fields from aerial searches. In the late 1980s and early 1990s, State Police Officer Lance King was assigned to CID where he worked as a spotter on numerous aerial marijuana searches and remembered how the officers spotted marijuana fields,

> Generally, you look for a bare spot or a place that has been tilled. That sticks out. In order for marijuana to grow it has to have sunlight. They can't just stick it under the canopy in a forest. It won't get enough light. So you will see areas of the forest that are cut out. Another thing is that marijuana growers typically use different methods to water it. You have to water marijuana. There is not enough rainfall here in northwest Arkansas for it to grow on its own so water is always a problem. Either the grower has to haul the water in—which is heavy and you burn calories that way, something they don't want to do—or you irrigate it off of a creek or a pond or use other means. Sometimes you can see the irrigation pipe. Also, they love these Wal-Mart kiddy wading pools. They would leave them out there by the patch and let them catch water, which they would then use to water the plants.[563]

As the State Police became more and more successful in spotting and destroying marijuana plots, the growers had to develop better methods of hiding their crop. Another change that then-Trooper King remembered,

> "When I first got into narcotics they were just starting to change their methods. Initially, they were planting fields of it that were very easy

to spot and that they couldn't hide. It changed from this farm type of operation to a guerrilla type of operation where small patches were scattered around. Instead of having a 120 plants growing in a field, they would have 20 or 25 plants per plot and scattered throughout an area. That way if the police found them they wouldn't get them all. They also moved to a higher grade of plant. They were using better seeds and taking better care of fewer plants. They would hit them hard with Miracle Gro and take better care of them that way. Another thing they started to do was grow them in bluff lines. Where the rocks came together and formed a gap, they would board the outside of the gap up and make it like a pot and fill it with potting soil. They also began to grow on the edges of fields instead of in the center.

Table 6.1–Results of the Arkansas State Police Marijuana Eradication Program[564]

Year	Plots	Plants	Arrests	Greenhouses	ASP manhours
1981	–	58,087	106	0	–
1982	–	61,201	127	0	–
1983	–	153,619	181	0	–
1984	812	92,291	266	0	–
1985	1,046	102,210	259	0	2,340
1986	1,449	101,938	377	19	3,976
1987	1,230	77,335	341	10	2,385
1988	1,219	118,352	250	15	2,245
1989	1,457	97,679	333	13	4,112
1990	1,540	117,061	256	22	2,872
1991	1,735	110,472	178	44	3,305
1992	1,973	110,294	200	33	3,614
1993	1,645	146,166	142	36	3,345
1994	1,471	217,208	146	37	2,852

The growers also began to move their marijuana plants inside greenhouses, which meant a smaller crop, but more secrecy. What the growers did not realize was that growing marijuana in a greenhouse required a substantial amount of electricity, which tipped off the electric company that something was amiss. One such incident occurred in north central Arkansas after residents tipped off Trooper Lyle Smith that a man was growing marijuana in a greenhouse behind his residence. So, Trooper Smith, contacted CID and DEA.

> They flew over at night with their infrared equipment and it lit up like a Christmas tree.... I asked [the electric company] to look at his electric bill and tell me what it had done in the last few months. It had doubled and tripled in the last few months and [the grower] had never complained about it. So the Drug Task Force got a warrant and found a big indoor grow operation.[565]

The State Police's eradication statistics confirm the increasing popularity of greenhouses, which grew from zero in 1981 to 44 ten years later. One particularly inventive grower in St. Francis County even went so far as to bury his marijuana operation. The man installed grow lights, an automatic water supply, ventilation, and a conveyer belt inside a tractor-trailer, which created an environment that mimicked a normal day/night cycle. Then, the man dug a deep pit, backed the trailer in, and covered it up with dirt. To complete his hidden pot farm, he had a mobile home moved in over the trailer and installed a hidden trap door in one of the bedrooms that connected the trailer with the mobile home via a ladder. When State and County officers raided the operation in 1990, he had 197 plants under cultivation.[566]

These operations would not be conducted without an element of tragedy. In July 1986, officers from the State Police, DEA, and local agencies were conducting spotter training in the Ozark National Forest. Two helicopters, each loaded with four officers, took off from a small airfield near Mount Ida to conduct a search. The first chopper cleared the tree line and headed into the distance just as the second began to rise in the air. At about 200 feet up, the second helicopter's rotor snapped off, sending the craft spinning to the ground as horrified officers looked on from the airfield. The helicopter hit the ground and burst into flames. The pilot and a DEA officer, Larry Carver, were pulled to safety with serious injuries, but Kevin Brosch, an investigator with the Jefferson County sheriff's office, Jim Avant, a detective with the Pulaski County sheriff's office and a former trooper, and Charles Bassing, a newly hired State Police narcotics officer, would not survive the crash.[567]

The State Police's efforts to stop narcotics trafficking in Arkansas also involved an aggressive interdiction tactic called the Criminal Apprehension Program or CAP. Arkansas's CAP program mirrored efforts by state police agencies in New Mexico, Louisiana, and Georgia, which used teams of officers dedicated to spotting and interdicting drug runners traveling on interstate highways. These dedicated teams were making large busts in their respective states, which raised interest within the Arkansas State Police for the creation of similar teams. The presence of large narcotics shipments traveling on interstates through Arkansas appeared to be confirmed in January 1985 when Trooper David Hyden and Sergeant Dale Best made a traffic stop on I-40 near Fort Smith that resulted in the seizure of 28.5 pounds of cocaine valued at $6.24 million.[568] This interest led to a meeting between officers from Arkansas, New Mexico, and Georgia after which the State Police came away convinced that the CAP program would work in Arkansas.

Colonel Goodwin assigned Major Ken McFerran to oversee the startup and operation of the program during the summer of 1986. The State Police created seven CAP teams, one in each Troop with an interstate highway running through its area of operations. They staffed each team with a sergeant and two troopers who went through a week-long training course provided by officers from the Louisiana State Police. Once finished, they were sent out on the road to focus solely on catching drug runners, as Trooper Billy Skipper remembered,

> It was just about getting criminal apprehensions.... You couldn't get out there and do good criminal apprehension work if you have to write tickets or go work a wreck every time you turn around. We had the freedom of knowing exactly what we were going to do and what area we were going to work. We just had to keep up with our court and our cases.[569]

During the CAP teams' first six months of operation, the 21 officers assigned made 5,381 traffic arrests and 981 criminal arrests, and seized $8.37 million in illegal narcotics, which included four pounds of methamphetamines, 22 pounds of cocaine, and 3,000 pounds of marijuana. The teams also recovered 23 stolen vehicles and more than $40,000 in stolen property.[570] Over the next year, CAP teams made several huge busts, including one that yielded 20 kilograms of 90% pure cocaine valued at $3 million and five pounds of heroin valued at $5 million.[571] Another instance involved Trooper Skipper and Trooper Scotty Dodd who were working CAP patrol on I-30. The troopers pulled over a car hauling eight pounds of methamphetamine valued at over a million dollars. "When I walked up, it just reeked and burned my nose. They had a duffel bag with two blocks of powder and they had two full bottles of P.2.P., which they use to make methamphetamines," Trooper Skipper recalled.[572] Another bust along I-40 near Forrest City led to a huge cash seizure. The arresting officer called Major McFerran who recalled,

> I could tell that he was excited. He said, "We need to see you." I asked him if I needed to come there and he said, "No, we need to come to Little Rock." I told him if it was important to come on over. He told me he would be here in an hour. They came up to my office on the second floor of the "new" headquarters. They had a four-wheel cart carrying a blue suitcase that zips in the middle. The thing looked like it couldn't hold anything else. It had just over $500,000 in cash! We weighed it and it weighed over 80 pounds.[573]

With this success came criticism from both within the department and from outside sources. Internally, some troopers grumbled about the CAP officers' freedom from working accidents and traffic enforcement. This was the same sort of criticism that dogged the Interstate Patrol in the early 1960s, which helped erode its support within the department and led to its downfall.

This criticism paled in comparison to the loud and sustained outcry against the program from defense attorneys and the *Arkansas Gazette*, which claimed the officers' tactics were unconstitutional since they relied in part on finding drivers who matched a specific profile. In 1987, several motorists who were pulled over and subsequently arrested by CAP officers when narcotics were found in their vehicles filed suit against the State Police. The CAP teams also suffered setbacks in local courts as a number of judges found the stops and searches to be unconstitutional and threw out evidence found by the officers. Spurred in part by the lawsuits, a federal court issued a consent decree in early 1988 that severely restricted the ability of the CAP teams to pull people over and mandated that written consent must be obtained before conducting a vehicle search. Before these changes could go into effect, the State Police had two of the largest cocaine seizures in State Police history. In December 1987, Trooper Steve Cook stopped a car on I-55 hauling 319 pounds of cocaine valued at $42 million.[574] A month later, Troopers Keith Eremea and John Scarberough stopped a car on I-40 with 175 pounds of cocaine valued at $21 million hidden in a side panel.[575] Despite the continued success of the program, the added restrictions essentially ended the CAP program as initially designed.

A more limited version restarted in 1991 when the department's first video cameras were installed in 15 patrol cars. The cameras provided proof that the driver had given an officer verbal consent to search his vehicle, but the mood at headquarters did not support a full-fledged return to seven separate CAP teams concentrating solely on interdicting drugs.[576]

The war on drugs was not the only issue that spawned new programs and units within the State Police during the early 1980s. This period also saw the creation of the first State Police S.W.A.T. teams. During the 1970s and early 1980s, police agencies throughout the United States began creating highly trained and well-armed units tasked with responding to a rising number of hostage and group violence situations. John Bailey, who was a lieutenant in the State Police at the time, played a large role in setting up and training the first State Police S.W.A.T. teams, remembering,

I happened to be at Little Rock Air Force Base.... I learned that the FBI had been using that facility to train their special response teams. After I looked into this, I found out that they had one of the best urban combat training facilities anywhere within this part of the United States. I saw an opportunity and went and met the head of this training group. I worked out an arrangement to use the facility and receive the training at no cost.... We took people from the 12 different troops to field a special response team. They got hands-on instruction on how to use equipment like tear gas, grenades, grenade launchers, M-16s, and how to conduct building and compass searches, which were used in marijuana eradication operations. It was an ideal training process.... Each [team] had between eight and 12 officers. We decided to include the snipers from each Troop since the two teams went hand in hand. We set up 12 separate teams because it was hard to get a team from Little Rock to the northwest part of the state quick enough to be effective.[577]

Lieutenant Colonel George Moye was also a firm believer in this program and used his considerable influence to ensure that S.W.A.T. team members were allowed time off to train and sufficient funds were provided to purchase equipment.

The S.W.A.T. teams were not created in time to respond to a particularly notable hostage situation that occurred in July 1982 on the Little Buffalo River Bridge in Jasper. On the morning of July 3, Keith and Kate Haigler boarded a northbound bus in Little Rock with a bizarre plan to fulfill a self-described prophesy that arose from a small cult in Newton County known as the Foundation of Ubiquity (FOU). The cult was led by Emory "Daddy FOU" Lamb who had convinced the Haiglers that he was the Messiah. The Haiglers were particularly enamored with Chapter 11 from the Book of Revelation in the Bible, which said that two people who witnessed the return of the Messiah would be slain 1,260 days later, but after three and a half days the two would rise from the dead. July 3, 1982, was 1,260 days after Keith Haigler had a vision of Daddy Fou as the Messiah, and he intended to fulfill the prophecy.

At 12:30 p.m., the bus and its 17 passengers were approaching Mt. Judea when, suddenly, Keith and Kate jumped from their seats and rushed to the front brandishing pistols. They stuck a gun to the bus driver's head and ordered him to turn west on state Highway 123 and then onto Highway 74, which ran to the small Newton County town of Jasper. When the bus arrived in town, the Haiglers ordered the driver to pull onto a narrow two-lane bridge spanning the Little Buffalo River and block both lanes. Eleven State Police officers and a handful of Newton County sheriff's deputies arrived shortly thereafter, blocking both ends of the bridge, and entered into negotiations with the pair.

The Haiglers' main demand was for an interview with a television news crew from a station in Springfield, Missouri, which they wanted to use to announce the coming of the Messiah. Until the news crew could arrive, they warned officers that they had wired the bus with dynamite, which they would detonate if police tried to rush the bus and free the 15 other passengers. Police would later determine this was a bluff and the "dynamite" they threatened officers with were actually sticks of wood painted to look like explosives. When the reporters arrived, the two told them that the "Messiah has arrived" and that when they left the bus they would kill everyone in sight, only saving a single bullet so they could commit suicide. The Haiglers had no qualms about murdering innocent police officers as long as they died and fulfilled their prophecy.

With this forewarning, the State Police began to formulate a plan that they hoped would allow them to take the Haiglers into custody without unnecessarily risking the officers' lives. Troop I, which based in nearby Harrison, dispatched its snipers to the scene where they were tasked with the difficult prospect of shooting to wound Kate and Keith. The snipers would aim for extremities—arms, legs, and shoulders—hoping to incapacitate the two and prevent them from firing their weapons at officers or themselves.

After Kate and Keith finished their interview at 2:30 p.m., they released seven of the hostages. Thirty minutes later, they released the remaining eight, leaving just the two of them on the bus. With pistols in hand, the two got off the bus and went down to their knees hoping to minimize the chances officers had in incapacitating them and not killing them. Twenty yards away, officers crouched behind their patrol cars and aimed their pistols, shotguns, and rifles at the pair. Slowly, the two edged forward on their knees as officers shouted for them to stop and throw down their weapons. The pair opened fire on the officers, forcing the snipers to return fire. The shots rang true, striking the two in their shoulders and knocking them to the ground. Sensing that this was their last opportunity, the two attempted to aim their weapons at one another to finish their pact, but Keith's wound prevented him from aiming his .22 caliber pistol at his wife. Kate's wound would not prove as debilitating. She raised her .38 caliber pistol to her husband's chest and pulled the trigger, killing him instantly. Then she placed the gun to her own chest and fired one final shot as stunned officers looked on helplessly. Kate would be pronounced dead on arrival at the Boone County Regional Hospital.[578] As Sergeant Jim Thomas, who was one of the negotiators there that day, correctly surmised, "They had no intentions of coming out of this alive," because "they were so firmly wrapped up in their religious belief that today was the day they were going to die."[579]

Fortunately, the S.W.A.T. teams were available in time to be used for what would become their largest deployment in State Police history, the standoff at the Covenant, the Sword, and the Arm of the Lord compound in Marion County in April 1985. This was an event that could indirectly trace its roots to the murder of an Arkansas State Police trooper outside DeQueen 10 months earlier.

On the afternoon of June 30, 1984, Trooper Louis Bryant patrolled Highway 71 a few miles outside of the southwest Arkansas town of DeQueen. The officer had conducted several traffic stops that afternoon to check driver's licenses, and when he pulled behind a van driven by Richard Wayne Snell, he had no reason to be particularly suspicious since it seemed to be just another routine stop. What Trooper Bryant could not know was that Richard Snell was an armed white supremacist with felony warrants for his arrest. As Trooper Bryant stepped out of his vehicle, Snell opened the door and got out of his van then raised a .45 caliber pistol and shot the officer twice. A passing motorist happened to look in his rearview mirror and saw Trooper Bryant lying on the ground and the van pulling away, so the man turned around and rushed to the officer's aid. When he arrived, he used Bryant's radio to summon help and pass along a description of the van. Snell was caught a short time later by officers in Broken Bow, Oklahoma, after he tried to run through a roadblock, engaging officers in a brief shootout before being wounded. Snell would be convicted of murdering Trooper Bryant and for the murder of a pawnshop owner in Texarkana, the latter of which earned him the death penalty.[580]

Bryant's murder would lead to a number of major changes within the department. First was the movement to provide officers with bulletproof vests. The State Police had been investigating such a move since the late 1970s, but had decided that the existing models were too cumbersome and ineffective to be of much use. By 1984, Bryant's murder combined with an improvement in bulletproof vest technology convinced the department to order 375 vests whose cost was covered by money from Governor Clinton's emergency fund.

The second major change was the first public calls for a new State Police radio system. Within the department, officers had begged for a new radio system for years since the current model relied on 1940s-era technology and reception proved spotty at best. Proponents argued that one reason why Trooper Bryant might not have called the traffic stop in on his radio was because the radio reception was so bad. Major Jim Tyler ran the State Police's Administrative Section at the time and recalled that,

> The system probably covered just 40% of the state … [and] the equipment was so old and obsolete that parts were not made for it anymore and were becoming impossible to find. Also, if one officer was talking, no one else in that area could talk. If someone stole a unit, which happened several times, all they had to do was key up on the radio and we could not communicate. As the department grew, there were more divisions with more personnel, and there were specialized units such as Narcotics, Rape Investigations, S.W.A.T.,

etc. Each division needed its own communications ... [and] its own frequency. We also needed something to allow portable communications as well.[581]

Installing such a high-tech system would require a massive financial commitment from a state that continued to face annual budgetary crises. The possibility of receiving funding got a boost when Governor Clinton acknowledged that the current system was in "very, very bad shape."[582] The legislature agreed, and in April 1985, Governor Clinton signed Act 817 that guaranteed fees from various licenses to fund a $30 million bond issue. The State Police selected Motorola as the supplier for the new radio system, which promised to provide a system with 90% coverage of the state for $25 million.

The Motorola 800 MHz microwave system, which became fully operational in 1991, was the largest of its kind and served as a model for agencies both within the United States and around the world. Although complaints of dead spots continued to plague the system, it vastly improved communications and provided a flexible platform that would be upgraded over the next few years to encompass new technologies. State Police officers who had suffered through the pitiful communications offered by the old radio system routinely cite the 800 MHz system as one of the most important improvements in the department's history.

Completion of the new radio system occurred seven years after Louis Bryant's murder publicized the necessity for a new system, but one aspect of the officer's 1984 murder led to an almost immediate change. Richard Wayne Snell's background as a survivalist/white supremacist awakened many in the state to the presence of such radical groups and the threat they posed to law enforcement. By the end of July of that year, the State Police began compiling a database of known survivalist movements and their members inside Arkansas. The results of this early investigation convinced Colonel Goodwin that the state "had a problem in north-central Arkansas" with these types of organizations.[583]

More specifically, Colonel Goodwin was referring to a small group of white supremacists belonging to The Covenant, the Sword, and the Arm of the Lord (CSA), which was headed up by Kerry Nobles and its "spiritual leader" Jim Ellison. The CSA occupied a 224-acre compound that abutted Bull Shoals Lake off State Highway 202 in rural Marion County. During the summer of 1984, the group defaulted on the property's loan, and despite repeated eviction notices and a public auction of the land, Nobles, Ellison, and the CSA refused to leave the compound. Instead, they argued that it was God's plan for them to occupy the land and that they would fight to defend themselves from forcible eviction by police, warning, "if 400 cops come in shooting, we would kill a lot of cops."[584] Police officials had no reason to doubt the seriousness of these claims. The CSA was organized on a semi-military basis with the men continually wearing camouflage and carrying weapons while they patrolled the perimeter of the compound and stood watch in sentry towers.

By September, the links between the CSA and Richard Wayne Snell were becoming more apparent. Oklahoma officers determined that Jim Ellison had manufactured pistol silencers found in Snell's van. Then in November, Kerry Nobles and Jim Ellison sat with Snell's family during his trial for the murder of Trooper Bryant. Still, Ellison claimed that Snell had merely visited the compound and was not a member of the CSA.

Just as frightening were the links that were appearing between the CSA and the neo-Nazi group, The Order. This group had been linked to two murders and two armored car heists in the previous few years. So when the Federal Bureau of Investigation found that the CSA and The Order were "friendly and cooperative" with one another, it raised even more concerns about the continued presence of the CSA.[585] The movement to raid the compound began to grow in early April 1985 when federal agents and State Police investigated a tip that led them to a buried cache in north central Arkansas containing $85,000 in cash along with guns and surveillance equipment. The FBI determined that the money was from The Order's armored car robbery in Seattle. From there, officers tracked down and arrested a member of The Order, Ardie McBrearty, in the northwest Arkansas town of Gentry.[586]

At least two other members of The Order were also in northwest Arkansas during April. Frank Silva was arrested in Rogers on April 16 without incident for a failure to appear warrant issued by a Grand Jury in Washington state. Silva's traveling companion, David Tate, would not go so quietly. The day before, Monday, April 15, Tate stopped his van at a Missouri Highway Patrol roadblock located near the intersection of U.S. highway 65 and state highway 86 near the Arkansas-Missouri border. The two troopers manning the roadblock, Jimmie Linegar and Allen Hines, were performing a routine check of driver's licenses and had no idea that they would come in contact with a cold-blooded killer. Trooper Linegar took Tate's driver's license to run a check from his patrol car radio. The check determined that the fictitious license actually belonged to Tate who was wanted for the same failure to appear warrant as David Silva. As Trooper Linegar approached the driver's side door and Trooper Hines approached the passenger side door, Tate jumped from his van and shot Linegar four times with a silenced pistol. Tate then ran around the front of the van where he shot Trooper Hines three times before fleeing on foot into the rugged Ozark Mountains. Allen Hines survived his wounds, but Jimmie Linegar would not. He died a few hours after being transported to the hospital.[587]

The murder of Trooper Linegar by a member of The Order forced federal, state, and local officers to move much more quickly than anticipated in sealing off the CSA's compound. They surmised that Tate was probably headed toward the CSA's compound in Marion County when he was stopped, and since he remained on the loose, they did not want him to make it there on foot. State Police S.W.A.T. teams were placed on standby while officers from Troop I and around the state headed north to set up 24 roadblocks near the scene of the murder and to assist local and federal officers in searching the woods where Tate fled. Missouri officers captured Tate without incident on Saturday, April 20, while he was sitting on a park bench in Forsythe, Missouri.

By the time Tate was in custody, the CSA compound had been sealed off. On the afternoon of Friday, April 19, federal officers from the FBI and Alcohol, Tobacco, and Firearms (ATF) along with more than 50 State Police officers moved into position, surrounding the compound on all sides and closing all roads leading in.[588] The reason for the operation was to serve arrest warrants on Jim Ellison for the manufacture, possession, and transportation of illegal weapons and silencers. Dan Kelly, the spokesman for the FBI, said, "We have no intention of invading the compound because there are women and children in there. We are not here to start a war," but the officers were prepared to do so if necessary. A member of Troop L's S.W.A.T. team remembered being issued several hundred rounds of M-16 ammunition, three boxes of .357 magnum rounds, and five boxes of shotgun shells, which prompted a fellow S.W.A.T. team member to half-jokingly remark, "Looks pretty serious doesn't it?"[589]

The State Police S.W.A.T. teams were assigned positions in the hills overlooking the compound, which they manned for 12-hour shifts before being relieved. The positions exposed the officers to the widely variable springtime weather in Arkansas. Officers working during the day shift ended their day soaked in sweat, while officers working the nightshift shivered and huddled together for warmth. Trooper Billy Skipper, a member of Troop K's S.W.A.T. team, recalled,

> Two of us at a time would watch the encampment. At night we would rotate in and out observing the encampment. We didn't have anything to get under except for some ponchos, so we lashed our ponchos together against a wind that seemed like it was blowing 50 or 60 miles an hour. It was so cold. What we would do is the last guy in line would roll out for his turn at watch and the guy he was replacing would roll in at the back. We were huddled up together and freezing to death.[590]

The State Police also sent a large number of Highway Patrol officers to setup roadblocks on all access points to the compound and establish roving patrols. The officers stopped everyone driving in the area to make sure members of The Order were not trying to slip into the compound to provide reinforcements or supplies. While such an event seemed remote, it remained a very real possibility. These patrol officers worked until exhaustion set in—and even beyond, as G. B. Harp experienced,

> We had our [bulletproof] vests on, and we never wore them until we got up there. It had a big metal plate that slid in the front of our vests. We put those in because we heard they had some pretty high-powered rifles. I remember we were sitting up there on this dirt road. I forget how long we had been there. It felt like days.... I was sitting there, and the next thing I remember was another trooper asking me if I couldn't hear the radio. It dawned on me that I had fallen asleep sitting up. The metal plate in my vest was so stiff that you could not fall over.[591]

Once the officers sealed the compound, the FBI and ATF began to negotiate for Ellison's surrender, but the CSA members' distrust of the federal government prevented any serious talks between the two. Therefore, the FBI relied heavily on State Police Investigator Gene Irby, who had developed a relationship with Ellison and Nobles over the past year that allowed him to initiate dialogue with the CSA and forestall an armed assault. Plus, the interaction between the State Police S.W.A.T. teams' members and the CSA remained cordial, as sniper Ron Lemons remembered, "The first day we were there, Kerry Nobles—who was the second in charge—drove up to get his mail and talked to some of the team members ... [and] got a drink of water from us."[592]

Through the weekend, negotiators made little headway with Ellison. "Finally," Gene Irby remembered, "we brought in the leader of a religious camp over at Elohim City in Oklahoma.... They asked to confer with him for spiritual reasons before they surrendered.... The U.S. Attorney at that time was Asa Hutchinson, and they asked at the end of the negotiations to have a written agreement between [Hutchinson] and James Ellison. It stipulated that Ellison would be treated fairly and that the members that came out that weren't involved in any of the criminal activity wouldn't be prosecuted." Hutchinson agreed, so on the morning of Monday, April 22, James Ellison surrendered to the FBI and State Police. Also inside the compound were four members of The Order, two of which were wanted on warrants related to the armored car robberies in the state of Washington. The compound also contained huge stockpiles of weapons and ammunition, including 15,000 rounds of rifle ammunition, dynamite, claymore mines, an anti-tank rocket, dozens of rifles and machine guns, and even two barrels of cyanide-based chemicals.[593]

The S.W.A.T. teams performed very well in their first major deployment at the CSA siege and would continue to prove their worth in marijuana eradication and in responding to hostage situations in the future, but they also had a few problems. Each Troop had its own S.W.A.T. team comprised of six or seven officers, which meant that for the units to be effective they had to train regularly. Allowing six or seven troopers time away from patrol placed a strain on the troop commanders who were already understaffed following the personnel cutbacks under Governor White. Also, equipping more than 80 S.W.A.T. officers with weapons and tactical gear proved expensive, but the largest blow came with the retirement of their original champion, Lieutenant Colonel George Moye in 1987.

During the 1987 legislative session, the General Assembly passed Act 187, which provided one-time retirement benefits for veteran State Police officers, which allowed officers to choose from several options including lifetime health insurance, a retirement bonus, and/or use of their highest annual salary as their retirement benefit instead of their average salary. In part, the legislation was meant to encourage the department's most experienced officers to retire so that younger officers would have additional opportunities for promotion. In this regard, it worked to perfection as more than 50 of the State Police's most senior officers retired. One of those was the Highway Patrol commander, Major Buren Jackson, who remembered, "They gave so many incentives that I couldn't afford to not retire ... [since] I could retire for as much or more money than I was making [working]."[594]

The State Police were able to pay for high-cost programs like the retirement incentives and new Motorola radio system through special funds established by the legislature. But the department's operating appropriations throughout the 1980s continued to fall far below what Colonel Goodwin had hoped. Arkansas troopers ranked last among state police agencies in starting salary at just $15,074 a year.[595] Plus, state employees had not received a raise in three years. Of equal concern was the department's deteriorating fleet of patrol cars. In 1989, the State Police had 109 cars with more than a 100,000 miles and 141 with more than 75,000 miles while the rest would surpass 75,000 miles within the next two years. The high-mileage cars made catching speeders more difficult and limited many to running radar in the direction the trooper was facing since they could not get turned around quick enough to catch someone traveling in the opposite direction.[596]

Governor Clinton attempted to obtain new funding to purchase patrol units in a special session of the legislature in the fall of 1989, but these efforts failed after he made the mistake of including it as part of a much larger "drug war" package. The plan's $6.4 million total cost soured many legislators on it and doomed the entire package. This failure forced Governor Clinton to designate 75% of the state's motor vehicle acquisition fund for the State Police, instead of their usual 50%. The $1.6 million in funding allowed the purchase of 134 new Chevy Caprices. Six months later, Clinton added another million dollars after the state's revenue exceeded forecasts, which allowed the State Police to purchase an additional 80 cars.[597]

The State Police were not the only police agency in Arkansas to suffer through the ill effects of poor finances. The Little Rock police department had much of the same complaints in 1989. Starting pay for city officers remained low at $17,022, and the recently approved budget offered little hope for the future since it froze pay and reduced benefits for the officers. At the same time, these men and women were battling with a huge increase in violent crime in the capital city, which made their jobs more dangerous. These factors convinced a large number of officers to participate in a "blue flu" protest during the first week of October. At the morning roll call on October 2, only five of the 30 officers scheduled to work showed up. At the mid-day roll call, 37 of the 80 officers scheduled to work actually reported for duty. The midnight shift fared the best when 25 of the 37 officers scheduled to work made it in.

For help, the Little Rock police department turned to the State Police and requested as many troopers as the department could spare to bolster the number of officers in the city. "Whether it's Little Rock or a small town," Colonel Goodwin said, "we are responsive to the problem."[598] Twenty-five troopers were called in from around the state to work the dayshift, and 25 additional troopers were brought in to work the nightshift. The LRPD gave each trooper a portable city radio so they could communicate with the city dispatchers, and the LRPD communications center was given a portable State Police radio to provide a second line of contact. Once the communication issues were resolved, the main issue facing the troopers was the almost complete lack of familiarity with the city streets. A problem they seemed to overcome fairly easily, as LRPD Lieutenant Jerry Smith said, "They've got maps and they're doing the job." Fortunately, the Little Rock Police's experience with the "blue flu" did not last long, and the troopers were released for their normal patrol duties.

The end of the 1980s would not be mourned in the State Police. The decade had seen a continual budget battle that forced the department to reduce the number of commissioned officers without a corresponding reduction in the level of responsibilities. Their attempts to implement new, aggressive drug interdiction plans had been stopped by the courts who viewed them as unconstitutional. Most tragically, the decade had been the deadliest in history for State Police officers. The murders of Glen Bailey in 1980 and Louis Bryant in 1984, along with the accidental death of Charles Bassing in 1986, were just half of the State Police officers killed in the line of duty during the 1980s.

The same year Richard Snell murdered Louis Bryant, another trooper fell victim to gunfire. On October 15, two prisoners from the Wrightsville facility, Steven Hill and Michael Cox, walked away from a work detail in Pulaski County around 3:00 p.m. That night, the two men wandered into a home, tied up the family, and stole their truck. An hour later, the couple squirmed free from their bonds and called police. Forty-five minutes later, Trooper Steve Pickens spotted the stolen truck parked in the driveway of a residence in south Pulaski County. The officer requested backup while he kept the truck under surveillance. In short order, Trooper Robbie Klein, Lieutenant Conrad Pattillo, and Trooper Phillip Valez arrived at the residence. Klein and Pattillo got out to search the truck while Pickens and Valez searched near the house. Klein and Pattillo found the truck empty, so they moved toward a station wagon parked in front of the truck. After a few steps, a deafening roar from a shotgun cut through the night air. The blast struck Trooper Klein, knocking him to the ground, while Lieutenant Pattillo returned fire. Klein was rushed to the hospital as additional officers arrived and set up a perimeter around the house. Tracking dogs led officers to a greenhouse behind the residence, which was quickly surrounded by officers from the S.W.A.T. team. After several hours of failed negotiation, the officers fired tear gas into the greenhouse and forced the two escapees to surrender. By the time Cox and Hill surrendered to police, tragedy had once again struck the department and a trooper's family when the injuries inflicted by the shotgun blast proved fatal for Robbie Klein.[599]

The final two years of the 1980s witnessed the deaths of two more State Police officers in almost the exact location and in almost the exact same manner. Trooper Wilson Atkins, a five-year veteran of the department, pulled a car over for speeding near Brinkley on I-40. Trooper Atkins had just written the motorist a ticket when a four-by-four pickup veered onto the shoulder, striking the officer, and killing him instantly.

Six months later, a new trooper named Clark Simpson was assigned to replace Atkins. Just after midnight on February 18, 1989, Trooper

Simpson pulled a semi-truck and trailer over at mile marker 209 on I-40 near Brinkley, which was roughly the same location where Trooper Atkins was struck and killed by the pickup truck in July. After writing the driver a speeding ticket, the officer pulled out onto the interstate and motioned for the semi-truck to pull out ahead of him while he blocked traffic. What Trooper Simpson did not see was another semi-truck and trailer barreling down I-40 right behind the young officer. The resulting impact was devastating. The gas tank on Simpson's patrol car exploded on impact and his car was knocked into a ditch beside the interstate. Both Trooper Simpson and the truck driver were killed in the collision.[600]

A new decade brought few major changes within the State Police. The continued presence of Colonel Goodwin as its director ensured stability and a continued adherence to policies and programs that already seemed to be working.

Within the department, Colonel Goodwin enjoyed widespread popularity and deep respect from his officers. Corporal Mickey Smith expressed a common sentiment when he recalled that "Tommy Goodwin sticks out as being a trooper's director, more than anyone else. He came up through the ranks and knew all of the headaches and heartaches. I really believe he had the troopers' best interests at heart. I knew of too many instances where he went the extra mile for a trooper."[601] Corporal Randy Toombs agreed, saying, "He was a highway patrolman's dream because he worked his way through the ranks. His door was always open, and if you didn't go by and speak with him, he would want to know what you were mad at him about."[602] Captain Bill Carver noted that Colonel Goodwin "was reserved, intelligent, trusting—he would just give you a job and tell you to go do it."[603] Major John Chappelle summed up the opinions of many troopers who served under Goodwin's command when he said, "The people of Arkansas really got some bang for their buck with that one."[604]

One decision made early in Colonel Goodwin's tenure that created much less agreement among officers was the choice to let officers wear short-sleeve uniform shirts during the summer months. Few things are as sacred in the State Police as its uniform, and the debate to allow short-sleeve shirts and no neckties had been bubbling among officers since the 1970s. Prior to this, it had been rumored among officers that Colonel Herman Lindsey refused to even consider the idea because he hated tattoos, which many troopers sported as a result of their time in the military. Soon after he became director in 1981, Colonel Goodwin allowed the transition to happen over the objections of more tradition-bound officers. One of those who did not favor the change was Sergeant Keith Ferguson who said long sleeves were "a tradition that I grew to admire. The State Police has one of the sharpest uniforms and I think it took away from the uniform."[605] Trooper Richard Hester supported the move, especially when he thought back to the early and mid 1960s when the State Police did not have factory air-conditioning in their patrol cars, "I was for the short sleeves. It was so bad. When I went to work, my first car was a 1967 Chevrolet with no air-conditioning, and I was assigned to south Arkansas. I had to wear a long-sleeve shirt, tie, and felt hat. We [literally] stunk."[606] Captain Conrad Pattillo echoed Hester's sentiment and recalled, "Wearing those long-sleeved shirts in the heat and humidity of summer was awful. Once I was manning a roadblock after a bank robbery, and by the end of the day I had perspiration running down in my boots."[607]

By 1993, a whole generation of troopers belonged to the department who never knew the feeling of driving a patrol car without air-conditioning while wearing long-sleeve uniform shirts, neckties, and felt hats at the height of an Arkansas summer. What they all shared though were a dozen years with Colonel Goodwin's steady leadership, but even this seeming constant presence appeared all too fragile in January 1993. On January 4, Tommy Goodwin felt a shortness of breath and checked into a hospital for tests. The doctors determined that the shortness of breath was symptomatic of a much more serious heart ailment that required coronary bypass surgery in March.

Soon after Colonel Goodwin checked into the hospital, a new governor took office in Arkansas. Bill Clinton's victory in the 1992

Presidential election elevated Lieutenant Governor Jim Guy Tucker to the governorship in January 1993, a change that would normally signal the entry of a new State Police director. This would not be the case when Governor Tucker took office. Both Tucker and Clinton were Democrats, so there was not the typical level of political pressure applied on a new governor to appoint a new director as a way of satisfying past campaign supporters. Plus, Colonel Goodwin enjoyed a strong reputation throughout the state, so his position as director remained secure. It would be continuing health issues that would lead to Colonel Goodwin's decision to retire from the State Police in the early summer of 1994. Goodwin's 13 years of continuous service as director ranks as the longest consecutive tenure of any commander the State Police has ever had. Herman Lindsey served as director for 16 years, with four coming during the McMath administration and 12 during the Faubus administration.

Under Colonel Goodwin, the State Police struggled financially as the state of Arkansas limped through trying economic times. Salaries remained low, and Troops and Companies around the state continued to be understaffed. Yet, the period saw critically important advancements in technology and tactics that would have an important influence on the department for the rest of its history.

The completion of the microwave radio system proved to be the most important of many technological advances, which included bulletproof vests and portable breathalyzers that were introduced during the Goodwin era.

Also, the creation of the CAP and S.W.A.T. teams continued to act as valuable resources for the State Police even though their design would be altered to better fit a police department operating in the 1990s.

Similarly, the marijuana eradication program and the continued efforts to reduce traffic accidents in the 1990s reflected strategies and ideas refined during the Goodwin era and bolstered by advances in technology and improved funding to produce the models in use today.

Chapter Seven

Reinventing the State Police, 1994-2000

"Ultimately, I lost my job at my friend's own hand."
—Colonel John Bailey on his replacement
as director of the State Police.

"About anyone can cook using this new method provided a little bit of training and the proper chemicals. You can get on the computer and find recipes, dangers, where to do it, and how to do it. These things came together to cause an explosion of 'mom and pop' meth labs."
—Lance King on the growth of small methamphetamine
manufacturing labs in Arkansas during the late 1990s.

On August 1, 1997, a farmer living near the small Washington County community of Lincoln climbed into a tree to retrieve a pair of pruning shears. The farmer, Hans Hoerler, was a Swiss immigrant who had moved to northwest Arkansas several years earlier to start a dairy farm, which he had expanded to include 125 milk cows and 400 acres of land by that hot summer day. After climbing up, Hoerler reached for a branch to steady himself only to hear the limb crack and then split in two. The breaking limb threw him off balance where he fell head first eight feet to the ground below. The resulting impact broke the dairy farmer's neck and left him paralyzed. Hoerler's 10-year-old son ran to their neighbor's house for help. Their neighbor for the past two years was State Police Trooper Ted Grigson, a five-year veteran of the department. Trooper Grigson called the accident in on his police radio and hurried to his neighbor's aid. When he arrived, his neighbor was conscious, but not worried so much about his own health as he was the future of the farm he had worked so hard to maintain. Grigson helped ease his friend's mind by promising to help keep the farm running so the Hoerlers could continue to pay their bills.[608]

As Hoerler lay confined in the hospital, Trooper Grigson set about fulfilling his promise. Rising at 5:00 a.m. every morning, the officer and his wife, Kecia, milked cows, mended fences, cut hay, and tended to the rest of the Hoerler's livestock until time for the officer's regular highway patrol shift came at 3:00 p.m. Once his shift ended at midnight, he had just five hours before he had to wake up and start all over again. Grigson quickly realized that the chores he thought might take an hour or two were actually lasting three to five hours, so he sought help from nearby farmers, friends, and volunteers. Six volunteers responded to the call and regularly showed up to help Grigson and his wife while another 30 pitched in intermittently over the next few months.

After Hoerler had spent a month in a local hospital, his doctors ordered him transferred to a rehabilitation facility in Denver, Colorado. The move prompted the farmer to reluctantly arrange an auction for his milk cows, which Grigson helped plan and carry out. Once the milk cows were sold, a portion of the workload dropped off, but there still remained hours of daily chores just to keep the farm ahead of Mother Nature. In time, a grateful Hoerler, now wheelchair bound, and his family would return from Denver and relieve Trooper Grigson from his double duty.

Slowly but surely, the story of Grigson's efforts on behalf of his neighbor began to travel around the state and the nation. In January, the officer was named the International Chiefs of Police Trooper of the Year for the southeast region. A month later, he was named the Arkansas State Police's Trooper of the Year. Also, the popular television show *America's Most Wanted* ran the story as a segment in its national broadcast. Additional television segments about Grigson ran soon after on *Real Stories of the Highway Patrol* and *Emergency*. As a result of his being named southeastern region Trooper of the Year by the

International Association of Chiefs of Police, Trooper Grigson was automatically one of four candidates for National Trooper of the Year. Each of the four worthy nominees had their stories dramatized by a nationally syndicated television program, which provided its viewers with call-in numbers to vote for their choice for Trooper of the Year. After watching the program, Grigson doubted his chances for winning, joking with a reporter that, "All I did was milk cows."[609] When he arrived at the award ceremony in August along with the other nominees, Grigson still did not believe he would be the winner since his table was located at the back of the hall and away from the other nominees. So, when the award was announced Grigson was actually talking with the people at his table and did not even hear his named called. It was only when everyone in the banquet hall turned to look at him that he realized something important had just happened, Ted Grigson had just become the first officer from Arkansas to be named National Trooper of the Year. He would add to that award the following year when the National Association of Police Organizations named him one of 10 "Top Cops" in the United States. In the State Police's history, only two other officers have ever earned such a prestigious designation.

* * *

In the spring of 1994, Colonel Goodwin was becoming worn down by the daily grind of overseeing the State Police. His health problems the previous year were only exacerbated by Goodwin's perception that "everything that happens in Washington comes right back to Little Rock" in the form of continued controversies resulting from President Bill Clinton's time as governor.[610] With these concerns in mind, Goodwin informed Governor Tucker that he would be retiring soon and that a search for his replacement should begin. A leading candidate quickly emerged in the form of John Bailey. Bailey spent almost 15 years in the State Police where he worked in Governor's Security, Highway Patrol, Internal Affairs, and Criminal Investigation before leaving the department in 1987 to head the State Highway Department's Highway Police. Governor Tucker approached Bailey in early May to get a feel for the officer's interest in the job and received a non-committal, but interested response. Then, Bailey remembered,

> A month or two later, we had the first-ever law enforcement summit where they got people from all of the law enforcement agencies in Arkansas together to talk about different issues. We were in the planning stage of that meeting. One of the Governor's aides came in the conference room of the Capitol and gave me a note saying the governor wanted to see me. I went in there to see him, and he said, "John it has just dawned on me that I have talked to you about this job and Colonel Goodwin is going to retire. It hasn't been made official yet, but I want to offer you the job and hope and pray that you say yes." This was on a Friday afternoon, and he told me that he understood if I needed to talk with my wife. I told him that I didn't need any time and told him I would take the job. I thought later that if I had really taken some time and analyzed it, I might not have taken it![611]

On June 1, 1994 Governor Tucker officially appointed John Bailey as the director of the State Police.

Colonel Bailey stepped from a position generally outside the purview of the state and national news media into a position that had become a maelstrom of controversy. The most damaging resulted from allegations made by several troopers in December 1993 that then-Governor Bill Clinton had used them to proposition women for him and assist in arranging trysts. The allegations, which first ran in the *Los Angeles Times* and the *American Spectator*, created a furor of publicity that became known as "troopergate." President Clinton denied the charges, and one of the original officers later backed away from his original statements, but the damage had already been done. The State Police's prestige suffered mightily as they became the punch line to numerous jokes over the next year. Amid this embarrassed atmosphere, Colonel Bailey became the department's director and began a movement to reinvigorate the State Police and reshape it as a 21st century police agency.

Some of the first and most visible efforts involved adopting a number of new technologies designed to improve the department's efficiency and its ability to respond to a changing world. This motivation led to the department's transition from the six-shot Smith and Wesson .357 magnum revolver to a .40 caliber Sig Sauer P229 capable of firing 12 rounds from a single clip of ammunition.[612] The search for a replacement to the tried-and-true Smith and Wesson wheel gun actually began during Colonel Goodwin's final year as director. A firearms evaluation committee was selected to test a number of semi-automatic pistols in November 1993. In April 1994, the committee recommended the Sig Sauer. Governor Tucker applauded the choice, telling the State Police Commission that, "There is a critical need that troopers have a firearm superior to the weapons they commonly encounter."[613] Colonel Bailey remembered that, "We were outgunned by the criminals, so police began to ride this emotional wave of 'we need better weapons.' ... We had an intensive experimentation process and ended up negotiating a deal with the gun makers that gave us the guns for free. They wanted to have our old ones to sell, because the used gun market was better than the new gun market."[614]

In actual deployment, though, the Sig would not perform as well as had been hoped. Complaints arose over firing pin failures, reduced knockdown power, a difficult trigger pull, and slide jamming. The weight of these complaints finally led to a change in 2000 when the State Police allowed officers to choose between a Glock Model 21, which was a .45 caliber semi-automatic, a Model 27, which was a compact .40 caliber semi-automatic, or a Model 35, which was a full sized .40 caliber semiautomatic.[615]

A few months after the department adopted the Sig, they introduced another brand new piece of technology. The legislature approved additional funding to purchase and staff an Automated Fingerprint Identification System (AFIS). This cutting-edge technology could scan a fingerprint and in less than 10 minutes compare it with almost a million prints in the Federal Bureau of Investigation's massive database. Without AFIS, this type of search could take days, so the new system proved to be an immensely valuable tool for CID and local investigators.

The AFIS system required 19 full-time staff members to run, which actually created a problem. As Colonel Bailey remembered,

> [W]e realized that we didn't have a place to put it. I was going to have to rent a building somewhere. At the same time, the crime lab was above and below us and they were saying they were out of space, too.[616]

The State Police had been in their headquarters on Natural Resource Drive since 1981 where they shared space with the crime lab and the lab's morgue, which was on the bottom floor. The presence of the latter proved to be a critical mistake due to the ever-present smell of dead bodies that permeated the building. The smell "just plagued the building," Colonel Bailey said and forced "everybody to have candles on their desk."[617] These two factors led Bailey to ask the governor what he thought about the State Police moving, and the governor thought it was a great idea.

> He told me he thought the State Police ought to be by a major highway so anybody with a map can find it. He told me he was glad to hear me recommend this and told me to talk with Chris Burls at State Building Services and see what we could find.... The first place I looked at was on the county line at a vacant outlet mall. I called them, and I was two weeks too late. They had already sold it. Later I went to lunch at El Chico's and looked out the window, and there was the old Target store, and a bomb went off in my head. It would be a perfect place. At the time we were just looking at one end of it, but we ended up buying the whole 28 acres. Teacher's Retirement invested money at a low rate for us to purchase and renovate the building.[618]

Originally, this southwest Little Rock location had been a retail mall that became vacant as its tenants moved to greener pastures in central Little Rock and North Little Rock. With 177,000 square feet, the facility offered enough space to consolidate both the State Police's Headquarters and Troop A headquarters at one location. Until this time, Troop A had remained at the old penitentiary buildings off Roosevelt Road when the main headquarters moved into the building on Natural Resources Drive. The state invested $14.8 million to renovate the abandoned mall, which was completed in March 1997.

One of the most important additions this new, larger space allowed was construction of the State Police training academy behind the Headquarters, which was funded by money from Governor Tucker's emergency fund. With this facility, the State Police no longer had to send its recruits a hundred miles south to the training academy at Camden. Plus, officers staying overnight in Little Rock could sleep in the new training academy's dorms instead of renting a hotel room.

After the new headquarters was dedicated in 1997, the State Police embarked on their next major upgrade: conversion of the analog Motorola microwave radio net to a digital system. The microwave system did a good job of handling the department's radio communications, but it was not advanced enough to handle electronic data transmissions, which was necessary if they were going to join the next wave of high technology policing. In the 1990s, in-car laptop computers rapidly gained in popularity as digital transmission technology became increasingly more advanced and affordable. The State Police estimated it would cost $20 million and take almost two years to equip its highway patrol cars with wireless laptops.[619] With the laptops, the officers could electronically file reports and access license and criminal databases without having to run the request through a dispatcher. According to State Police Lieutenant Jim Tudor, the new technology would relieve a major "bottleneck" between dispatchers and officers.[620]

The hope for all of these changes was to make its officers more efficient and better prepared to accomplish their jobs. Yet none of these changes could stop a speeder, arrest a drunk driver, investigate a crime, or make a drug bust. To do this, the State Police needed men and women in patrol cars, working undercover, and interrogating suspects. This would be difficult since the 488 commissioned officers in the State Police in 1994 was well below its peak of 573 in 1980. Help, though, would be coming from an unexpected source.

In 1994, President Clinton unveiled his Community Oriented Policing (COPs) program that promised to put 100,000 new police officers on the streets. In Arkansas, the State Police would be the largest recipient of this federal largesse. Colonel Bailey remembered that,

> David Pryor was the Senator, and he called me from the Senate floor and said they were trying to get some COPs money for Arkansas.... He asked me if I could give him a statement to make when he gave his presentation, and I said, "If you get me that COPs money, the people in rural Arkansas are going to see that money everyday because that is where I am going to put it. It is not going to some printed material or in a grade school. I am going to hire a trooper that is in the community." There were stipulations. We had additional reporting requirements and these new COPs troopers had to spend so many hours a month in community-oriented tasks. It was such a great deal. We got five years with 75 percent of the officer's cost covered. After the five years, you had to figure out how to fund them. It was really just seed money."[621]

By 1996, the State Police had been awarded $5.6 million in COPs grants that required matching funds of $1.8 million and allowed the State Police to hire 75 new officers.[622] By the end of the decade, COPs grants would provide funding for more than a hundred new officers whose presence on the highways would begin to be reflected in increasing arrest statistics and falling fatality rates.

Arkansas Traffic Fatality Rates, 1994-2000

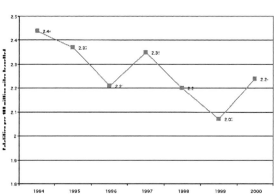

Table 7.1–Comparison of Highway Patrol Activity, 1997-1998[623]

	1997	1998
Driving While Intoxicated	5,884	6,509
Speeding Tickets	82,170	106,371
Officer-Violator Contacts	342,568	471,070

These additional officers, along with increased seatbelt usage and other advances in automobile safety, helped achieve the lowest traffic fatality rate in Arkansas history in 1999 with just 2.07 deaths per 100 million miles traveled. This was a more than 30% decrease from just 10 years earlier.

The State Police also continued their efforts to rein in drug use in Arkansas by focusing on interdiction, marijuana eradication, and undercover narcotics operations. Interdiction efforts relied primarily on the continued operation of a reduced-force CAP program, now known as an Intensified Patrol Unit. The Intensified Patrol Unit essentially consisted of two officers, John Scarberough and Les Cook, and Cook's K-9 partner, Charlie. The unit worked primarily in Pulaski County where they had a good success rate in seizing drugs and making criminal arrests. In 1997, Scarberough, Cook, and Charlie confiscated 1,702 pounds of marijuana, 19 pounds of cocaine, three pounds of methamphetamine, and $26,100 in cash. They also recovered five stolen cars and made 98 total arrests.[624] But, the State Police's ability to commit additional officers to drug interdiction remained low, as Colonel Bailey remembered, "I intended to increase this unit, but you can't take a guy out of rotation in a district and put him somewhere else without giving them a replacement. You can't rob Peter to pay Paul."[625]

On September 2, 1998, Corporal Scarberough was on Intensified Patrol along I-30 near Benton where he pulled over a motorist. As the officer and the driver were sitting in Scarberough's car, a tractor-trailer driver's moment of inattention allowed his rig to drift onto the shoulder where it smashed into the police car. The horrific impact killed Scarberough and seriously injured the truck driver. Colonel Bailey called John Scarberough "the epitome of an Arkansas State Police trooper," a compliment attested to by the 32 letters of commendation the officer had accumulated over his 22-year career.[626]

Another way the State Police attempted to reduce the flow of drugs through Arkansas was through an expansion of the department's canine program (K-9). They purchased their first dogs in 1994, one of which was a Labrador Retriever named "L.B." In March 1995, "L.B." and his handler, Trooper Karl Byrd, were working a speed enforcement program known as "Operation Safe Speed" on I-30. Over the course of a week, the pair made four separate drug busts, which yielded a total of 895 pounds of marijuana valued at $1.3 million.[627] The early successes of these teams lead to the program's expansion to 25 K-9s by 1998. This corresponded to higher activity levels. In 1998, State Police K-9s and their handlers conducted 453 searches, confiscated 1,050 pounds of marijuana, 45 crack rocks, and 6.5 pounds of methamphetamine.[628]

It was methamphetamine's explosive growth in the 1990s that quickly solidified it as the main target of the State Police. The State Police first noted the rise in meth's popularity in the mid 1980s as officers began to bust an increasing number of small manufacturing laboratories. The labs posed a dangerous new problem for officers. Cleaning them up exposed officers to a number of toxic and flammable chemicals that few people had the training or experience to dispose of safely. Therefore in 1990, the State Police began training officers to dismantle meth labs. This training came none to soon as the number of labs seized exploded from 24 in 1995 to 433 in 1998. During this period, CID Investigator Lance King worked closely with the DEA to locate and destroy meth labs and explained the reason behind this huge increase,

> In the past, methamphetamine was produced … [using a] method of production known as the PA method or the phenyl acetic acid method. You didn't have to be a chemist, but you had to have a pretty

good understanding of chemistry and be able to follow a complicated recipe. The cook took at least 72 hours to complete. Also, you had to have high-grade scientific glass and a helper to watch temperatures and control the process. The main people that were trafficking methamphetamine at that time were outlaw motorcycle gangs in Texas and California. Texas got tired of all the labs, and they started enacting some tough state laws. When they did that, the cooks started moving into Arkansas where there weren't as many controls and state laws limiting the availability of the chemicals.... At that time, the federal government jumped in and did things like make possession of a triple neck flask a felony offense. Plus, a lot of the cooks had been caught and jailed ... [then] the method of production began to change from the PA method to the ephedrine method. About anyone can cook using this new method provided a little bit of training and the proper chemicals.... You can get on the computer and find recipes, dangers, where to do it, and how to do it. These things came together to cause an explosion of "mom and pop" meth labs.[629]

In addition to finding increasing numbers of meth labs, the CID continued to have success using undercover narcotics officers targeting other drugs. In 1996, undercover officers infiltrated a large crack cocaine ring in Jonesboro, which they busted in January 1997, making 55 arrests.[630]

Narcotics investigations were not the only crimes CID officers worked in the mid 1990s. State Police Investigators assisted FBI agents in their investigation of powerful state Senator Nick Wilson on corruption charges.

The largest and most high-profile investigation CID officers made during the 1990s was the blue light rapist case. The rapist first struck in November 1995. Using a dash-mounted blue light, the man pulled a woman over on a deserted stretch of highway in east Arkansas. The man walked up to her car, pointed a gun in her face, and forced her into his car after which he drove to a remote area and raped her. Over the next few weeks, he repeated his crime twice, although in one fortunate instance, the woman was able to escape before being violated. As media attention focused on his heinous crimes and state and local officers feverishly worked to stop him, the rapist seemingly disappeared—at least until January 1997 when he once again used a blue light to pull over a Lonoke County woman, abduct her, and then rape her.

The commander of the State Police's Sex Crime Unit, Lieutenant Mary Kesterson, assigned two of her investigators to work the case full time while Colonel Bailey set up a meeting with 50 local law enforcement officers from the area where the rapes occurred to disseminate information and establish dialogue between the various agencies.[631] The case also prompted the state legislature, which was in session at the time, to get involved. They passed a law making the use of a blue light by anyone other than a law enforcement officer a felony. Meanwhile, State Police spokesmen Wayne Jordan and Bill Sadler worked with the media to remind women to only pull over in well lit areas and to keep their windows rolled up until the police officer presented some sort of identification. The department also committed $5,000 to a reward fund, which was matched by $5,000 from an anonymous donor and several thousand raised locally, for information that led to the arrest of the blue light rapist.[632]

Despite hundreds of tips and several suspects, the investigators could not find the rapist who had once again gone into a period of inactivity. This brief respite ended in July when he abducted and raped a 17-year-old girl. This time, instead of raping her in a remote location, he took her to a building. A deviation that Lieutenant David Rosegrant, the CID commander in nearby Forrest City, called "a mistake" and noted that "we plan to capitalize on every mistake he makes."[633] Based on testimony by the victim, the investigators believed that the building was located in Woodruff County, so 35 troopers descended upon the area. Spokesman Bill Sadler described the effort, saying, "We're just driving around looking and talking to people, looking for anything that might give [the investigators] a break."[634] Understandably, the residents of the area were terrified. One woman told reporters, "If I was on the highway at night, I don't know that I would pull over."[635]

Police were also getting worried that the blue light rapist would soon start killing his victims. Fearing that such an escalation in violence was imminent, the State Police created a task force comprised of 10 State Police investigators, a Cross County sheriff's office detective, and a Wynne police department officer. CID Sergeant J. R. Howard coordinated the task force as it worked through a "mountain of leads."[636] Investigators also hoped that a separate task force might keep the course of the investigation a secret since the rapist might be connected in some way with law enforcement.

In mid September, the task force caught a break from a seemingly unrelated case, as Lieutenant Rosegrant remembered,

> We caught him through a home invasion case. We had DNA from our stops out on the highway. Then we had some home invasions around the Wynne and Forrest City area, and we compared the DNA and found that the two people were the same. We had a suspect on the home invasion.[637]

The match convinced officers to obtain a blood sample from their suspect in the home invasions. The break in the case presented officers with their best lead yet, but publicly they remained wary as State Police Investigator Barry Roy remarked, "We feel upbeat about it, but we felt good about the [other suspects], too."[638] When the test results came back the next day, they positively linked the suspect in the home invasion with the blue light rapist. Also, investigators were able to link the suspect to the remote building he used to rape his final victim. With such strong evidence in hand, Sergeant Howard proudly proclaimed, "I can say that the blue light rapist is finally in jail."[639]

In addition to regular Highway Patrol and CID responsibilities, the 1990s were defined by a myriad of additional duties being placed under the State Police's umbrella of responsibility. In addition to traditional duties like the fire marshal's section, security guard licensing, and driver's testing, the legislature added concealed handgun licensing, background checks for handgun purchases, and oversight of used car dealerships. The largest and most controversial new duty was the legislature's decision to include civilian social workers within the State

Police. In March 1997, State Representative Carolyn Pollan introduced a bill giving the State Police authority over all child abuse cases in the state.[640] At the time, the Department of Human Services used 58 caseworkers to investigate complaints of abuse, but Representative Pollan and others questioned the ability of the DHS to adequately investigate such cases. The commander of the department's Sex Crimes Unit, Lieutenant Kesterson, opposed the inclusion of civilian caseworkers in the State Police and instead argued for an increase in the number of commissioned police officers assigned to her unit. Colonel Bailey supported the inclusion of civilian investigators, saying, "This gets into a philosophical debate on whether sex crimes and child abuse are social or criminal. In my opinion, when you do certain things to a child, that is not a social problem. That is something that people have to be held accountable for."[641]

Whether the department thought it was a good idea or not did not really matter since the legislature approved Pollan's bill for the creation of a new Family Protection Unit within the State Police. The new unit, which included 15 commissioned officers and 39 civilian investigators, struggled initially to develop a sense of cohesion between civilian and commissioned personnel.[642] Also, differing attitudes on how investigators should approach cases created conflict within the unit and resulted in declining performance. As the unit became more experienced and additional investigators were added, its performance improved, but the tension between civilian and commissioned investigators remained in the background.[643]

Another important change instituted during Colonel Bailey's tenure as director was the reemergence of a State Police S.W.A.T. team. The State Police's S.W.A.T. teams lost their most vocal supporter when Lieutenant Colonel George Moye took the special retirement incentives in 1987. As a result, the various Troop S.W.A.T. teams fell into disuse due to their high maintenance cost and the regular training requirements for team members. When Colonel Bailey returned to the State Police as director in 1994, it only seemed natural that some sort of S.W.A.T. team would be revived since he was also a key driving force behind their initial creation in the early 1980s.

To be successful and cost effective, though, the old formula of a S.W.A.T. team in each Troop had to be reworked. After much consideration, the decision was made to establish a single Special Response Team (SRT) comprised of approximately 30 officers from around the state. Also, the newly designed SRT would allow officers from any division in the State Police to join instead of limiting participation to only Highway Patrol officers like the S.W.A.T. teams did. Corporal Buddy Acoach was one of the officers who led the reorganization effort and remembered that the reason for the single team approach was, "one, it was cheaper, two, so we wouldn't rip the heart out of a Highway Patrol Troop, and three, we could use people from different backgrounds."[644] Also, with team members spread around the state instead of being centrally located in Little Rock, the SRT still allowed a rapid response. As Colonel Bailey remembered, "If we needed a five-man team in Texarkana, we would call up members from southwest Arkansas and get them there quickly. If we needed specialized people, like an attack dog, we had the ability to airlift them because I now had airplanes and helicopters. Within an hour or two we could have whatever we needed on site."[645]

Qualifications for the new SRT began in December 1994, and over the next six months 19 officers were selected. The team members underwent extensive training and received cutting-edge tactical equipment over the next year before becoming officially active in 1996. Over the next four years, the State Police's SRT would grow to include 30 officers and a K-9 and responded to an average of 100 calls each year.[646]

While the State Police was reinventing itself by adding new programs and restarting old ones, the state government was going through a crisis. In 1996, Governor Jim Guy Tucker, along with James and Susan McDougal, was convicted of fraudulently obtaining and using Small Business Administration loans to fund the infamous Whitewater real estate venture. Arkansas law prevents anyone with a felony conviction from serving as governor. Therefore, Tucker announced that he would be stepping down as the state's chief executive.

The transition between Governor Tucker and Lieutenant Governor Mike Huckabee proved to be just as controversial as the investigation. On the day Tucker was supposed to submit his resignation and leave office, he changed his mind and argued that he should wait until the outcome of his appeal had been settled. Colonel Bailey and his administrative assistant went to the Capitol to watch the transition that day not knowing that Tucker had changed his mind. A decision Bailey later called "a mistake," since,

> Within 10 minutes it turned into a riot. I am thinking, 'I should not be here.' People were telling me, 'He is in there and he won't come out. Are you going to go get him?' Now the news media is in my face. Mike Huckabee is down the hall ready to make this big change in command. I had no idea what to do. I was just praying to God that somebody would come to their senses. They did in about 45 minutes. When Tucker did finally leave, "Say" Macintosh went crazy. He incited the crowd. I got on the cell phone and called the Highway Patrol commander to get as many of the biggest troopers over here as fast as he could. I knew that we were fixing to have a problem, and I wanted a show of force there. Fortunately, it all fizzed out and everybody went on their way.[647]

Normally with a new governor in office, the State Police director begins to update his resume and prepare for the inevitable change in leadership. But in this instance, Governor Huckabee and Colonel Bailey had met and become friends 10 years earlier during a Christian police officer's program.[648] So when Governor Huckabee became the state's chief executive, John Bailey remained the director of the State Police. Yet this relationship was not destined to last as Bailey would write later, "Ultimately, I lost my job at my friend's own hand."[649]

The relationship between Bailey and Huckabee began to sour early in 1998. The news media in the state began reporting allegations of criminal activity by a member of Governor Huckabee's family and began questioning why the State Police was not investigating the matter. In

Bailey's view, "this wasn't State Police business ... [and] the only way my department would be involved would be if a request came through the Attorney General's office to investigate."[650] An official request for an investigation was submitted, by a local prosecutor, which created a dilemma for Bailey. Would he accede to the prosecutor's request or follow the governor's request to deny it? Bailey refused to officially deny the request for investigation, which greatly upset the governor, but before the issue could be investigated, the election for governor had been held and the prosecutor decided to let the matter drop.

Before the damage between Bailey and Huckabee's relationship could be repaired, another controversial issue intervened to push them even farther apart. A few weeks after the election, word began to seep out of the governor's mansion that Governor Huckabee wanted to move his official residence out of Little Rock to his personal home in western Arkansas. To do this would require the State Police to upgrade the security at the governor's lakefront home, a project that Bailey refused to sign off on.[651] A few smaller points of contention between Bailey and Huckabee followed soon after, and as a result, whatever trust that had existed between them was irreparably damaged.

The governor's anger over these perceived slights led him to ask for Bailey's resignation the first week of December. "Never had I been caught so totally off guard," Bailey would write. "I wanted to be angry ... but I was too hurt."[652] Bailey acquiesced with the governor's wishes and on December 8 publicly announced his retirement. Colonel Bailey was not the only one surprised by the turn of events. Captain Bill Young worked in the State Police's Special Services section and recalled, "Everybody was shocked for a few days. You don't know what to expect. You are worried about changes and if you would still be doing what you are doing. It was a madhouse around there for a while."[653]

Governor Huckabee's choice for director only exacerbated the worry of many State Police officers. On December 11, 1998, Huckabee tapped Tom Mars, a prominent Fayetteville attorney, as the director of the State Police. The two men had become friends after

Mars provided legal guidance to the governor on ethics complaints, which arguably was the same sort of issue that the governor felt John Bailey had not supported him on. The main source of worry for many State Police officers was Mars's lack of law enforcement experience. Mars's background included a degree in Criminology from Arkansas State University, two years as a police officer in Lynchburg, Virginia, and a law degree from the University of Arkansas Law School. The fear was that without extensive experience in law enforcement, or more specifically, State Police experience, Mars could not understand the unique challenges that face troopers and investigators and that this would lead to policies and procedures that might make their jobs more difficult.

Both Mars and Huckabee "worried" about how State Police officers might react to an outsider being named head of their department.[654] So, when Mars agreed to be appointed director, he did not plan on making it a long-term position, remembering,

> The agreement with my law partner was that I would leave everything in my office just like it was because I would probably be back in a year. I told the governor that I would only commit to it for a year because it involved a move to Little Rock and a significant change in income ... and [I] had two kids. One was 16 and the other was 12 or 13. That was a pretty significant consideration for me. My kids are very important to me, and it was a big factor in agreeing to only do it for a year. As time wore on it became an even bigger issue to my kids and me.[655]

With this focus on short-term results, Mars set out to accomplish two main tasks, increasing the department's efforts to catching drunk drivers and gaining national accreditation for the State Police.

Arresting drunk drivers has always been an important State Police function, but under Colonel Mars it became the key measuring stick of an active trooper. Instead of gauging activity by the traditional yardstick of one officer-violator contact per hour, Highway Patrol Commander Jim Elliott noted that "we are placing more emphasis now on quality," which meant giving more credit for arrests like DWIs.[656] This understanding allowed troopers to dedicate more time to finding drunk drivers and conducting sobriety checkpoints. There were penalties, though, for officers who still failed to make enough DWI arrests. Officers ranking in the bottom 20 percent of DWI arrests were "invited" to a month-long training session on DWI enforcement in Little Rock.[657]

For those officers who exceeded expectations, the department partnered with Mothers Against Drunk Driving (MADD) to create a special program of recognition that Colonel Mars remembered gave "troopers ... a sticker showing a wine glass with a hash mark through it for every five or 10 DWI arrests." Also, Bill Sadler created a competition among the troopers that awarded a plaque and designation as "Blue Knight" to the officer who made the most DWI arrests each year.[658] This change in emphasis led to an increase in the number of DWI arrests. In June and July 1999, troopers made a respective 57% and 64% more arrests than they did the previous year.[659]

Colonel Mars's second major effort involved gaining national accreditation for the State Police. To earn such a designation, Colonel Mars turned to the Commission on Accreditation for Law Enforcement Agencies, or CALEA. CALEA was a respected national commission formed in 1979 by the International Association of Chiefs of Police, National Organization of Black Law Enforcement Executives, National Sheriffs' Association, and the Police Executive Research Forum to "develop a set of law enforcement standards and to establish and administer an accreditation process through which law enforcement agencies could demonstrate ... that they meet professionally-recognized criteria for excellence in management and service delivery."[660] Colonel Mars's intent was,

> to bring [the State Police] up to the standards that many law enforcement agencies ... aim for. I don't think anybody questions that CALEA represents those high standards. There may be more efficient or less costly ways to reach those high standards, but I knew that I

didn't have the credibility in law enforcement to come in and sell my ideas. Therefore, I needed a tool to sell them. It didn't take me long to find this tool in CALEA, which provided me with a credible source to promote these ideas. No one could question the rationale behind them because the source was impeccable.[661]

To become accredited, the State Police had to meet 436 standards related to "agency role and responsibilities; organization and administration; personnel administration; operations and support; prisoner and court-related issues; and auxiliary and technical services."[662] The accreditation quickly ran into resistance, as Mars remembered, "the opponents of accreditation were savvy enough to point out that the expenses and stress such changes put on the organization would be harmful. Also, there wasn't buy-in at the troop commander level, which is crucial for any initiative that occurs in the State Police.... Getting the commanders to agree and then enforce a standard policy was a challenge."[663]

Ultimately, the accreditation process would be canceled after Colonel Mars left the State Police in 2001, but one surviving piece of the process gave Mars a measure of satisfaction. "It did allow us to get a manual put together," Mars remembered. "The State of Washington had a State Police director who was a lawyer at the time and she was a female, which made it even more interesting. She had managed to get that agency through the CALEA process, and we used them as a model for our manual."[664]

A continuing issue the State Police faced during the final years of the 20th century was the continued growth of methamphetamine production and use inside the state. The year Governor Huckabee appointed Tom Mars as director, law enforcement officers seized 443 meth labs in Arkansas. By 2001, the number of labs seized almost doubled, with 853 destroyed during the year.[665] The State Police provided assistance to local agencies in detecting, raiding, and cleaning up meth labs, with one of its most intensive efforts occurring in August 1999 with the launching of Operation Checkmate.

Operation Checkmate targeted Madison County, a predominately rural county located in northwest Arkansas that had become a haven for meth labs. The initial spark for the operation was the shooting of State Police Corporal Tracy Spencer. On August 25, Corporal Spencer and Madison County Chief Deputy Sheriff Herb Marshall knocked on the door of a recreational vehicle parked on a lonely dirt road. They were seeking the arrest of a man in connection with a recent shooting. The investigation turned deadly when the trailer's occupant, Charles Nevels, reached into a closet and grabbed an assault rifle. As the officers retreated toward cover behind Deputy Marshall's car, Nevels opened fire. One of the rounds struck Spencer in the right arm, fracturing the bone. Both officers returned fire and killed Nevels. A subsequent search determined that Nevel's vehicle contained a meth lab.

As additional State Police officers responded to the scene of the shooting, they noticed that several residences "looked out of place in that area." Major Elliott noted that, "This guy (Charles Nevels) is not the only one in this area [with methamphetamine]. We knew that already. But we didn't know it was so prevalent."[666] Amply motivated, the State Police pulled in 75 troopers and investigators from around the state where they began knocking on residents' doors asking for tips and assisting the sheriff's office serve more than 500 outstanding warrants in hopes of simultaneously uncovering additional meth labs. The sweep had some success. State Police officers uncovered two meth labs, two marijuana patches, and arrested 44 people for a wide range of violations.

The year 2000 would find little changed within the State Police, but renewed financial difficulties appeared on the horizon. In subsequent years, the State Police would see a reduction in COPs grants and declining state revenues, which forced a return to economy measures that included limiting officers' mileage and leaving vacancies unfilled. Plus, Colonel Mars had not been successful in winning over many of the department's officers or the State Police Commission. The resulting conflict would ultimately lead to Colonel Mars's resignation in 2001.

As the State Police would find once again, no matter who occupied the director's office, the troopers, investigators, radio operators, and administrators would continue to do their very best to fulfill the responsibilities that had been assigned to them. Just like their predecessors had been doing since 1935.

Chapter Eight

The Lighter Side

"If you don't have some humor in your work, I promise you,
you won't make it through your career."
—Captain Win Phillips[667]

The physical, mental, and emotional demands placed upon a trooper, or any police officer for that matter, can be tremendous. The physical dangers are the most obvious since every time an officer makes a traffic stop, he or she runs the risk of death. This threat has the potential to inflict physical scars and extinguish lives, but there are also the mental and emotional demands that inflict a pain that is often hidden, but no less painful or capable of destroying a life.

One way of mentally surviving the job and coping with the stress is by realizing the humor and light-heartedness that can occur at any moment. The goal of this chapter is to relate some of that light-heartedness—not just to entertain the reader, but also to show how overworked and underpaid men and women tried to make it through a 20 or 30 year career with their sanity intact and their bodies whole.

The Infamous Radio Incident

Most everyone will know who the participants in this incident are because it has been an oft-told warning to young troopers concerning the "dangers" of the State Police radio system.

One morning in the late 1970s, Trooper John [not his real name] was working patrol in north Arkansas. While on patrol, Trooper John happened to pass Trooper Bill [not his real name] on the highway, and as police officers are bound to do they decided to stop and have a chat about their day. Trooper Bill pulled in behind John's patrol car, got out, and slid into John's front seat. As Bill was doing this, Trooper John laid his radio mic down beside him and shifted in his seat to better face his friend. The two troopers began their conversation innocently enough, talking about their daily activity, but then, again as troopers are bound to do, the talk turned to more juicy topics. The two began to relate in great detail their gripes with the promotional system and their dislike of departmental politics. For 28 minutes, the two men named names and left no one out. Their discussion was quite surprisingly interrupted when a deputy's patrol car roared past them and slid to a stop in front of John's cruiser. Trooper John asked his partner, "What in the heck is his problem?" Before Bill could answer, the deputy was out of his car and running toward the cruiser yelling, "JOHN, YOUR MIC IS KEYED!" As the realization dawned on the two troopers that their entire conversation was being beamed out over the whole State Police radio network, Trooper John uttered a final and quite fitting epithet and pulled the mic out from under his leg, which cut off the signal. During the discussion, two local sheriff's deputies had recognized John's voice and had been looking for the two troopers since they couldn't reach them by radio because their mic was keyed. At the same time, the radio room at Little Rock headquarters was growing crowded as the radio operators called more and more officers in to listen to these two troopers discuss personnel and policies with a candor that is not always conducive to a patrolman's career. Luckily for the two officers, neither suffered anything other than acute embarrassment over the incident, but their example serves to warn rookie officers to always know where you mic is.

Out of Gas

This story also involved using the radio, or at least the decision to not use the radio.

In the late 1960s, a rookie trooper was assigned to the Fort Smith Troop, which was commanded by the legendary and intimidating

Damon "Slick" Wilson. Captain Wilson's reputation for being a very gruff and stern commander was well known within the State Police, and the last thing a new trooper wanted to do was embarrass Captain Wilson. Along with a new post came a new car for the trooper, or at least new to this man since the car was actually a hand-me-down from another officer.

On his first day of patrol the officer headed out, no doubt ready to single-handedly catch every criminal and arrest every drunk that threatened the citizens of his county. The trooper's first day was going as well as could be expected with only routine traffic stops dotting his activity log. Late in the day, he pulled over a gentleman for another routine traffic stop and had the man come sit in his car while he finished the paperwork. As the he was finishing the stop, his patrol car started to shudder a little bit. The trooper looked at his gauges and made sure that he still had gas and the oil pressure was fine, both of which showed adequate levels. Despite what the gauges told him, the patrol car continued to shudder until it finally sputtered one last time and died. As the trooper and his passenger sat in the car listening to the now still engine clicking and popping as it cooled, the passenger turned to the trooper and said, "I think you just ran out of gas." Once again the trooper read his gas gauge, which still showed a quarter of a tank, but unbeknownst to the rookie officer, the gas gauge was broken and he had indeed run out of gas on his very first day in "Slick" Wilson's Troop. The thought of getting on the radio and calling headquarters for help and then being forced to admit he had run out of gas was not a pleasant thought, so the trooper asked the man he had stopped if he would take him to the nearest gas station. The man agreed, and the two set off in the man's car to the nearest gas station, which was some distance away. When they arrived, the trooper borrowed a gas can with five gallons of gas and bummed a ride back with the station's tow truck driver.

> During the trip back, the trooper was sure that no one would ever be the wiser about his mistake. This thought was quickly banished when the two drove up to his car and saw deputy sheriff's cars and State

Police cars pulled over around the officer's stranded unit with lights flashing and police officers combing the side of the highway. The trooper remembers, "You can imagine what an empty State Police car parked on the side of the road might look like to another officer. Since I hadn't called it in, they thought I was in serious trouble. After this I knew that the next time I saw Captain Wilson, I was probably going to be fired." Fortunately for this trooper, Captain Wilson proved to be understanding and told him that there was no shame in running out of gas because everyone has done it once, but he also made it known in no uncertain words that he better use the radio if it ever happened again. Advice the man never forgot and faithfully followed until he retired more than 30 years later.

When Monkeys Attack

Walking up to a vehicle, the officer never knows what awaits.

A trooper working in Pulaski County was passing the Mabelvale overpass when he saw a car pulled over on the side of the interstate. The trooper pulled in behind the car to check out the situation and see if he needed to render assistance. Within a few minutes of the initial stop, he realized that the man and the woman in the car were highly intoxicated, so he decided to arrest them. The situation was complicated by the fact that the couple was in a high state of agitation with one another, and when he began to place them in handcuffs, this anger swung onto the officer, as well. Such a scene would be complicated by itself, but this particular arrest had another factor that worked to ratchet up the opportunity for mayhem—a visibly angry monkey. The monkey was the driver's pet, and just like a dog, it sported a collar and a leash. Apparently, when the monkey saw the trooper attempting to put the two intoxicated, angry people in his car, it decided to come to their rescue. With only the subtle rattle of a trailing dog chain on concrete as a warning, the monkey charged out of the car and up the trooper's back. The monkey started clawing and biting the trooper's back and head, while the officer continued to try to manhandle the couple into his patrol car. With one hand on his prisoners, he used his other to swat at the enraged monkey and finally succeeded in hitting it only to have the primate bite down on his hand. With this final indignity, the monkey leaped off the trooper's shoulders and ran into the nearby field. The trooper remembers, "If I could have found it, I would have shot it on the spot." With the prisoners in the back of the car and the monkey in hiding, one would think that the incident was over, but when things start going downhill it can be impossible to stop. While in route to the jail, the couple continued to argue until the woman, who had her hands cuffed in front of her, started beating the man in the head with her fists and handcuffs. When the trooper reached back to separate them, the woman started hitting the officer, too. Needless to say, the officer quickly pulled over and cuffed her hands behind her back before going to the jail and to the hospital for a tetanus shot.

Red Plymouth

Sometimes things are not what they appear.

A sergeant and two troopers were working radar on I-40 in the western part of the state. The three wanted to try something different, so the sergeant decided to take his radar up the road to an overpass where he could clock vehicle speeds from a relatively hidden position. He would then radio a description of the cars and their corresponding speeds to the waiting troopers who would then pull them over when those cars passed. The sergeant set up his position and started clocking speeds and calling them down, "Green Oldsmobile, 85 miles an hour." "Black Ford, 80 miles an hour." This went on for 10 minutes or so, and the whole time the troopers down the road from the sergeant's position were growing more and more frustrated. Every time the sergeant would radio down a description of a speeding car, they would peel their eyes for the violator to pass, but none of the cars ever went past their position. The string of no-shows finally ended after the sergeant radioed, "Red Plymouth, 85 miles an hour." A short time later a red Plymouth sped by the waiting troopers, who pulled him over and issued a citation. Thinking that their plan was finally working, the troopers grew even more perplexed when the pattern of missing speeders began again. As time passed, it became apparent that the only speeders identified by the sergeant that actually passed the troopers drove red cars, thus it dawned on one of the troopers that "he is colorblind! The only colors he recognized were the red ones. We told him to just send us the fast red ones. Then, lo and behold, he gets assigned a fire-engine red Plymouth patrol car."

The Sanctity of the Uniform

The State Police uniform is an almost holy thing within the department, and appropriate attire is one of the Ten Commandments of a successful trooper, especially when it comes to the hat. If troopers forgot to put their hat on and they were caught, it could result in a verbal reprimand, time off, or worse. More than one trooper has rushed out of their car responding to a serious accident, forgotten to put their hat on, been photographed by the local newspaper in such a compromising position, and suffered the consequences the next morning when their troop commander reads the paper.

A Pulaski County trooper was working his run on Highway 10 west of Little Rock and happened to see white bass breaking along the dam at Lake Maumelle. The officer was an avid fisherman, and such a sight proved too tempting for him to simply ignore. Luckily, he was carrying his rod and reel in the trunk of his unit, so he quickly pulled off the road, turned on his flashers, and grabbed his fishing gear, but in his hurry he forgot to slap on his hat. In short order, the trooper had two good-sized white bass on the bank, and a third was bowing his rod trying to keep from joining them. Decades later the trooper would vividly remember what happened next. "Then I hear this whining noise. There was one thing that emitted that sound: the loudspeaker on an unmarked Ford. I knew it was unmarked because the loudspeaker wouldn't sound that way if it came from the bar light speaker. The grill speaker gave it a distinctive squeal. I looked up, and the sun was setting right behind this midnight blue Ford, and there is Captain Gene Donham. And he is wearing his hat! He reaches down and picks up his microphone, and I am thinking that I am done and I will be working nights on the worst run in the state from now on. Captain Donham said, 'TROOPER! GET YOUR HAT ON!" Then he put the microphone down and drove off, and I never heard another word about it. I ran and got my hat and caught two or three more."

Hats were not the only thing that could cause troopers some embarrassment if they were not wearing them. Pants had a way of doing that, too.

In 1994 the State Police was in the midst of its transition from Smith and Wesson revolvers to Sig Sauer automatics. The change had generated a general level of upset among members of the department who preferred wheel guns to automatics. Still, the change was mandatory, and in an effort to instill a sense of urgency for every trooper to switch and become qualified with the new weapon, there were warnings of dire consequences for those who failed to do so. It was under this pressure that a female trooper arrived at the range to qualify with her new automatic. The trooper wore her fatigues to the range that day, and per her usual practice did not wear a belt. She stepped up to the line with five of her fellow officers and 15 more waiting for their chance behind them. The range master barked the order to commence firing, and after a few shots the trooper's Sig misfired and ejected the cartridge. While she was reaching to catch the round, her pants unceremoniously proceeded to slide down around her ankles. Scared that if she stopped she wouldn't qualify and thus would suffer the dire consequences, she caught the round, jammed it back in her weapon, and finished firing all while her pants were pooled at her feet. When she finished and successfully qualified with the weapon, she was finally able to pull her pants up, and the only comment she heard about the incident was from the range master who simply asked, "Did your britches fall down?"

This next incident does not directly involve the uniform as much as what got on the uniform.

In the 1960s, the State Police would transport the state penitentiary's bloodhounds from their home at Cummins Prison to various manhunts around the state. The duty was not a particularly popular one because the dogs had a tendency to tear up a patrol car since the units were just standard cruisers with no special equipment to keep the dogs confined. In this particular instance, a trooper had just pulled out on Asher Avenue to take the dogs back to Cummins from Little Rock when another car pulled out in front of him. The officer swerved to miss the car and in doing so lost control and ended up running into a building. The crash sent the officer into the windshield and the two bloodhounds over the top of the officer. The trooper went to the emergency room to get a couple of cuts stitched up, which was accomplished fairly quickly. As the man was getting ready to leave, he noticed the nurse looking at his head with a huge grin on her face. Confused, he ran his hand through his hair and found the source of her delight: a parting gift of droppings from the bloodhounds had gotten smeared in his hair during the accident. From then on, everyone simply referred to the trooper as "Dog."

My Car is Faster

One of the few things a trooper loves more than a new car is a fast car.

During the 1970s, the State Police's fleet of patrol cars was not of a unified make or model. As a result, competitions often developed between officers who drove different makes and models in an effort to settle the age-old question of whose car was the fastest. Just such a competition developed when a trooper in western Arkansas was assigned a new car. The trooper was justifiably proud of his new cruiser and challenged another officer to pit his older Plymouth against his shiny new patrol unit. The Plymouth, though older, boasted a 383-cubic-inch engine that produced quite a bit of horsepower, and if the new car could outrun the Plymouth, it would be quite an impressive achievement. The two waited until late one night when the interstate was completely clear of traffic and decided to settle it once and for all. They pulled side by side and mashed the pedals to the floor, and the Plymouth easily won the race. Unfazed, the trooper with the new car argued that he had gotten a bad start and that they should do it again. The officer with the Plymouth agreed, so they lined up once again and took off. Apparently, the trooper's brand new car had had enough, and the transmission seized up forcing him to pull over on the side of the road. For obvious reasons, he was worried about how the captain was going to react when he heard that the patrol car's transmission had been destroyed while two troopers were drag racing. The trooper in the Plymouth told him to just call in a pursuit on the radio, wait a minute, and then call in that his car had broken down and he was calling off the pursuit. That way, no one would know what happened and he would have an acceptable reason for breaking his car. Seeing the logic in this ploy, the trooper radioed that he was in pursuit of a red Oldsmobile on I-40. Then he got back on the radio and said he stopped the pursuit because he was having problems with his car and that he needed a tow truck. All seemed to be going according to plan until about 15 minutes passed and a local police officer radioed the trooper to say he had the driver of the red Oldsmobile pulled over and for him to come by and identify the driver! The trooper quickly got on the radio and told the officer that he had not gotten close enough to provide an accurate identification and told the officer to let the man go.

The Browns

Working for the State Police is often a family affair with sons, daughters, brothers, and sisters following in the footsteps of another family member. One such family was the Browns. Carlton Brown was a trooper assigned to Benton County in northwest Arkansas, and Kenneth was a trooper assigned to Russellville in central Arkansas. The Browns also had a brother who was a city police officer in their hometown of Hot Springs. One stubborn tourist got to meet each of them on a single day. On this particular day, the man headed south from Missouri on Highway 71 for a vacation in Hot Springs. Apparently, he was in a hurry to arrive since Carlton Brown stopped him for speeding when he passed through Benton County and wrote him a ticket. Then, as Kenneth Brown remembered, "This guy comes through [my] area, and I stop him and write him a ticket. Then he got down to Hot Springs and my brother down there stopped him and wrote him a ticket. [The motorist] asked him, 'Is every damn cop in Arkansas named Brown?'"

A Shootout?

During the 1950s, a group of inmates escaped from Cummins Prison and stole a car in an effort to outdistance their pursuers. The State Police responded by setting up a number of roadblocks in the area. The escapees ran through a roadblock manned by two troopers, one of whom was armed with a carbine and the other a pistol. The two troopers threw a storm of fire at the rapidly fleeing car, but were unable to stop it. One of the troopers got on the radio and called to the next roadblock to warn them that the escapees were heading their way. When the trooper manning the other roadblock asked them what the escapees were driving, he responded, "I don't know, but the whole ass end is going to be shot out of it!" The escapees never arrived at the next roadblock, and when the State Police found the car, it had run off into a ditch and the prisoners had fled on foot. When the officers approached the car, they expected to find it filled with bullet holes from the troopers' previous fusillade, but upon closer inspection could locate only a single bullet hole on the bumper.

Driver's Test Nightmares

It has often been argued, quite convincingly, that giving drivers' tests is the most hazardous job in the State Police. The following stories show why this is not only funny, but also pretty true.

A trooper was giving driver's tests in Magnolia where he would typically ask the applicant to drive a short, simple route around the courthouse square followed by a parallel parking test. The traffic around the square was controlled by yield signs to allow east-west traffic on Highway 82 to pass freely on the south side of the courthouse. The route was fairly simple and would not normally present too many critical decisions to the driver. On this particular day, the trooper got in a car with a woman and asked her to take the standard route while he observed her signals and her overall skill. He noticed that the woman gave a yell when she passed the first yield sign around the square. The trooper asked her if something was wrong. The woman replied, "No, Mr. Big Hat," and continued around the square and approached the intersection for Highway 82, which also used a yield sign to stop southbound traffic. The trooper saw a semi truck and trailer approaching the intersection and at the same time realized that the woman was not making any attempt to slow down. The driver of the truck realized this as well and locked up his brakes while the woman yelled again and went right through the yield sign without slowing. As the trooper sat with a seemingly crazy woman yelling on his left and a semi truck bearing down on his right, his time on this earth seemed short. Luckily, the truck was able to stop before hitting the car with 18 inches or so of room to spare. The trooper ordered the woman to pull around and stop, which she did without incident, and he asked, "What in the world are you doing, and why were you hollering like that?" She said, "Mr. Big Hat, that [yield] sign says 'yell,' and I hollered as loud as I could!" She did not pass the test.

In the 1960s and 1970s it was fairly common for elderly women to have never owned a driver's license or learned how to drive. Often their husbands had done all of the driving, and when they died, the widow would have to learn to drive in order to survive. It is often this situation that created some of the most hazardous tests.

An elderly lady came in to take a driver's test after her husband died. She easily passed the written test and earned her learner's permit, which allowed her to practice driving with a licensed adult for 30 days, after which she could come back and take the driving portion of the exam. The woman immediately went out and bought a brand new Pontiac and asked her kids to teach her to drive. After the proscribed period, the woman came back driving a Pontiac with two dented fenders. The trooper soon learned why those fenders were dented and politely failed her. He recommended that she practice for another 30 days and come back to retest. Apparently, she had scared off her kids because she had to hire someone to help her drive this time. In another 30 days, the woman came back driving the Pontiac with all four fenders dented. Once again, the trooper had to politely fail the woman whose skills had not greatly improved. The third time proved the charm as the woman found a person from her church to teach her to drive and she was able to pass the exam, although the same couldn't be said for her previously shiny, new Pontiac which was a near total wreck by the time she got her license.

An Act 300 Marriage

All troopers carried a very thick, nicely bound book containing all of the state's traffic regulations, which are outlined in Act 300 of the Arkansas Code of Law. The book provided one of the most commonly cited instances of levity.

A trooper comes upon a parked car and upon inspection finds two young lovebirds contained within. The trooper gets them out of the car and finds that they are intoxicated and also not married. He decides to play a joke on the two and grabs the Act 300 book and begins what seems to be an official wedding ceremony for the two, which concludes with the trooper pronouncing them man and wife on the way to jail for public intoxication. Most of the time when the young couple sobers up, they realize they were not actually married, but not every time. In one instance a young couple actually moved out of the county and were trying to apply for a loan as husband and wife when they found out that they were not married. Needless to say, when word reached the trooper's commander about what had happened, it was not a pleasant conversation.

The State Police Lie Detector

The State Police's radio system prior to 1983 was a low-power system that required the patrol cars to have fairly strong transmitters to get a signal back to headquarters. Also, these radios needed long whip antennas to send the signal. Whenever a trooper would key the mic, the antenna would conduct enough of an electrical charge from the radio to light a fluorescent light bulb. This oddity would prove very useful as a mobile "lie detector" for officers. A trooper would ask a clearly intoxicated driver if he had been drinking, and the driver would invariably answer "no." So, the trooper would have the driver get out of the car to take a "lie detector test." He would give a fluorescent bulb to the drunk driver and have him hold to the whip antenna, which he called a "lie detector." Then the trooper would hold the mic in his hand and ask a series of questions that he knew the driver was telling the truth to, like "what is your name" or "when were you born." Then he would again ask the driver if he had been drinking, and if the driver said, "no," he would key the mic thus sending a charge to the antenna and lighting up the bulb. When the bulb lighted up, the trooper would tell the driver, "See, you are lying!"

Yes.

In the mid 1960s, the State Police were tasked with overseeing the state's driver's license program, which including revoking the license of drivers with poor records. This new restriction caused more than a few stubborn Arkansans to resist any attempts to take their driver's license, which led to the follow story.

Bill Miller (who later would become director) was in charge of the newly created Safety Division of the State Police in the mid 1960s. One of his duties was to oversee the issuance and revocation of driver's licenses in the state. One particular Arkansan who lived in the northeast part of the state had racked up an impressive tally of violations, so the Safety Division decided to revoke his license before he killed someone through his negligence. Lieutenant Miller wrote the man a letter ordering him to mail his license into the Safety Division until his period of probation was complete. A few weeks later, a reply letter from the man arrived on Lieutenant Miller's desk. In the letter, the man cussed the State Police and Lieutenant Miller and took great care to ensure both were well aware of the man's feelings toward any attempt at taking his driver's license. He then closed by writing, "There is not a goddamned State trooper in the state of Arkansas big enough to take my license." Clearly, such a challenge could not go unanswered. Miller took the man's letter and wrote across the bottom, "Can you handle this?" Then he mailed the letter to Buren Jackson, who was a trooper in northeast Arkansas known for his impressive stature. For four days, Miller did not hear a peep about this incident, and just as it was beginning to slip his mind, a letter from Jackson landed on his desk. Lieutenant Miller opened the letter to find the driver's license in question enclosed along with Miller's original letter asking Jackson, "can you handle this." Now, though, there was something else written on the letter. To the question of "can you handle this," Trooper Jackson had simply written, "Yes."

A Bombing

In April 1968, the State Police sent almost 40 officers to Pine Bluff following an outburst of vandalism, shooting, and firebombing due to the black community's anger over the assassination of Martin Luther King. Part of the deployed force included a mobile communication trailer that allowed the troopers to communicate with local officers. Despite the stressfulness of the situation, several troopers saw an opportunity to play a joke on a fellow officer, as described in the instigator's own words.

"The radio operator, who later became a troop commander, was operating the communication van set up outside of town. Another trooper and I had gotten some cherry bombs from some kids, and we told the operator that we had information that they (rioters) might try to blow this van up. We told him to keep his eyes open. We snuck back there two or three hours later and threw those cherry bombs in there, and he came out of there in a panic. It was really funny."

The First State Police Test for Marijuana

Upon his retirement in 1978, State Police Officer Jim Rowell related a story to an Arkansas Gazette *reporter about what might be the first marijuana arrest made by a State Police officer.*

In 1954, Trooper Jim Rowell was on patrol in Clark County when he pulled over a car for speeding. During a brief chase, the men tossed a bag out of the car. After the trooper arrested the men, he took them back to pick up the bag and see what they had thrown out. Instead of finding a gun or knife, the officer found 30 pounds of some sort of plant-like material. In 1954, marijuana was just beginning to creep out of the big cities, and no one in the State Police had much experience with it. He had his suspicions, though. Rowell called his supervisor to tell him about his find and ask what he needed to do next. His supervisor recommended that Rowell run a test to see if the substance was indeed marijuana before he called the FBI out to investigate. The only way—unofficially of course—that the State Police had to test for marijuana in 1954 was to roll it in cigarette paper and smoke it and then wait to see if it had any effect on him. So, Trooper Rowell dutifully rolled it and smoked a little bit of it—undoubtedly to the shock and amazement of his four arrestees. As a result of the experiment, Rowell said, "I felt a little perked-up." Proof enough for the trooper to turn the men and the 30 pounds of marijuana over to the FBI, who later confirmed the findings of Rowell's field test![668]

Epilogue

Often, historical narratives have a logical ending point. If someone is writing about combat operations in the Civil War, the surrender at Appomattox provides a convenient conclusion for a reader who can then close the book without wondering what happened next. For an organization like the Arkansas State Police, it is impossible to write anything resembling a true "conclusion." Each and every day, a trooper will get into a patrol car or an investigator will open a new case that has the potential to not only create new history, but to overshadow everything that has come before it. Therefore, any attempt at reaching a "conclusion" for such an ever-changing, perpetual entity remains merely conjecture. What is possible though is a comparison of past and present and an analysis of how society and the State Police have interacted to create its most recent version.

Arguably, the State Police as an organization can be viewed in two different phases. The first began in 1935 with the creation of the Rangers and ended in 1966 with the election of Winthrop Rockefeller. This 31-year period can be defined by the ever-present influence of state politics within the department and on their operations. To get hired, troopers had to have political influence, and to keep from being transferred or even fired, the trooper had to make sure he did not cross the local political structure.

Despite the consequences of politics, the State Police remained a close-knit family of officers whose dedication and commitment to the job are legendary. As one current State Police officer testified, "I can remember my father working those six-10s and on his day off go riding with another trooper." As a result of this dedication and commitment, troopers were counted on and looked up to by the communities they served, which often only had a handful of local officers to call on in times of need.

The absence of local officers during this period also placed troopers far outside the reach of assistance if a confrontation turned violent. Even if troopers had local officers they could count on, it was hardly certain that the signal from their outdated radios could reach a dispatcher. On the other hand, officers were provided more leeway on how they did their jobs. If they wanted to search a car, they searched it. If a confrontation turned physical, they did not have to worry too much about repercussions. Another benefit to working during the early years of the State Police was the tremendous amount of respect the judicial system placed on the State Police. Judges and prosecutors relied heavily on a trooper's integrity to establish the guilt or innocence of suspects.

After the election of Winthrop Rockefeller, the State Police began a lengthy transition into the force they are today—an agency that is more professional and business-like than any previous incarnation. This does not mean that the State Police as a whole became better or worse, just different in important ways.

The most critical change was the declining influence of politics on the average trooper and investigator. It became more and more rare for an officer to be moved from a post simply because he angered the sheriff or local politician by arresting a political supporter. Also, a blatant disregard of state laws like those occurring in Hot Springs came to a halt and would not be repeated as officers were allowed to enforce laws without political pressure to look the other way.

State Police personnel witnessed major changes as well. The workweek went from a minimum of 60 hours a week with no compensatory time to a standard 40-hour week with comp time for anything over 40 hours. In part to offset the reduction of hours troopers spent on the highway, the department greatly expanded its ranks and increased its pay to attract more and better qualified recruits. Hand-in-hand with this expansion, the State Police began to more closely resemble the population they were charged with protecting as black and female officers began to join the department in increasing numbers. Also, these new officers underwent a more rigorous and lengthy training academy before earning their commission. And, once commissioned, officers enjoyed equipment and technology far superior to anything their pre-Rockefeller predecessors could have hoped to use.

Offsetting all of these seeming improvements within the State Police was a dramatic increase in the danger an officer faced on a daily basis. In the 31 years encompassed by the founding of the State Police and the election of Winthrop Rockefeller, three State Police officers were killed in the line of duty. In the ensuing 39 years, 13 officers have died in the line of duty.

A more subtle and less definable change has been in the relationship between officers and the community. In the 21st century, it seems that officers are not as likely to experience the "our trooper" phenomenon that existed during the 1950s, 1960s, and even into the 1970s. By the year 2000, fewer and fewer residents know a State Police officer by name, or even by sight. In part, this distance developed as local and county law enforcement agencies grew larger, better trained, and more capable of responding to calls for service. This often limits the interaction of State Police officers and the public to brief traffic stops or accident investigations.

Another factor was the shorter workday. An officer is only on the highway for eight hours in a shift during which he or she has to work accidents, run traffic, and complete paperwork. This limits the opportunities the officer has to interact with the community, both socially and professionally. When officers worked six-10s, they had the time to stop by the barbershop or corner diner to talk with residents and learn about problems they might be having, which encouraged a closeness between police and public that is less likely to exist today.

Whether the State Police will transition into a new and definable third phase at some point in the future is not certain. One of the major influences on the State Police during their second phase was the impact of illegal narcotics, which began to consume a major portion of the department's budget and manpower in the mid 1970s. So the real possibility exists that the next phase of the State Police's history will be triggered by the presence of another major threat. After September 11, 2001, one need not look far to find one very likely candidate for an organization-altering threat.

Acknowledgements

At its very core, the history of the Arkansas State Police is about the men and women who don the uniform and go to work everyday. It is about the troopers, the investigators, the radio operators, and the administrators and how they tried to do their jobs every day and go home to their families when their shift ended. Consequently, the big events simply represent mileposts along the way where the reader can observe the reaction of the State Police and see the reflection of the society they are charged with protecting. In the State Police's nearly 70 years of existence, society has changed quite dramatically, and the State Police's history clearly reflects this change. Therefore, the study of the State Police provides more than just the story of a law enforcement organization. It also highlights the transition of a Southern state from the Old South to the New.

Since my personal experiences provided such a limited basis for writing a history of the State Police, I am deeply indebted to a number of people for their help, encouragement, guidance, and energy. First and foremost, I want to thank Don Melton, Steve Dozier, Dale Saffold, Mae Humphries, Diana Goodwin, and Larry Slamons for their support, assistance, and encouragement in getting the project moving forward and ensuring I had everything I needed to keep it going.

Another critical cog in this project was the more than 70 retired and active-duty State Police personnel who agreed to share their experiences, files, and pictures with me. These interviews form the base of this history and are immensely valuable resources for anyone interested in writing about the State Police in the future. Therefore, I want to thank:

Buddy Acoach, John Bailey, James Beach, Hansel Bradford, Les Braunns, Jim Bray, Elton Brown, Kenneth Brown, Ray Carnahan, Bill Carver, John Chambers, Howard Chandler, John Chappelle, Dave

Davidson, Jerry Davis, John Paul Davis, Lynn Davis, Jim Elliott, Dean Friend, Terrie Grace, Ted Grigson, Paul Halley, Doug Harp, G. B. Harp, Mel Hensley, Thomas Henson, Richard Hester, Gene Irby, Buren Jackson, Jesse Jones, John Kidwell, Lance King, Ron Lemons, Harold Luter, Tom Mars, Ken McFerran, Freddie McKinley, Bill Miller, Dale Miller, Glenn Minton, Tom Morrow, Robert Neel, Conrad Pattillo, John Purcell, Jerry Reinold, David Rosegrant, Leroy Sitton, Billy Skipper, Billy R. Skipper, Lyle Smith, Mickey Smith, Wayland Speer, M. L. Tester, Jim Thomas, Buddy Thompson, Mack A. Thompson, Mack E. Thompson, Randy Toombs, W. A. Tudor, Jim Tyler, Travis Ward, Charles Webb, John Westmoreland, W. A. Wren, and Bill Young. In addition to these interviews, I have talked informally with a number of other officers who graciously shared their time and experiences, as well.

I am thankful to Leroy Sitton and the late Herschel "Plug" Eaton for their histories of the State Police. Both of these well-written and insightful texts provided a base of knowledge to build from and helped guide me during my research. Anyone interested in the history of the State Police would be well served by reading either of them.

Last, but in no way least, is my family. My wife, Lara, and my two children, Bailey and Amelia, were very understanding and supportive when I had to spend time away conducting interviews, searching through archives, and reading microfilm. Also, the support and encouragement provided by my mother, Joyce, and father, Uvalde, proved immensely valuable.

Portions of the expenses incurred during my research were paid through the generosity of the University of Arkansas's History Department in the form of a Mary Hudgins Research Grant.

Additionally, a condensed and edited version of the first chapter of this book was original published in the Winter 2005 edition of the *Arkansas Historical Quarterly* under the title "Localism and the creation of a state police in Arkansas."

Notes

Chapter One

1 W. A Reid to J. M. Futrell, October 20, 1935, Junius Marion Futrell Papers, Departmental Papers—Attorney General, Arkansas History Commission, Little Rock.

2 *Mountain Echo*, October 30 and November 6, 1935

3 Gene Mooney to A. G. Albright, October 28, 1935, Futrell Papers, Departmental Papers—Attorney General.

4 Ibid.

5 A. G. Albright oral interview conducted by Leah S. McCloughan, July 28, 1973, University of Central Arkansas Library, Special Collections.

6 Mooney to Albright, October 28, 1935.

7 William Link, *The Paradox of Southern Progressivism: 1880-1930* (Chapel Hill: University of North Carolina Press, 1992), 9, and Edward Ayers, *Vengeance and Justice: Crime and Punishment in the 19th Century American South* (New York: Oxford University Press, 1984), 252.

8 David E. Rison, "Arkansas During the Great Depression" (Los Angeles: University of California at Los Angeles PhD Dissertation, 1974), 95-103, and Timothy Donovan, ed., et al, *The Governors of Arkansas: Essays in Political Biography*, 2nd Edition, (Fayetteville: University of Arkansas Press, 1995), 185-189.

9 David R. Johnson, *American Law Enforcement: A History* (St. Louis: Forum Press, 1981), 9.

10 "Ordinance No. 129—City of Little Rock, 1859," *Arkansas Gazette*, May 14, 1859. (Hereinafter referred to as the *Gazette*)

11 *Gazette*, December 6, 1865.

12 *Gazette*, March 5, 1873.

13 Ibid, March 5, 1873.

14 *Arkansas House Legislative Journal* and *Little Rock Republican* April 3, 1873.

15 *Gazette*, March 22, 1873.

16 Ibid, April 3, 1873.

17 Ibid, also see the *Arkansas House Legislative Journal*, April 3, 1873.

18 Ibid, February 1894. Little Rock Police Chief Frank McMahon noted that rivers and railroads were easy avenues of travel for criminals.

19 Ibid, June 21, 1883.

20 Ibid, June 25, 1884.

21 Ibid, February 10, 1894.

22 Weldon Cooper, "The State Police Movement in the South," *Journal of Politics*, Vol. 1 No. 4 (1939), 424.

23 H. Kenneth Bechtel, *State Police in the United States: A Socio-Historical Analysis* (Westport, CT: Greenwood Press, 1995), 34. Also see Robert Utley, *Lone Star Justice: The First Century of the Texas Rangers* (New York: Oxford University Press, 2002), x,

Johnson, 155, and Cynthia Morris and Bryan Vila, *The Role of Police in American Society: A Documentary History* (Westport, CT: Greenwood Press, 1999), 29.

24 Ann Patton Baenziger, "The Texas State Police During Reconstruction: A Reexamination," *Southwestern Historical Quarterly*, Vol. 72, No. 4, (April, 1969), 491.

25 Utley, 287.

26 D. Johnson, 160.

27 Grif Stockley, *Blood in Their Eyes: The Elaine Race Massacres of 1919* (Fayetteville, AR: University of Arkansas Press, 2001), and Jeannie M. Whayne, "Low Villians and Wickedness in High Places: Race and Class in the Elaine Riots," *Arkansas Historical Quarterly*, Vol. 58, No. 3, (Fall, 1999), 285-313.

28 *Harrison Daily Times*, "Citizens Must Get Protection or Lose All," January 13, 1923.

29 Ralph R. Rea, *Boone County and Its People* (Van Buren, AR: Press-Argus, 1955), p. 174. Also, see J. K. Farris, *The Harrison Riot or The Rein of the Mob on the Missouri and North Arkansas Railroad*, (Wynne, AR: Self Published, 1924), and Walter Bradley, *An Industrial War: History of the Missouri and North Arkansas Railroad Strike* (Harrison, AR: Bradley & Russell Publishing, 1926), p. 98.

30 Rea, 175.

31 *Harrison Daily Times*, January 23, 1923.

32 Rea, 179.

33 George Murrell Hunt, *A History of Prohibition in Arkansas* (Fayetteville, AR: Master's Thesis, 1933), 48-50 and 142-150. Ben Johnson, *John Barleycorn Must Die: The War Against Drink in Arkansas* (Fayetteville, AR: University of Arkansas Press, 2005), 36.

34 Cynthia Morris and Bryan Vila, *The Role of Police in American Society: A Documentary History* (Westport, CT: Greenwood Press, 1999), 138.

35 "Arkansas Chiefly Dry Says Official," *Gazette*, February 21, 1931.

36 "State's Prohi Sentiment is Strong, Report," *Arkansas Democrat*, February 21, 1931. Hereinafter referred to as *Democrat*.

37 Ibid.

38 Arkansas Highway and Transportation Department, *Historical Review of the Arkansas State Highway Commission and the Arkansas State Highway and Transportation Department: 1913-1992* (Little Rock, AR: Arkansas Highway and Transportation Department, 1992), 236-240.

39 "A Good Move," *Gazette*, February 11, 1914.

40 "Speed That Endangers Lives," *Gazette*, November 11, 1917.

41 Arkansas Highway and Transportation Department, *Eighth Biennial Report*, p 20 and p 99.

42 *Arkansas Almanac: 1956-1957* (Little Rock: Arkansas Almanac Co., 1957), 122. Annual vehicle miles traveled are provided by AHTD, *Historical Review*, 237.

43 *Boone County Headlight*, January 10, 1935.

44 *Gazette*, January 26, 1935.

45 National Highway and Transportation Safety Administration, "Arkansas: Toll of Motor Vehicle Crashes, 2001," http://www.nhtsa.dot.gov/stsi/State_Info.cfm?Year= 2001&State=AR, (November 8, 2003).

46 "Governor Argues for Traffic Safety Laws," *Gazette*, February 19, 1935.

47 Samuel Walker, *A Critical History of Police Reform: The Emergence of Professionalism* (Lincoln, NE: University of Nebraska Press, 1977), 139-152. Also see H. Kenneth Bechtel, *State Police in the United States: A Socio-Historical Analysis* (Westport, CT: Greenwood Press, 1995), 57, and August Vollmer and Alfred E. Parker, *Crime and the State Police* (Berkley, CA: University of California Press, 1935).

48 *Biennial Reports of the Attorney General of the State of Arkansas*, 1925-1934.

49 Attorney General of the State of Arkansas, *Biennial Report: 1925-1926*.

50 Attorney General of the State of Arkansas, *Biennial Report: 1929-1930*, 104.

51 *Gazette*, June 21 1935. The source cited by the *Gazette* was *The Spectator*.

52 "100 Texarkana Citizens Will Aid in Checking Crime," *Gazette*, January 27, 1933, and "Texarkana Moves to Check Crime," *Gazette*, February 1, 1933. Also see James S. Parker, "A Deeper History: The Oil Boom of the 1920s in Union County Arkansas" (Fayetteville, AR: University of Arkansas Master's Thesis, 2000).

53 Bruce Smith, *The State Police* (Montclair, NJ: Patterson Smith, 1925), 9.

54 *Annals of the American Academy of Political and Social Science*, Vol. 146, November 1929.

55 Bryan Vila and Cynthia Morris, *The Role of Police in American Society: A Documentary History* (Westport, CT: Greenwood Press, 1999), 141.

56 Vollmer and Parker, 143.

57 Bechtel, 43-44.

58 "In the Senate," *Gazette*, March 6, 1923.

59 Arkansas Highway Commission, *Seventh Biennial Report: 1924-1926*, 8.

60 J. E. Richards, ed., *The Arkansas Sheriff: The Official Organ of the Arkansas Sheriffs' Association* (Little Rock: Arkansas Sheriffs' Association, 1927), 6.

61 Arkansas Highway Commission, *Eighth Biennial Report: 1926-1928*, 15.

62 "Would Have State Take Over College," *Gazette*, January 30, 1929.

63 Ibid.

64 J. M. Futrell to S. L. Cooke, April 15, 1935, Futrell Papers.

65 A. G. "Gray" Albright Interview.

66 Arkansas Secretary of State, *Legislative Journal*, February 19, 1929.

67 "Act 299," *Acts of Arkansas*, 1929, 1289.

68 *Legislative Journal*, March 6, 1929.

69 "Senate Bills are Rushed by House," *Gazette*, March 12, 1929.

70 *Meeting Minutes of the Arkansas Highway Commission*, April 18, 1929.

71 Arkansas Highway Commission, *Ninth Biennial Report: 1928-1930*, 3.

72 "Expense of State Road Patrol Analyzed," *Gazette*, January 17, 1933.

73 Arkansas State Highway Audit Commission, *Report on the Audit of the State Highway Department of Arkansas*, Volume 1, (1933), 71.

74 Audit Commission, Volume 1, 72.

75 Earl R. Wiseman, *Third Biennial Report of the Department of Revenue, 1932-1934*, Arkansas Department of Revenue, 40-41.

76 "Listening in on the Legislature," *Democrat*, March 4, 1931 and *Acts of Arkansas-1931*, 234.

77 "In the Senate," *Gazette*, March 7, 1933.

78 "Legislative Calendar," *Democrat*, February 15, 1931.

79 Futrell Papers.

80 *Democrat*, February 15, 1935.

81 "Senators Receive 18 More Measures," *Gazette*, January 16, 1935.

82 "Measure Provides for State Police," *Gazette*, January 17, 1935.

83 "Planning Board's Bill Passes House," *Gazette*, January 23, 1935.

84 "New Measure Provides for State Police," *Gazette*, February 5, 1935.

85 "New Measure Provides for State Police," *Gazette*, February 5, 1935.

86 "Governor Gets a Few Things Off His Chest," *Gazette*, February 6, 1935.

87 "17 Bills Passed by Senate in Busy Day," *Gazette*, February 8, 1935.

88 "State Police Bill Up for Final Passage," *Democrat*, February 14, 1935.

89 "Governor Argues for Traffic Safety Laws," *Gazette*, February 17, 1935.

90 "State Police Bill Approved in the House," *Gazette*, February 19, 1935.

91 Johnson, *John Barleycorn*, 42-43.

92 J. M. Futrell to Senate Judiciary Committee, March 5, 1935, Futrell Papers.

93 *Legislative Journal*, March 8, 1935, 692.

94 *Legislative Journal*, March 8, 1935, 693.

95 "Senate Passes Bill Creating State Police," *Democrat*, March 8, 1935.

96 "Act 120," *Acts of Arkansas*, 330.

97 "House Responds to Request for Enforcement," *Democrat*, March 13, 1935.

98 "Letter from Attorney General Carl Bailey to Grady Forgy," January 13, 1936,
Papers of Governor J. M. Futrell and Arkansas State Police, *Annual Report-1935*.

Chapter Two

99 *Democrat*, March 28. The Marion Hotel was the epicenter of politics in
Arkansas during this time. Its banquet rooms were used as meeting places for sub-
committees, and its lobby was the preferred station for job seekers and lobbyists.

100 *Gazette*, March 28, 1935.

101 A. G. Albright oral interview by Leah McLoughan, University of Central
Arkansas Special Collections, Conway, Arkansas.

102 *Democrat*, March 28, 1935. Also see Herschel Eaton, *History of the Arkansas
State Police* (unpublished, 1985).

103 Grady McCall, "Letter to Grady McCall from Bob Morehead, March 8, 1935,"
Arkansas State Ranger Materials, University of Central Arkansas Special Manuscript
Collection, Conway Arkansas.

104 A. G. Albright, "Letter to J. M. Futrell from A. G. Albright, April 30, 1935,"
Futrell Papers, AHC.

105 Personnel Records for E. E. Frazier. A representative question might be the
one that asked, "What would you do if you were told of a gambling house outside
your region and the sheriff and local authorities weren't stopping it?"

106 Albright Interview, 14.

107 *Democrat*, June 17, 1935.

108 "Albright Interview," p 12. Lieutenants were authorized a salary of $2,100 versus a Ranger salary of $1,800.

109 *Arkansas State Police Annual Report*, 4/1/35-7/1/36, 13.

110 Ibid, 5-6.

111 *Gazette*, August 2, 1935.

112 *Democrat*, February 15, 1936.

113 *Arkansas State Police, Biennial Report, 1936-1938*.

114 H. L. Mitchell, *The Mean Things Happen in this Land* (Montclair, NJ: Allanheld Osmun Publishing, 1979), 104.

115 Ibid, p 89-91. The account refers to a State Police captain and the only captain in the State Police at this time was C. T. Atkinson.

116 *Sharecropper's Voice*, June 1937.

117 Albright interview, 18.

118 *Democrat*, January 28 and February 2, 1937.

119 Ibid, February 11, 1937.

120 Ibid, February 12, 1937.

121 Ibid, April 1, 1937.

122 Ibid, May 19, 1937. Lilburn R. Briggs would be promoted to Lieutenant and take over the Investigation Division in 1940 when its former commander, Neil Shannon, left to join the Secret Service.

123 Ibid, July 21, 1937.

124 Ibid, August 16 and 17, 1937. James Atkinson, "Clifford T. Atkinson Personal History," *The Arkansas Trooper*, (Summer 2003), 15.

125 Ibid, September 12 and September 14, 1937.

126 Orval Allbritton, *Leo and Verne: The Spa's Heyday* (Hot Springs: Garland County Historical Society, 2003). Allbritton argues that Governor Bailey was won over by the Hot Springs political machine shortly after his election, and this is the reason for the reduction in pressure from the State Police on gambling in the city.

127 Arkansas State Police, *Biennial Report, 1936-1938*, 15.

128 Albright interview.

129 *Democrat*, January 31, 1939.

130 Ibid, August 20, 1939.

131 Arkansas State Police, *Biennial Report, 1938-1940*. The report alternately called them Districts and Troops, but the official designation would be Districts.

132 *Democrat*, May 31, 1940.

133 Ibid, October 3, 1940.

134 Ibid, January 3 and January 5, 1942.

135 Ibid, May 14, 1941.

136 Ibid, June 1, June 15, July 20, 1941.

137 Ibid, December 11, 1941.

138 Ibid, February 23, February 27, March 5, 1941.

139 Ibid, April 24, 1941.

140 Ibid, July 17, 1941.

141 Ibid, June 29, 1941. The school was the State Police's fourth school. There was a full four-week course in 1937 and 1938. A third course that lasted just a week

was given in 1939. Captain Lindsey Hatchet was in charge of the 1941 training school and, interestingly, former Assistant Superintendent Bob LaFollette returned to be a guest instructor. He had recently been appointed by Governor Adkins to head up the Highway Department's Traffic Safety Division.

142 Ibid, January 18, 1942.

143 Ibid, August 19 and August 31, 1942.

144 Ibid, July 12, 1941.

145 Ibid, September 14, 1941.

146 Ibid, October 1, October 6, October 12, 1941.

147 Ibid, October 16 and October 17, 1941.

148 Ibid, October 18 and October 19, 1941.

149 Ibid, January 25, 1942.

150 Ibid, February 1, March 11, and March 22, 1942.

151 Ibid, November 8, 1942.

152 Ibid, November 9, 1942.

153 Ibid, January 27, 1943.

154 Ibid, February 19, 1943.

155 Ibid, March 9 and March 15, 1943.

156 Ibid, March 15, 1943.

157 Ibid, June 18, June 19, June 20, 1943.

158 Ibid, July 3, 1943.

159 Ibid, July 29, 1943.

160 Ibid, August 12 and August 20, 1943.

161 Ibid, August 18, August 19, and August 20, 1943.

162 Ibid, September 18 and September 24, 1943.

163 Ibid, September 26, 27, 1943.

164 Ibid, October 17, October 19, and October 23, 1943.

165 Ibid, November 15 and November 16, 1943.

166 Scott Wood to Homer Adkins, January 28, 1944, Papers of Governor Homer Adkins, Arkansas History Commission, Little Rock.

167 Homer Adkins to F. L. Hurst, May 15, 1944, Adkins Papers.

168 Herschel Eaton, *History of the Arkansas State Police* (unpublished manuscript, 1985), 23-25.

169 *Democrat*, November 26, 1944.

170 J. C. Smith to Ben Laney, January 26, 1945, Papers of Governor Ben Laney, AHC.

171 *Democrat*, January 5, 1945.

172 Ibid, January 9 and January 10, 1945.

173 Ibid, January 3, 1945.

174 Eaton, 27.

175 *Democrat*, January 18, 1945.

176 Ibid, January 24, 1945.

177 Ibid, January 27, 1945.

Chapter Three

178 *Democrat*, August 9, 10, 11, and September 11, 1946. Add Shug would retire as a Lieutenant in the State Police.

179 Ben Johnson, *Arkansas in Modern America: 1930-1999* (Fayetteville, AR: University of Arkansas Press, 2000), 59.

180 Ibid, July 26, 1946.

181 Ibid, December 31, 1945.

182 Ibid, August 11, 1946.

183 Ibid, July 15, 1946.

184 Glenn Minton, "Oral Interview with Glenn Minton by Michael Lindsey, February 12, 2004." Also see, *Democrat*, March 15, 1948.

185 *Democrat*, December 19, 1945, January 5 and 13, 1946.

186 Ibid, April 8, 1946. Travis Ward retired as a Lieutenant with the State Police.

187 The best accounts of the Phantom Murders are provided by Wayne Beck, www.geocities.com/txkphantom/index2.htm.

188 Ibid, *Democrat*, March 30, 1946.

189 "Letter to Governor Ben Laney, May 7, 1946," Papers of Arkansas Governor Ben Laney, Arkansas History Commission, Little Rock, Arkansas.

190 *Democrat*, May 11 and May 15, 1946.

191 Beck, www.geocities.com/txkphantom/index2.html.

192 The conviction was overturned because the Appeal Court determined he did not have adequate representation.

193 *Democrat*, November 23, 1946.

194 Ibid, June 24, 25, and 26, 1946.

195 Ibid, June 30, 1946.

196 Ibid, July 5, 1946.

197 Ibid, July 8, 1946.

198 Ibid, August 14, 1946.

199 Ibid, March 3, 1946 and the *Arkansas Almanac, 1957-1958*, 165.

200 Ibid, February 4, 1946.

201 Ibid, February 16 and 22, and March 3, 1946.

202 Ibid, February 27, March 2 and 3, and July 7 and 13, 1946.

203 Ibid, June 4, 1948.

204 Ibid, August 30, 1948.

205 Ibid, August 20, 21, and 22, 1948.

206 Arkansas State Police Commission, *Commission Meeting Minutes: September 18, 1948.*

207 *Democrat*, September 25, 26, 27, 28, 29, 30 and October 1, 6, 7, 8, 9, 1948 and May 14 and June 22, 1949. Also see Eaton, pp. 30-33.

208 Ibid, December 12, 1948, and January 16, 1949.

209 Ibid, December 17, 1948. The proposed bill also called for graduated salaries based on seniority, which was a new policy intended to reduce personnel turnover.

210 Ibid, January 15, 1949.

211 Arkansas State Police, *Biennial Reports*, 1936-1949. The 1949 Biennial Report

provides the 225,000 criminal prints data, 32. Also, in 1949 the State Police had 125,000 civilian prints on file. This followed a nationwide drive to fingerprint Americans as a sort of patriotic obligation.

212 Arkansas State Police, *Biennial Report–1949*. The seven officers were G. D. Morris, W. T. Bowling, Guy Grant, J. H. Porterfield, O. E. Bowden, Bernard Young, and Tom Smalley. *Democrat*, April 17, 1949.

213 *Democrat*, February 20, 1949.

214 Ibid, March 15 and 24, 1949. The money in the slot machines was donated to charity and then the equipment was burned in a public ceremony in May.

215 Ibid, June 18 and July 13, 1950.

216 Ibid, August 10, 1950.

217 Ibid, May 5, 1951.

218 Ibid, February 15, 1951.

219 Ibid, May 21, 1950.

220 Leroy Sitton, "Oral Interview of Leroy Sitton by Michael Lindsey, December 10, 2003."

221 *Democrat*, April 22, 1949.

222 Ibid, August 21, 1949.

223 Ibid, August 28, 1949 and Eaton, 35-36.

224 Ibid, October 20, 1949.

225 Ibid, September 25, 1950.

226 Ibid, July 27, 1950.

227 Ibid, January 1, 1950.

228 Ibid, January 2, 3, 4, and 5, 1950.

229 Ibid, January 18, 1950.

230 Ibid, July 1, 1951.

231 Arkansas State Police, *Annual Report–1949*.

232 *Democrat*, October 12, 1951.

233 Ibid, October 20, 1951.

234 Ibid, October 31, 1951.

235 Ibid, January 1, 1952. There were 37 fatalities in December 1951 compared to 50 in December 1950.

236 Ibid, April 6 and June 12, 1952.

237 Ibid, October 5, 1952.

238 Ibid, August 17, 1952.

239 Ibid, November 29, 1952.

240 W. A. Tudor, "Oral Interview with W. A. Tudor by Michael Lindsey."

241 *Acts of Arkansas–1953*.

242 Arkansas State Highway Audit Commission, *Arkansas State Highway Department Reports—July 1947 to June 1951*, 49.

243 Ibid, p 13.

244 *Acts of Arkansas–1953*, 419. Also see *Democrat* April 2, 14, and 16, 1953.

245 *Democrat*, August 9, 1953.

246 Ibid.

247 Ibid, September 29, 1953.

248 Ibid, October 18, 1953. Also see May 31 and September 9, 1954.

249 Ibid, January 7, 1954.

250 Ibid, February 14, 1954.

251 Ibid, January 17, 1954.

252 Ibid, February 5, 1954.

253 Ibid, December 24, 1954.

254 Ibid, December 12, 1953.

Chapter Four

255 Mrs. Norman Wright to Orval Faubus, December 1, 1960, Faubus Papers, University of Arkansas Special Collections, Fayetteville.

256 Buren Jackson, "Oral Interview with Buren Jackson conducted by David Chastain," David Chastain's Personal Collection, University of Arkansas at Little Rock.

257 *Gazette*, September 6, 10, 12, 18, and October 3, 4, 5, 6, 8, 9, 12, 13, and November 8 and 19, 1960, and October 6, 1962. Also see Howard Chandler, "Oral Interview with Howard Chandler conducted by Michael Lindsey, October 9, 2003."

258 Paul McDonald, "Report to Herman Lindsey from Paul McDonald, October 8, 1962," Faubus Papers.

259 The details of this account are provided by the previously cited report prepared by Paul McDonald. Also see *Gazette*, October 6 and 7, 1962.

260 Arkansas State Police, *Biennial Report, 1954-1956.*

261 *Acts of Arkansas–1955.*

262 *Democrat*, July 18, 1955.

263 Ibid, June 23, August 1, 2, 3, 4, and 5, 1955.

264 Ibid, November 15, 1954.

265 Ibid, December 30, 1955, January 2, 3, 4, and 5, 1956.

266 Ibid, May 28 and December 29, 1955.

267 Buren Jackson, "Oral Interview with Buren Jackson conducted by Michael Lindsey."

268 *Democrat*, November 14, 1955.

269 *Arkansas Almanac—1957 to1958*, 165.

270 *Democrat*, June 8, 1955.

271 Ibid, November 22, 1955.

272 Ibid, January 15, 16, and 24, 1956.

273 Ibid, January 12 and 13, 1956.

274 Ibid, November 16, 1955, and January 13, 1956.

275 Ibid, February 17 and 30, 1956.

276 Ibid, February 28, 1956.

277 Ibid, March 1 and March 3, 1956.

278 Ibid, March 28, 1956.

279 Ibid, March 29, 1956.

280 Ibid, March 14 and 18, 1956.

281 Ibid, March 19, 1956.

282 Ibid, June 4, 1956.

283 Ibid, January 7, 1957.

284 Ibid, January 23, 1957. Also see Act 474 of 1957, *Acts of Arkansas*, 1267.

285 Wayland Speer, "Oral Interview with Wayland Speer by Michael Lindsey, January 13, 2004."

286 Ibid, June 7, 1957.

287 Dwain Thompson, "Oral Interview with Dwain Thompson conducted by Michael Lindsey, December 17, 2003."

288 Numan Bartley, *The New South: 1945-1980*, (Baton Rouge: Louisiana State University Press, 1995), 200-204.

289 *Democrat*, September 2 and 7, 1956.

290 N. V. Bartley, "Looking Back at Little Rock," *AHQ*, Vol. 25, No. 2 (Summer 1966), 102-103.

291 Ibid, p 103.

292 C. Fred Williams, "Class: The Central Issue in the 1957 Little Rock School Crisis," *AHQ*, Vol. 61, No. 3 (Autumn 1997), 340.

293 David Wallace, "Orval Faubus: The Central Figure at Little Rock Central High School," *AHQ*, Vol. 39, No. 4 (Winter 1980), 329.

294 Virgil Blossom, *It Has Happened Here*, (New York: Harper and Brothers, 1959), 54.

295 Brooks Hays, *A Southern Moderate Speaks*, (Chapel Hill: University of North Carolina Press, 1959), 132.

296 Wallace, 326.

297 Hays, 133.

298 Wallace, 327.

299 Alan Templeton to Herman Lindsey, September 4, 1957, Faubus Papers.

300 *Democrat*, September 5, 1957.

301 Mack Thompson, "Oral Interview with Mack Thompson conducted by Michael Lindsey, August 4, 2003."

302 Melba Pattillo Beals, *Warriors Don't Cry: A Searing Memoir of the Battle to Integrate Little Rock's Central High* (New York: Washington Square Press, 1994), 48.

303 *Democrat*, September 4, 1957.

304 Beals, 2.

305 Ibid, September 20, 1957.

306 Ibid, September 22, 1957.

307 Herman Lindsey, "Letter to File by Herman Lindsey, September 22, 1957," Faubus Papers.

308 Alan Templeton to Herman Lindsey, September 23, 1957, Faubus Papers.

309 W. D. Davidson, "Oral Interview with W. D. Davidson conducted by Michael Lindsey, January 9, 2004."

310 Templeton, "Report, September 23, 1957."

311 *Democrat*, September 23, 1957.

312 Davidson, "Oral Interview." Also see Thompson, "Oral Interview."

313 Templeton, "Report, September 23, 1957."

314 *Democrat*, September 23, 1957.

315 Davidson, "Oral Interview." Also see Templeton, "Report."

316 *Democrat*, September 24, 1957.

317 Templeton, "Report, September 23, 1957."

318 Alan Templeton, "Report to Herman Lindsey, September 24, 1957," Faubus Papers.

319 *Democrat*, September 25, 1957.

320 Bill Miller, "Oral Interview with Bill Miller conducted by Michael Lindsey, August 12, 2003."

321 Ibid, September 29, 1957. Also see Bill Miller, "Oral Interview."

322 Alan Templeton, "Report to Herman Lindsey from Alan Templeton, September 25, 1957," and "Report to Herman Lindsey from Alan Templeton, September 27, 1957," Faubus Papers.

323 See CID reports dated November 10, 1958 and December 10, 1958 in Faubus Papers. Also see "Letter from Howard Chandler to Herman Lindsey, February 25, 1964." Faubus Papers.

324 "Letter from Howard Chandler to Herman Lindsey, June 19, 1961." Faubus Papers.

325 *Gazette*, October 12, 1960.

326 Ibid, June 3, 1979.

327 "Letter from Howard Chandler to Herman Lindsey, October 2, 1962," Faubus Papers.

328 *Democrat*, December 7, 8, and 10, 1957.

329 Ibid, October 12, 1957, and Bill Miller, "Oral Interview."

330 Ibid, December 22, 1957.

331 Arkansas State Police Commission Meeting Minutes, November 1, 1957.

332 Ibid, July 2, 1958.

333 Thompson, "Oral Interview."

334 *Democrat*, August 18, 1958.

335 Arkansas State Police, *Biennial Report, 1956-1957*.

336 John Chappelle, "Oral Interview."

337 "Letter from Mack Thompson to Herman Lindsey, June 9, 1962," Faubus Papers.

338 "Letter from Herman Lindsey to Orval Faubus, April 25, 1963," Faubus Papers.

339 Ibid, July 18 and November 2, 1959.

340 *Gazette*, December 16, 1960.

341 Ibid, February 1, 1960.

342 Ibid, May 4, 1960.

343 Ibid, November 1, 1962.

344 Ibid, March 14, 15, 26, and 31, 1963.

345 Jim Bray, "Oral Interview with Jim Bray conducted by Michael Lindsey, May 19, 2004,"

346 *Democrat*, August 6, 1957.

347 "Letter from Herman Lindsey to Carl Burger, April 4, 1963," Faubus Papers.

348 *Gazette*, May 2, 1963.

349 "Letter from John Miller to Orval Faubus, December 11, 1963," Faubus Papers.

350 *Gazette*, April 21, 1963.

351 Ibid.

352 Herman Lindsey to Orval Faubus, May 3, 1963, Faubus Papers.

353 *Gazette*, March 28, 1964.

354 Ibid, June 12, 1962.

355 Ibid, June 17, 1962.

356 Henry Alexander, *Sources of Revenue for Community Services and Facilities in Hot Springs, Arkansas* (University of Arkansas Fayetteville: February 1962), 5.

357 Ibid, January 6, 12, 1963, and February 19, 1964.

358 Ibid, January 13, 1963.

359 Ibid, June 19, 1963.

360 Ibid, January 24, 1963.

361 Ibid, February 15, 1963.

362 Ibid, February 17, 1963.

363 Ibid, February 22 and 24, 1963.

364 Ibid, February 24, 1963. Also see February 17, 1963.

365 Ibid, March 20, 1963, and February 19, 1964.

366 Orval Allbritton, *Leo and Verne: The Spa's Heyday* (Hot Springs, AR: Garland County Historical Society, 2003), 594.

367 *Gazette*, March 27, 1964.

368 Ibid, September 19, 1964.

369 Ibid, October 14, 1964.

370 *Historical Report of the Arkansas Secretary of State*, 160. A total of 592,113 votes were cast in the general election for governor in 1964, which was more than in any previous election. Faubus received 337,489, Rockefeller received 254,561, and Garland County Senator Q. Bynum Hurst received 63.

371 *Democrat*, March 18, 1965.

372 H. H. Atkinson to Herman Lindsey, March 8, 1965, Faubus Papers.

373 "Report by Howard Chandler to Herman Lindsey, May 3, 1965," Faubus Papers. Also see Charles Winn to Howard Chandler, May 3, 1965, Faubus Papers.

374 *Gazette*, October 10, 1962.

375 Herman Lindsey to Mack Sturgis, January 8, 1963, Faubus Papers.

376 Carl Miller to Carl Burger, September 18, 1963, Faubus Papers.

377 Eaton, 51.

378 "Act 493" and "Act 548," *Acts of Arkansas–1965*.

379 Douglas Harp, "Oral Interview with Douglas Harp conducted by Michael Lindsey, February 12, 2004."

380 *Gazette*, December 26, 1960, and Elton Brown, "Oral Interview with Elton Brown conducted by Michael Lindsey, September 25, 2003."

381 Ibid, December 26, 1960.

382 Arkansas State Police, "General Informational Bulletin—August 1965," Faubus Papers.

383 Freddie McKinley, "Oral Interview with Freddie McKinley conducted by Michael Lindsey, January 14, 2004."

384 *Democrat*, June 23, 24, and 26, 1965.

385 Ibid, June 24, 1966.

386 Arkansas State Police, "Tucker Prison Farm Report," 1966.

387 Ibid, p 61.

388 *Gazette*, September 2, 3, and 6, 1966. Also see Jim Bray, "Oral Interview with Jim Bray conducted by Michael Lindsey, May 19, 2004."

Chapter Five

389 David Rosegrant, "Oral Interview with David Rosegrant conducted by Michael Lindsey, December 9, 2003."

390 *Gazette*, October 20 and 21, 1977.

391 *Gazette*, January 21, 1967.

392 Mack Thompson, "Oral Interview." Also see, "Memo to File from Orval Faubus, November 17, 1966," Faubus Papers.

393 *Gazette*, February 28, 1967.

394 Winthrop Rockefeller, "Letter to officials in Garland and Pulaski County, February 22, 1967," Winthrop Rockefeller Papers, University of Arkansas at Little Rock.

395 Ibid, March 2, 1967.

396 Ibid, March 19, 1967.

397 Ibid, March 14, 1967.

398 Ibid, March 29 and 30, 1967.

399 Ibid, April 1, 1967.

400 Ibid, February 7, March 3, April 1, and May 6, 1967.

401 Eaton, 55-56.

402 Dean Friend, "Oral Interview with Dean Friend conducted by Michael Lindsey, February 12, 2004."

403 *Gazette*, June 2, 1967.

404 Mack Thompson, "Letter to Winthrop Rockefeller, May, 29, 1967," Rockefeller Papers, University of Arkansas at Little Rock.

405 Lynn Davis, "Oral Interview with Lynn Davis conducted by Michael Lindsey, August 18, 2003."

406 Ibid.

407 *Gazette*, August 2, 1967.

408 Davis, "Oral Interview."

409 *Gazette*, August 18, 1967.

410 Mickey Smith, "Oral Interview with Mickey Smith conducted by Michael Lindsey, October 21, 2003."

411 Ibid, September 1, 1967.

412 Ibid, October 5, 1967.

413 Glenn Minton, "Oral Interview with Glenn Minton conducted by Michael Lindsey, February 12, 2004."

414 *Gazette*, October 8, 1967. Also see Davis, "Oral Interview."

415 Ibid.

416 Ibid, November 25, 1967 and Davis, "Oral Interview."

417 Ibid, December 6, 1967.

418 Davis, "Oral Interview."

419 *Gazette*, December 6, 1967.

420 Ibid, December 7, 1967 and Davis, "Oral Interview."

421 Ibid, December 19 and 20, 1967.

422 Ibid, December 21, 1967.

423 Ibid, February 9 and 17, March 14, 1968.

424 Bill Miller, "Oral Interview with Bill Miller conducted by Michael Lindsey, August 12, 2003."

425 Winthrop Rockefeller, "Letter to Ralph Scott, February 6, 1968," University of Arkansas at Little Rock, Rockefeller Papers.

426 Ibid, February 29, 1968.

427 Ibid, April 5, 1968.

428 *Democrat*, April 6, 1968.

429 *Gazette*, April 6 and 7, 1968.

430 Ibid, April 19, 1968.

431 *Gazette*, August 10 and 11, 1968.

432 Ibid, August 4, 1968.

433 Ken McFerran, "Oral Interview with Ken McFerran conducted by Michael Lindsey, September 11, 2003."

434 Robert Neel, "Oral Interview with Robert Neel conducted by Michael Lindsey, May 19, 2004."

435 *Gazette*, March 19 and March 22, 1969.

436 Ibid, April 22, 1969.

437 Ibid, April 4, 1969.

438 Ibid, March 21 and 23, 1969.

439 Ibid, July 3, 1969.

440 Ibid, July 23 and 20, 1969.

441 W. A. Tudor, "Oral Interview with W. A. Tudor conducted by Michael Lindsey, August 13, 2003."

442 *Gazette*, August 21 and 22, 1969.

443 *Gazette*, August 23, 1969.

444 Tudor, "Oral Interview."

445 *Gazette*, August 23, 1969.

446 Ibid, August 24 and 26, 1969.

447 Ibid, August 27, 1969.

448 Ibid.

449 Ibid.

450 Ibid, September 19, 1969.

451 Ibid, September 21, 1969.

452 Ibid, September 8 and 10, 1970.

453 Mel Hensley, "Oral Interview with Mel Hensley conducted by Michael Lindsey, August 13, 2003."

454 *Gazette*, September 12, 13, and 17, 1970.

455 Hensley, "Oral Interview."

456 Bill Miller, "Oral Interview."

457 Tudor, "Oral Interview."

458 G. B. Harp, "Oral Interview with G. B. Harp conducted by Michael Lindsey, June 7, 2004."

459 *Gazette*, January 29, 1968.

460 Cathy K. Urwin, *Agenda for Reform: Winthrop Rockefeller as Governor of Arkansas, 1967-1971* (Fayetteville, AR: University of Arkansas Press, 1991), pp. 99-100.

461 Ken McFerran, "Oral Interview with Ken McFerran conducted by Michael Lindsey, September 11, 2003."

462 The independence of troop commanders is well documented in multiple interviews. The "God" quote is from Les Braunns, "Oral Interview with Les Braunns conducted by Michael Lindsey, July 8, 2004."

463 *Gazette*, March 15, 1974.

464 *Gazette*, July 28 and 29, 1969.

465 Dale Bumpers, *The Best Lawyer in a One-Lawyer Town* (New York: Random House, 2003), pp. 220-221.

466 Eaton, p 61.

467 *Gazette*, February 19, 1971.

468 Ibid, February 20, 1971.

469 Ibid, February 23, 1971.

470 Ibid, April 2, 1971.

471 Bill Miller, "Oral Interview."

472 Ibid.

473 *Gazette*, June 17 and July 17, 1971.

474 Eaton, p 61.

475 Ibid, August 7, 1971.

476 Ibid.

477 Ibid.

478 Ibid, August 10, 1971.

479 Dale Miller, "Oral Interview with Dale Miller conducted by Michael Lindsey on January 10, 2004."

480 *Gazette*, August 11, 1971.

481 Ibid, March 17 and April 18, 1972.

482 Neel, "Oral Interview."

483 *Gazette*, April 22, 1976.

484 Chandler, "Oral Interview."

485 Conrad Pattillo, "Oral Interview with Conrad Pattillo conducted by Michael Lindsey on March 18, 2004."

486 "Act 719," *Acts of Arkansas–1973*, p 745.

487 McFerran, "Oral Interview."

488 Ibid.

489 Anonymous interview.

490 McFerran, "Oral Interview."

491 Jerry Reinold, "Oral Interview with Jerry Reinold conducted by Michael Lindsey on May 12, 2004."

492 Keith Ferguson, "Oral Interview with Keith Ferguson conducted by Michael Lindsey on August 17, 2004."

493 *Gazette*, October 17 and 19, December 3, 1975, and May 19, 1976.

494 Reinold.

495 *Gazette*, September 27 and October 4, 1972.

496 Ibid, March 10, 13, 15 and November 8, 1973.

497 Ibid, November 8, 1973.

498 Ibid, April 20, 1974.

499 Eaton, p 64. Also see *Gazette*, February 28 and March 1, 1975, and February 26, 1976.

500 Doug Harp, "Oral Interview with Doug Harp conducted by Michael Lindsey on February 12, 2004."

501 *Gazette*, ibid, May 7, 9, 13, 1975.

502 Ibid, May 18, 1975.

503 Ibid, May 7, 9, and 13, 1975.

504 Eaton, p 64, also see McFerran, "Oral Interview."

505 David Rosegrant, "Oral Interview with David Rosegrant conducted by Michael Lindsey on December 9, 2003."

506 Eaton, p 65.

507 *Gazette*, September 14, 1977.

508 Ibid, September 15, 1977.

509 Arkansas State Police Commission, "Meeting Minutes for November 10, 1977."

510 Ibid, January 11, 1978.

511 McFerran, "Oral Interview."

512 Arkansas State Police Commission, "Meeting Minutes, June 20, 1980."

513 *Gazette*, March 2 and 17, 1977.

514 Eaton, p 71.

515 Ibid, p 66.

516 John Purcell, "Oral Interview with John Purcell conducted by Michael Lindsey on January 9, 2004."

517 *Gazette*, February 13 and March 2, 1979.

518 John Robert Starr, *Yellow Dogs and Dark Horses: Thirty Years on the Campaign Beat*, (Little Rock: August House, 1987), p 164-175.

519 Harp, "Oral Interview."

520 Starr, p 165.

521 *Gazette*, August 28, 1979. Also see Reinold, "Oral Interview."

522 Buren Jackson, "Oral Interview with Buren Jackson conducted by Michael Lindsey on January 9, 2004."

523 *Gazette*, September 26, 1979.

524 Eaton.

525 Harp, "Oral Interview."

526 Bill Young, "Oral Interview with Bill Young conducted by Michael Lindsey on October 9, 2003."

527 Changing from the designation of Districts to Troops occurred on April 23, 1976. See Commission Meeting Minutes.

528 Arkansas State Police, *Annual Report–1980*, p 3.

529 Harp, "Oral Interview."

530 *Commission Meeting Minutes*, July 21, 1978, March 16 and April 20, 1979.

531 *Gazette*, March 13, 1980.

532 *Annual Report–1980*, p iv.

533 Reinaldo Arenas, Dolores Koch, trans., *Before Night Falls* (New York: Penguin Books, 1993), p 283.

534 *Southwest Times Record*, "Insight 2000: Changing Faces."

535 Ibid.

536 *Chaffeegram*, May 19, 1980.

537 Ibid, May 27, 1980.

538 Gene Irby, "Oral Interview with Gene Irby conducted by Michael Lindsey on July 16, 2004."

539 *Gazette*, May 26 and 28, 1980.

540 Ibid, May 28, 1980.

541 *Southwest Times Record*, June 3, 1980.

542 *Gazette*, May 30, 1980.

543 Arvel "Buddy" Acoach, "Oral Interview with Arvel Acoach by Michael Lindsey on June 9, 2004."

544 For media coverage of the event, see the *Gazette*, June 2, 3, 10, and 14, 1980. For personal remembrances, see oral interviews provided by Buddy Acoach, Gene Irby, and Tom Morrow.

545 Les Braunns, "Oral Interview with Les Braunns conducted by Michael Lindsey on July 8, 2004."

546 *Gazette*, June 2, 1980.

547 Harp, "Oral Interview."

548 Tom Morrow, "Oral Interview with Tom Morrow conducted by Michael Lindsey on August 9, 2003."

549 *Gazette*, October 4, 1980.

550 Lyle Smith, "Oral Interview with Lyle Smith conducted by Michael Lindsey on March 11, 2004."

551 Braunns, "Oral Interview."

552 See Oral Interviews with Mel Hensley and Dale Miller, along with Eaton, pp. 68-69. Also see *Gazette*, September 6 and 7, 1980.

553 Purcell, "Oral Interview."

Chapter Six

554 Keith Ferguson, "Oral Interview with Keith Ferguson conducted by Michael Lindsey on August 17, 2004."

555 *Gazette*, November 6 and 7, 1984. Also see *The Springdale News*, November 6, 1984.

556 Ibid, May 29, 1981.

557 Ibid, May 22 and August 29, 1981, July 2, 1982.

558 State Police Commission, *Meeting Minutes*, July 16, 1982, and June 17, 1983.

559 Ibid, June 26, 1988.

560 Ibid, July 31, 1977.

561 Ibid, June 9, 1977.

562 Ibid, November 16, 1983.

563 Lance King, "Oral Interview with Lance King conducted by Michael Lindsey on July 20, 2004."

564 Arkansas State Police, *Marijuana Eradication Reports 1984-1994.*

565 Lyle Smith, "Oral Interview with Lyle Smith conducted by Michael Lindsey on March 11, 2004."

566 *Gazette*, May 22, 1990, and ASP Commission, *Meeting Minutes*, June 15, 1990.

567 Ibid, July 25, 1986.

568 Ibid, January 29, 1985.

569 Billy R. Skipper, "Oral Interview with Billy R. Skipper conducted by Michael Lindsey on February 12, 2004."

570 Ibid, May 17, 1987.

571 Arkansas State Police Commission, *Meeting Minutes*, November 21, 1986, and July 17 and October 29, 1987.

572 Skipper, "Oral Interview."

573 McFerran, "Oral Interview."

574 *Gazette*, December 20, 1987.

575 Ibid, January 30, 1988.

576 Ibid, October 18, 1990, and March 22, 1991. Also see *Commission Meeting Minutes*, October 19, 1990.

577 John Bailey, "Oral Interview with John Bailey conducted by Michael Lindsey on March 11, 2004."

578 *Gazette*, July 4 and 5, 1982.

579 Ibid.

580 Ibid, July 1, 1984.

581 Jim Tyler, "Oral Interview with Jim Tyler conducted by Michael Lindsey on December 9, 2003."

582 *Gazette*, July 8, 1984.

583 Ibid, April 25, 1985.

584 Ibid, September 5, 1984.

585 Ibid, April 17, 1985.

586 Ibid, April 5, 1985.

587 Ibid, April 16 and 17, 1985.

588 Purely by coincidence, the date of April 19 is infamous in the anti-government movement since it is the anniversary of the battles at Lexington and Concord, which triggered the Revolutionary War in 1775. Also, the 19th is the day of the tragic final raid on the Branch Davidian compound in Waco Texas in 1993.

589 Braunns, "Oral Interview."

590 Billy R. Skipper, "Oral Interview." Also see Dale Miller, "Oral Interview."

591 G. B. Harp, "Oral Interview with G. B. Harp conducted by Michael Lindsey on June 7, 2004."

592 Ron Lemons, "Oral Interview with Ron Lemons conducted by Michael Lindsey on July 21, 2004."

593 Gazette, April 23, 1985, and Irby, "Oral Interview."

594 Buren Jackson, "Oral Interview."

595 Gazette, May 2, 1989.

596 Ibid, November 2, 1989.

597 Ibid, November 2 and 4, 1989, and June 2, 1990.

598 Ibid, October 3, 1989.

599 Ibid, October 17, 1984.

600 Ibid, February 19, 1989.

601 Mickey Smith, "Oral Interview with Mickey Smith conducted by Michael Lindsey."

602 Randy Toombs, "Oral Interview with Randy Toombs conducted by Michael Lindsey."

603 Bill Carver, "Oral Interview with Bill Carver conducted by Michael Lindsey."

604 John Chappelle, "Oral Interview with John Chappelle conducted by Michael Lindsey."

605 Ferguson, "Oral Interview."

606 Richard Hester, "Oral Interview with Richard Hester."

607 Conrad Pattillo, "Oral Interview with Conrad Pattillo."

Chapter Seven

608 Gazette, January 14, 1998.

609 Ibid, April 5, 1998.

610 Ibid, June 1, 1994.

611 John Bailey, "Oral Interview."

612 Bob Herron, "Weapons of the State Police," (unpublished internal State Police document).

613 Arkansas State Police Commission, "Commission Meeting Minutes," April 15, 1994. Also see minutes from November 30, 1993.

614 Bailey, "Oral Interview."

615 Herron. Also see John Purcell, "Oral Interview."

616 Bailey, "Oral Interview."

617 Gazette, March 6, 1997.

618 Bailey, "Oral Interview."

619 Arkansas State Police Commission, "Meeting Minutes," June 5, 1997.

620 *Gazette*, August 16, 1996.

621 Bailey, "Oral Interview."

622 *Gazette*, February 29 and October 1, 1996. Also see Commission, "Meeting Minutes," November 17, 1995.

623 Highway Patrol Monthly Reports for 1998 and Arkansas State Police, "Biennial Report for 1996-1997."

624 Arkansas State Police, "Crime Information Bulletin," Vol. 4, No. 2 (February 1998), p 2.

625 Bailey, "Oral Interview."

626 *Gazette*, September 3, 1998.

627 Ibid, March 26, 1995.

628 Arkansas State Police, "Biennial Report, 1996-1997."

629 Lance King, "Oral Interview."

630 *Gazette*, January 30, 1997.

631 Ibid, January 22, 1997.

632 Ibid, February 1 and 5, 1997.

633 Ibid, July 23, 1997.

634 Ibid, July 13, 1997.

635 Ibid.

636 Ibid, September 10, 1997.

637 David Rosegrant, "Oral Interview."

638 *Gazette*, September 13, 1997.

639 Ibid, September 16, 1997.

640 Ibid, March 22, 1997.

641 Bailey, "Oral Interview."

642 Terrie Grace Simpson, "Oral Interview."

643 *Gazette*, November 24, 1999.

644 Buddy Acoach, "Oral Interview."

645 Bailey, "Oral Interview."

646 *The Arkansas Trooper*, Summer 2003, p 191. The SRT K-9 was killed during an operation in 1999.

647 Bailey, "Oral Interview."

648 John Bailey, *Integrity on Patrol: 101 Stories of the Arkansas State Police* (Kinsman, OH: Virginia Pines Press, 2002), p 213.

649 Ibid.

650 Ibid, p 214.

651 Ibid, p 223. Also see *Gazette*, February 11, 1999.

652 Ibid, p 226.

653 Bill Young, "Oral Interview with Bill Young conducted by Michael Lindsey."

654 Tom Mars, "Oral Interview with Tom Mars conducted by Michael Lindsey."

655 Ibid.

656 *Gazette*, June 23, 1999.

657 Mars, "Oral Interview."

658 Ibid.

659 *Gazette*, August 4, 1999.

660 Commission on Accreditation for Law Enforcement Agencies, http://www.calea.org/newweb/accreditation%20Info/Accred%20Program%20Info.htm, January 27, 2005.

661 Mars, "Oral Interview."

662 CALEA, http://www.calea.org/newweb/accreditation%20info/time_to_take_ another_look_at_law.htm, January 27, 2005.

663 Mars, "Oral Interview."

664 Ibid.

665 Arkansas State Crime Laboratory, http://www.arkansas.gov/crimelab/sections/ illicit, January 27, 2005.

666 *Gazette*, August 28, 1999.

Chapter Eight

667 Oral Interview, Win Phillips with Michael Lindsey, July 22, 2003. University of Arkansas Special Collections, Fayetteville, Arkansas.

668 *Gazette*, August 9, 1978.

Index

About the Author

Michael Lindsey researched and wrote *The Big Hat Law: Arkansas and Its State Police, 1935-2000* while earning a master's degree in history from the University of Arkansas. He received the Violet J. Gingles award for the best paper on an Arkansas history subject in 2005 and has been published in the *Arkansas Historical Quarterly*. Michael was born and raised in Harrison, Arkansas, and resides in Fayetteville with his wife, Lara, and two daughters, Bailey and Amelia, where he works as a public finance banker with Morgan Keegan.